Aim High

Workbook 5

Paul Kelly   Susan Iannuzzi

OXFORD
UNIVERSITY PRESS

OXFORD
UNIVERSITY PRESS

Great Clarendon Street, Oxford, OX2 6DP, United Kingdom

Oxford University Press is a department of the University of Oxford.
It furthers the University's objective of excellence in research, scholarship,
and education by publishing worldwide. Oxford is a registered trade
mark of Oxford University Press in the UK and in certain other countries

© Oxford University Press 2011

The moral rights of the author have been asserted

First published in 2011

2015 2014 2013 2012 2011

10 9 8 7 6 5 4 3 2 1

Links to third party websites are provided by Oxford in good faith and for
information only. Oxford disclaims any responsibility for the materials
contained in any third party website referenced in this work

ISBN: 978 0 19 445318 9   WORKBOOK
ISBN: 978 0 19 445330 1   STUDENT'S CD-ROM
ISBN: 978 0 19 445329 5   PACK

Printed in China

This book is printed on paper from certified and well-managed sources

ACKNOWLEDGEMENTS

The publisher would like to thank the following for permission to reproduce photographs:
Alamy Images pp.7 (Flooded forest/Jan Carroll), 8 (Cruise ship/Chris Pearsall),
19 (Students in exam/VStock), 28 (Bluewater shopping centre/PCL), 29 (Pasting
advertising poster on billboard/Jeff Morgan 03), 31 (Women in coffee shop/
Kumar Sriskandan), 32 (Electronics department/British Retail Photography),
36 (Placebo medicine/mauritius images GmbH), 43 (Homeopathic and Herbal
Medicine mortar/INSADCO Photography), 51 (Fashion model/Marcin Jamkowski/
Adventure Pictures), 53 (Wheat seeds and plant/Li Ding), 54 (Preparing food/
Chris Rout), 60 (Coconut drink/Miguel Sobreira), 68 (Freecycle logo/Art
Directors & TRIP), 73 (Tourists in Barcelona/Carlos Rios); Corbis pp.7 (Capsule
hotel/George Steinmetz), 9 (Gondola on Grand Canal, Venice/Sylvain Sonnet),
17 (Group of teenagers/Jutta Klee), 38 (Playing basketball/Mika), 39 (MRI scan
of the brain/Owen Franken), 52 (Svalbard Global Seed Vault/Global Crop Diversity
Trust/epa), 55 (Boiled egg with toast soldiers/Williams, Paul/the food passionates),
57 (Portrait of Queen Margherita/Underwood & Underwood), 59 (Burritos/
Roulier/Turiot/photocuisine), 61 (FC Barcelona's team celebration/Toni Albir/
epa), 71 (Electrical plugs in socket/moodboard), 76 (Portrait of English poet
John Keats, by J. Severn/Lebrecht Music & Arts), 77 (Pianist David Helfgott/
Siemoneit Ronald/Corbis Sygma), 78 (Soccer players sitting on bench/Kevin
Dodge), 81 (Young boy playing violin/LWA-JDC), 83 (Helen Keller); Getty Images
pp.4 (Bottle-nosed dolphin leaping/Stephen Frink), 8 (Liverpool Street station/
Andrew Holt), 13 (Teenager in library studying/Jupiterimages), 22 (Benz Three-
Wheeler/Library of Congress/digital version by Science Faction), 25 (Birmingham
pen factory in 1823/SSPL via Getty Images), 27 (Bacteriologist Alexander Fleming/
Time & Life Pictures), 30 (Newscaster/Blend Images/Kim Steele), 40 (Soccer
game/Andrew Hetherington), 41 (Outdoor swimming pools/David Greedy),
44 (Historic Einstein Papers), 44 (Handwritten note by Picasso/Gjon Mill/Time
Life Pictures), 63 (Immigrants arriving in New York/Superstock), 64 (Businessman
at hotel reception/Alistair Berg/Digital Vision), 65 (Little Brazil, Manhattan/
Leanna Rathkelly), 79 (Teenager doing homework/Thinkstock Images), 85 (Family
with electronics/OJO Images/Robert Daly), 86 (Restaurant waitress/William
West/AFP); Oxford University Press pp.67 (Golf/Photodisc), 87 (Fireworks over
city/Comstock); Photolibrary pp.14 (Tailor/Antenna/FStop), 46 (Friends in ski
gear/Laurence Mouton/Photoalto), 56 (Busy restaurant/Beau Lark/Fancy),
62 (Businessmen greeting/Image Source), 72 (Woman with backpack and MP3
player/Cultura); Rex Features pp.20 (Aquaduct concept vehicle/Tony Kyriacou),
23 (Muslim Heritage exhibition/Nils Jorgensen).

Cover: Photolibrary (Glider flying/Michael Turek/White)

Illustrations by: Paul Daviz pp.6, 16, 24, 75, 88; Carl Pearce pp.11, 12, 33, 35, 47,
49, 70, 84

1 The great escape

1 Match the words in the box with the definitions.

excursion   guide   itinerary   ~~representative~~   resort

1 A person who has been chosen to act or speak for a company. _representative_

2 A place where people go to have a holiday. _____

3 A plan of a journey, including the route and the places that you will visit. _____

4 A person who shows tourists or travellers where to go. _____

5 A short journey or trip that a group of people make for pleasure. _____

2 Read the text quickly. How has the relationship between the Azorean 'vigia' and whales changed?

Face to face with nature

Some people go on holiday to see historical sites, to visit famous cities or to find idyllic places to relax in. But others are choosing their holiday destinations because they want to get closer to the wildlife around them.

The Azores is a group of islands in the middle of the Atlantic Ocean, about 1,500 miles west of the coast of Portugal. The waters around the Azores islands make the perfect location for whale and dolphin watching, and 24 of the planet's 80 species of whales and dolphins have been sighted there. Some travel companies are now helping an ever-increasing number of adventure-seeking tourists to fulfill their dreams by arranging excursions to the islands to swim with wild dolphins.

Dolphin Connection, a travel company based in the UK, creates itineraries for holidaymakers to see dolphins in their natural habitat. They arrange boats to take tourists to the areas where the dolphins gather. Tourists wishing to remain dry watch the dolphins from the boat deck, while those wishing to interact with the dolphins can swim and snorkel. Each group is accompanied by a Dolphin Connection representative who is a trained

guide or marine biologist. The guide ensures that no dolphins are harmed or stressed by their encounters with humans. The experience involves local people too. In the past, the Azorean watchmen (vigia) used to spot whales for hunting. Now they are using their knowledge to guide tourists in their close encounter with nature.

Swimming with dolphins is popular in other parts of the world, too. Dolphin Connection also arranges trips to a beautiful eco-village resort on the Red Sea coast of Egypt. Guests are taken to a nearby coral reef, where the dolphins come every year to raise their young away from the dangers of the open sea. Dolphins are very playful animals and they are also curious, so swimmers simply need to wait for the dolphins to approach them and they will enjoy a truly magical and amazing experience.

3 Are the sentences true or false? Correct the false sentences.

1 The Azores is a peninsula in the Atlantic Ocean. _F_
   The Azores is a group of islands in the Atlantic Ocean.

2 More than 25% of the world's whale and dolphin species have been seen near the Azores. ____

3 A lot of tourists dream of swimming with dolphins. ____

4 Dolphin Connection takes dolphins to the tourist resorts. ____

5 Some Dolphin Connection employees are trained to look after dolphins. ____

6 Local people can be stressed by the arrival of so many tourists. ____

7 The Azores isn't the only place where people can swim with dolphins. ____

8 Dolphins take their young away from the dangers created by the tourists. ____

4 Tick the things that Dolphin Connection does.

1 Organizes holidays to historical sites. ☐
2 Offers trips for animal lovers. ☐
3 Organizes trips to the dolphins' natural habitat. ☐
4 Trains marine biologists. ☐
5 Employs local people. ☐
6 Raises young dolphins at a special resort. ☐

Unusual holidays

1 Complete the sentences or answer the questions.

1 Which verb talks about a light that shines and seems to shake slightly?
   a shimmer **b** surpass **c** marvel

2 If you tell a good *gag*, people will …
   a cry. **b** laugh. **c** shout.

3 What does a *comedian* do? Tell …
   a stories. **b** jokes. **c** lies.

4 What is a *chalet* usually made of?
   a concrete **b** steel **c** wood

5 If you *crave* something, you really ___ it.
   a hate **b** want **c** don't care about

6 Which verb means *to come together in large numbers*?
   a shimmer **b** surpass **c** flock

7 A *multitude* refers to a ___ number of people or things.
   a large **b** small **c** surprising

8 A person who is relaxing away from home is called a …
   a guide. **b** travel agent. **c** holidaymaker.

9 *Meteorology* involves the study of the …
   a oceans. **b** weather. **c** planets.

10 If something is a *marvel*, it fills you with great surprise and …
   a anger. **b** disappointment. **c** admiration.

11 If you have a good *vantage point*, you can ___ things clearly.
   a talk about **b** hear **c** see

12 A ___ hunts and kills other animals.
   a predator **b** participant **c** guide

13 If you are friendly and welcoming to visitors, you are …
   a entertaining. **b** disposable. **c** hospitable.

14 *To surpass* expectations means to do something ___ than expected.
   a worse **b** better **c** slower

15 *Rustling* is the sound that ___ things make when moving.
   a dry **b** metal **c** wet

Onomatopoeia

2 Complete the sentences with the correct form of the words in the box.

| clatter | creak | gurgle | hiss | ~~rustling~~ | screech |

1 I heard a _rustling_ in the leaves but fortunately I didn't see any rats.

2 There was a _____ of dishes in the kitchen as my brother laid the table.

3 The actors' terrible performance resulted in boos and _____ from the audience.

4 There was a _____ on the stairs and then suddenly the bedroom door started to open slowly!

5 I listened to the _____ of the rainwater as it went down the pipe next to the window.

6 The baby let out a loud _____ and then started to cry.

Idioms with *off* and *on*

3 Put the words in the box in the correct columns.

| ~~tenterhooks~~ | the boil | the cuff | the go | the hoof |
| the off chance | the record | the wall |

on	off
tenterhooks	

4 Correct the mistake in each sentence.

1 I hadn't prepared a speech, so I just said a few words off the ~~tenterhooks~~. _cuff_

2 My brother applied for the job on the off hoof but he didn't really expect to get it. _____

3 We've been on the record all day and we're really tired. _____

4 Jane gets her exam results tomorrow. She's been on hoof all week. _____

5 The boss's business ideas are a bit off the go. He says we should be rude to our customers! _____

6 What the player said is off the boil and can't be published in the newspaper. _____

7 Once the surprise has worn off, it will be difficult to keep people's interest on the chance. _____

8 I haven't got time to sit and have lunch so I'll eat a sandwich on the wall. _____

GRAMMAR

Stative verbs

1 Which verb in each group can change its meaning when used in a continuous form?

1	**a** hate	**b** like	**c** taste	**d** agree
2	**a** see	**b** love	**c** prefer	**d** contain
3	**a** possess	**b** believe	**c** depend	**d** weigh
4	**a** want	**b** understand	**c** think	**d** belong

2 Put the verbs in exercise 1 in the correct categories.

senses and appearances	emotions and feelings	having and being	thinking and perception
1 taste	4 _____	9 _____	14 _____
2 _____	5 _____	10 _____	15 _____
3 _____	6 _____	11 _____	16 _____
	7 _____	12 _____	
	8 _____	13 _____	

3 Choose the correct answers.

1 This milk (tastes) / **is tasting** off. How long has it been in the fridge?

2 Mike sent a text message and he says he **has** / **'s having** a good time on the school trip.

3 My dad is going on a diet. He **weighs** / **'s weighing** over 90 kilos!

4 We **think** / **'re thinking** about where to go on holiday but we haven't decided yet.

5 I **'m weighing** / **weigh** all the ingredients really carefully because I want this cake to be perfect.

6 I don't like wearing my glasses, but I **see** / **'m seeing** much better with them on.

7 The pudding is nearly ready to go into the oven. Mum **tastes** / **'s tasting** it to check that it's sweet enough.

8 I've **had** / **been having** this camera for ages.

9 I'm not going to school this morning because I **see** / **'m seeing** the dentist at 10 a.m.

10 I **don't think** / **am not thinking** violence can ever be justified.

4 Complete the dialogue with the correct simple or continuous form of the verbs in brackets.

Dad Come on, Jack!

Jack Just a minute, Dad. I [1] **'m weighing** (weigh) my suitcase. I don't want to have to pay more at the airport for excess baggage.

Dad But you're late! Look, I'll take this bag down to the car. Oops … It [2] _____ (weigh) a ton!

Jack That's not mine! It [3] _____ (belong) to Jane.

Dad How long [4] _____ she _____ (think) you're going for? A year?

Jack Well, she [5] _____ (like) to be prepared for any situation! Anyway, it's small so we'll take it on the plane.

Dad But yesterday she [6] _____ (agree) to take just a few things. You're not going on holiday; you're going to visit your sick grandad!

Jack Don't worry. We [7] _____ (think) of getting a taxi from the airport to Grandad's house.

Dad Isn't Mum going to meet you at the airport?

Jack No. Grandad [8] _____ (see) the doctor this afternoon and Mum is going with him.

Dad OK. Now remember to tell your mum if she needs anything, I'll bring it at the weekend. Now, where's Jane? You're going to miss that plane!

●●●●● **CHALLENGE!** ●●●●●

Write a short email to a friend. Tell them:

• what you love / hate about holidays.

• where you prefer to spend your holidays.

• what you want to do for your next holiday.

_____

_____

_____

_____

Feeling at home

1 **Match the words (1–8) with the definitions (a–h).**

1 frosty
2 uninviting
3 atrocious
4 homely
5 stark
6 charming
7 lavish
8 extravagant

a of very bad quality
b pleasant and attractive
c costing too much money
d freezing, with a thin layer of white ice covering everything
e plain or ordinary, but pleasant
f designed to impress and expensive
g empty, without decoration
h not attractive or hospitable

2 **Complete the sentences with the words in the box.**

cosy dreadful enchanting five-star ~~luxuriant~~
opulent sparse unassuming

1 The room was filled with the perfume of exotic plants, whose luxuriant_____ leaves trailed across every surface.
2 The _____ decor and expensive furnishings were very different from those of the cheap and simple hotels that I usually stayed in.
3 It was a _____ room with just a bed and a table.
4 It was a _____ hotel but the service would have been very poor even for a hotel of a lower category.
5 The restaurant we went to was awful. The food was bad and the service was _____.
6 The café was in an _____ building that you wouldn't notice if you didn't know it was there.
7 My study is small but it's nice and _____ in the winter when the fire is lit.
8 Venice is the most magical, _____ city that I've ever visited.

3 **Read the text. Are the sentences true or false? Correct the false sentences.**

1 Most hotels are very different from each other. F
   Most hotels are very similar.
2 A lot of the workers in Tokyo and Osaka do not live in the centre of these cities. ___
3 Japanese office workers are expected to work in the evenings. ___
4 The capsule hotel rooms don't have washing facilities. ___
5 Men are using capsule hotels as home during the working week. ___
6 The building techniques for Ariau Towers were designed by Jacques Cousteau. ___
7 Wild animals can be seen from Ariau Towers hotel. ___
8 Ariau Towers is eight kilometres from the jungle. ___

Fitting in with the environment

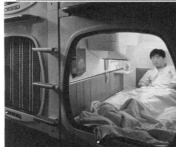

Most of the world's hotels offer very similar services. However, there are a few that specialize in providing their clients with something very unusual. Here we look at just two examples of the world's most remarkable places to stay.

Capsule hotels
Japan is a nation where everybody is constantly on the go. Every day, thousands of commuters flock to the country's two biggest cities, Tokyo and Osaka. But as well as working long hours, Japan's office workers are also expected to socialize in the evenings with their colleagues, so there is often no point in making the long journey home for only a few hours' sleep. The solution? Capsule hotels. Capsule hotels offer 'rooms' that are two metres long, one metre high and one metre wide: just enough space for a bed. The rooms have a small TV and internet connection but bathroom facilities are shared. Some of the hotels have 700 capsules and their popularity is growing. In fact 30% of the men at the Capsule Hotel Shinjuku 510 in Tokyo stay there all week, only returning home at the weekends.

Tree house hotels
If the capsule hotels seem to fit in perfectly with the Japanese city environment, then tree house hotels do the same thing but in the more attractive setting of tropical forests. One of the best examples is the Ariau Towers hotel in the Amazon jungle in Brazil. The idea for such a hotel came from the world-famous conservationist Jacques Cousteau. Cousteau suggested following the building techniques of the local inhabitants of the jungle, who constructed houses raised above the ground on long pieces of wood. Staying in a building that is 22 metres off the ground keeps guests safe from wild animals and also provides them with a vantage point from which they can enjoy the spectacular views of the trees and the jungle wildlife. There are eight kilometres of aerial walkways that connect the different tree houses and provide guests with a unique opportunity to experience the jungle.

● ● ● ● ● **CHALLENGE!** ● ● ● ● ●

Create a unique hotel that fits the environment of your home town. Write a few lines about the following points:

• location   • type of clients   • rooms – size / facilities

_____
_____
_____

Expressing trends with simple and continuous forms

1 Answer the questions with the words in the box. Which tense describes trends that:

> present perfect continuous   present continuous
> past continuous

1 have stopped? _____

2 are occurring now and might change in the future? _____

3 started in the past and are still happening or important now? _____

2 Complete the text with the present continuous, past continuous or present perfect continuous form of the verbs in brackets.

Going places

Not very long ago, travelling was an expensive activity enjoyed by a lucky few. Today, thanks to falling prices, more and more people ¹ *are visiting* (visit) the four corners of the planet.

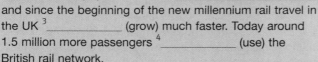

Rail travel

The number of rail passengers ² _____ (increase) slowly at the end of the 1990s but the arrival of private rail companies changed everything. They increased the frequency of trains on more popular routes, and since the beginning of the new millennium rail travel in the UK ³ _____ (grow) much faster. Today around 1.5 million more passengers ⁴ _____ (use) the British rail network.

Cruises

Cruises used to be an exclusive form of travel for the very wealthy but during the eighties the number of rich people taking cruises ⁵ _____ (decline) so fast that the cruise lines had to do something. They dropped prices and today they ⁶ _____ still _____ (fall). As a result, since the beginning of the 1990's the number of people taking cruises ⁷ _____ (rise) quickly and 1.5 million British people now take a cruise every year. Furthermore, the cruise lines ⁸ _____ (currently increase) capacity by building over 40 more ships that will carry over two million passengers every year in the future.

3 Choose the correct answers.

1 Bookings for our hotel have **been falling** / **fallen** for some time.

2 Prices for cruises have **been falling** / **fallen** by 50% in the last ten years.

3 Airport security have **been stopping** / **stopped** people from taking liquids onto planes for some years now and some people say they should also stop people from taking on food.

4 The trend for long holidays has **been stopping** / **stopped** because of the financial crisis.

5 The number of people using the internet to organize their holidays has **been increasing** / **increased** steadily for some time and a lot of high street travel agencies will have to close.

6 The number of passengers on this airline has **been increasing** / **increased** from 40,000 in 2001 to 250,000 this year.

7 Phone calls for information about our trips to the Arctic have **been decreasing** / **decreased** to just five a day.

8 After a dramatic increase in visitors to the museum at the beginning of the decade, numbers have **been declining** / **declined** gradually over the last few years.

> ●●●●●● **CHALLENGE!** ●●●●●●
>
> **Write about the trends in tourism in your country.**
>
> What are the primary tourist destinations in your country now?
> _____
>
> What is the perception of foreign tourists in your country now? Does this represent a change from past years?
> _____
>
> Where do most people from your country like to holiday now? Has this changed in recent years?
> _____

A persuasive essay

Preparation

1 Read the essay. Number the paragraphs in the correct order.

Winter time travel

A ☐ To conclude, there are few people who do not find Venice an incredible city when they visit it for the first time. However, visitors should plan their trips to the city for the winter months, when the city has been abandoned by the large crowds of camera-carrying tourists. It is then that you can take advantage not only of its wonderful architecture and art, but also of its unique atmosphere, a feature that cannot be photographed or filmed, but that has to be experienced.

B ☐ As well as offering a more relaxed visit, the winter also provides the visitor with the chance to experience what life might have been like in an ancient city. The absence of large groups of tourists, added to the fact that there are no cars and few of the other elements that we associate with a modern city, make the visitor feel that they have gone back in time. That impression is reinforced if you leave the main sites and stroll along some of the smaller canals. Then it's time to sit at the terrace of a café, have a coffee and watch the gondolas float past the magnificent palaces of the 14th century.

C ☐ Venice's unique location, its fantastic architecture and its artistic heritage means that it is visited by tourists all year round. However, there are a number of reasons that make the winter the best time of the year to go there. Firstly, there are far fewer tourists then. As a result, it is much easier to visit the many wonderful buildings and art exhibitions. Furthermore, the cooler winter temperatures mean that it's a far more comfortable time of the year to see the city.

D ☐ Venice is one of the world's most beautiful cities. The 'city of canals' lies on 117 small islands in a lagoon on the coast of the Adriatic Sea, and it is the perfect place to escape from the modern world. The city has no streets and the only way to get around is along the narrow footpaths or on the water buses that go up and down the canals. Going on a trip to Venice is like travelling into the past, especially if you go in the winter.

2 Which paragraph ...

1. sums up and repeats the writer's opinion? ____
2. provides the writer's main argument? ____
3. sets out the writer's opinion of the topic? ____
4. provides the writer's supporting argument? ____

3 Complete the mind map about Venice.

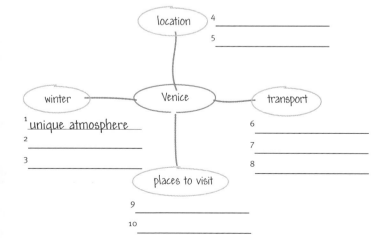

Writing task

4 Think about the following questions and make notes. Use a mind map to organize your ideas.
- Why do people visit your city? Is it to visit places or exhibitions, or to participate in festivals?
- When is the best time to visit the city? Is that because of the weather, or the timing of events?

5 In your notebook write a persuasive essay about the best time to visit your city. Use your notes from exercise 4 and the writing plan to help you. Write 200–250 words.
- Think about your own opinion on the topic.
- Make a list of examples to support your argument.
- Decide which example is the strongest and use it as your main argument.
- Organize your material into four paragraphs.

Check your work

Have you
- ☐ used a mind map?
- ☐ organized your arguments?
- ☐ used a paragraph plan?

1 Answer the questions.

1 Which tense describes a trend that started in the past and continues now?

_____

2 Which category of stative verbs do the verbs *like, agree, love, hate* and *prefer* belong to?

_____

3 Write three stative verbs that are verbs of thinking and perception.

_____

4 Which verb do we use to say something stops changing and stays the same?

_____

5 Which tense describes a trend that has stopped?

_____

6 Which tense do we often use to show that a trend started in the past but now it is completed?

_____

7 Write three stative verbs that are verbs of senses and appearance.

_____

8 Write an example of a stative verb that can also be used in the continuous form.

_____

9 Which tense describes a trend that is happening now?

_____

10 Which category of stative verbs do the verbs *possess, belong, depend, want* and *contain* belong to?

_____

Your score [   ] /10

2 Complete the dialogue using the correct simple or continuous forms of the verbs in brackets.

Mark So, what [1]_____ (you / think) of doing for your holidays?

Liam Well, we [2]_____ (want) to visit Europe by train.

Mark That sounds great. Are you going by Inter Rail?

Liam Yes, we [3]_____ (have) special student tickets for all the high-speed trains like the ICE in Germany and the TGV in France. They [4]_____ (change) the railways a lot in these countries in recent years and they [5]_____ (introduce) more and more of these fast trains all the time.

Mark Hey, that sounds cool! I [6]_____ (think) they're as quick as going by plane.

Liam They can be if you take into account the time spent going to and from airports.

Mark And I bet you don't have to worry if your suitcase [7]_____ (weigh) too much!

Liam No, if you can carry it, you can take it! Anyway, what are you doing?

Mark At the moment I [8]_____ (have) a hard time studying for my exams. The problem is I [9]_____ (not understand) anything I wrote in my notes.

Liam Why don't you ask Tom for his? He writes very clearly.

Mark I'm going to but he [10]_____ (see) his Maths teacher at the moment. I hope they're easy to understand, because if I don't pass the exams, I won't be going on holiday!

Your score [   ] /10

3 Some of the sentences in these pairs are incorrect. Tick the ones that are correct.

1 a Mum thinks that you've made a mistake. ☐
  b He says they are thinking of buying a new car. ☐

2 a The value of houses in the area has risen by 30%. ☐
  b The number of students going to university has been rising by 15% this year. ☐

3 a My bag is weighing a lot. Can you carry it for me? ☐
  b They're weighing the suitcases before they go on the plane. ☐

4 a Mobile phones were growing in popularity at the end of the 1990s. ☐
  b Adventure holidays have been growing in popularity from 2000 to 2005. ☐

5 a The hotel is costing $120 a night. ☐
  b A week at the resort costs $850. ☐

6 a The woman is tasting the food before giving it to the baby. ☐
  b This pizza tastes really good! ☐

7 a Do you believe he'll win the election? ☐
  b I'm not believing a word they said! ☐

8 a We have a good time at the restaurant. I'll phone you again when we leave. ☐
  b Jack has tickets for Saturday's football match. ☐

9 a The trend for exotic holidays has been stabilizing in the last few months. ☐
  b The trend for exotic holidays has stabilized in the last few months. ☐

10 a These flowers are smelling very nice. ☐
  b Why are you smelling that milk? Has it gone off? ☐

Your score [   ] /20

Total [   ] /40

1 Complete the vocabulary quiz with words from Unit 1.

QUIZ

1 If something is off the _____, it is unusual.

2 Which sound is made by bubbling water? _____

3 Who make their living by telling gags? _____

4 Which adjective means ordinary but pleasant? _____

5 A wooden house in the mountains is called a _____.

6 If you really want something, you _____ it.

7 _____ is a synonym for *dreadful*.

8 When you do something off the _____, you do it without planning it.

9 _____ has the opposite meaning of *sparse*.

10 _____ is the scientific study of the weather.

11 What do we call an animal that hunts, kills and eats other animals? _____

12 The verb _____ means to show surprise and admiration.

13 A person who is always on the _____ is always busy.

14 Which word is the sound made when two objects hit against each other? _____

15 If you are on _____, you are nervous about something that is going to happen.

16 When it's very cold and there is a thin layer of white ice everywhere, we say it's _____.

17 To do something on the _____ is to do something while you're moving.

18 A _____ is the sound made by a snake.

19 A _____ is a noise made by a door or a wooden floor.

20 If you say something off the _____, you don't want it to be reported.

Your score ___ /20

2 Complete the article with the correct words (a–d).

At last, your summer holiday has arrived! You've booked two weeks in a ¹_____ hotel that the travel agent's website describes as a marvel ²_____ modern architecture. A ³_____ room with lavish decoration and an opulent en-suite bathroom awaits you. You imagine enjoying the spectacular views of the beach from the ⁴_____ that the big hotel room balcony will offer you. Two wonderful weeks of living an ⁵_____ lifestyle and forgetting about day-to-day problems. It sounds perfect, doesn't it? Unfortunately, many ⁶_____ discover that the difference between the travel agent's descriptions and reality is often great.

Most of us ⁷_____ to holiday resorts at the same time of the year so many holidays start with delays and stressful journeys. And when we do finally arrive at our destination, we discover that neither the hotel nor the ⁸_____ resort are anything as nice as they appeared on the travel agent's site. Furthermore, the photos of deserted beaches are replaced by the sight of a ⁹_____ of holidaymakers fighting for a few centimetres of sand. The descriptions of the relaxing sound of the sea are replaced by the ¹⁰_____ of shouting children and screaming parents and after only a few days in your holiday 'paradise', you are already beginning to look forward to going home!

	a	b	c	d
1	five-stars	stark	uninviting	five-star
2	of	in	at	on
3	modest	hospitable	frosty	dreadful
4	place	vantage point	landscape	sights
5	uninviting	atrocious	extravagant	extreme
6	predators	comedians	holidaymakers	travel agents
7	crave	surpass	escape	flock
8	charming	humorous	disposable	frosty
9	gang	multitude	process	commuter
10	gurgle	rustling	hiss	screech

Your score ___ /10

Total ___ /30

2 Talking the talk

READING

Before reading: Language learning

1 Complete the sentences with the correct form of the words in the box.

> consonant   mother tongue   native speaker
> syllable   tone   ~~vowel~~

1 The five letters that represent _vowel_ sounds are *a, e, i, o* and *u*.
2 All the English teachers at our school are _____ from Britain and Ireland.
3 He used a sympathetic _____ of voice to give me the bad news.
4 885 million people speak Mandarin Chinese as their _____.
5 There are 21 letters that represent _____ sounds in the English alphabet.
6 The word *interesting* has got three _____.

2 Read the text quickly. Which three continents do the three languages mentioned come from?

3 Read the text again. Which language ...

1 is the mother tongue for a very small group of people?
Sentinelese
2 is spoken in two countries? _____
3 has sounds that are particularly difficult for adults to reproduce? _____
4 uses written letters that other languages use?
_____
5 replaces consonants with different types of sounds?
_____
6 is spoken by people whose way of life has changed very little over the years? _____

4 Are the sentences true or false? Correct the false ones.

1 Thai speakers find English easier to learn than speakers of Chinese. _F_
Thai speakers find Chinese easier to learn than speakers of English.
2 A foreign language that is difficult for the speakers of one language might be easy for the speakers of another language. ____
3 Basque is related to very few languages. ____
4 It's extremely difficult for adults to learn how to speak click languages. ____
5 Sentinelese is known to be difficult to learn because of the research that has been done on the language. ____
6 Sentinelese is one of the world's least common languages. ____

What is the most difficult language in the world to learn? Everyone has their opinion about it, and very often our opinions are based on the language we speak as a first language. For example, many native speakers of English believe that Chinese is a difficult language to learn. However, speakers of Thai, which is a Chinese-influenced language and also relies on changes in tone to express meaning, do not find Chinese as difficult to grasp. So, without considering one's mother tongue, is it possible to say which languages are the most difficult to learn? Here are three possibilities ...

Basque

Basque is spoken by about 650,000 people in a region that spans Spain and France. Despite using a Roman alphabet, it isn't related to any other language spoken in the world today. This means that no one already speaks a language that is like it, so it is equally difficult for everyone.

African click languages

Click languages, which use a variety of clicking sounds instead of consonants, are spoken in southern and eastern Africa. The clicking sounds are made by sucking in air while the tongue is in contact with the roof of the mouth, and then releasing it quickly. These sounds can change the meaning of a word in the same way that changing the first sound of *big* to a *d* sound creates a different word in English. These languages are especially difficult because it is almost impossible for most people to master the clicking sounds beyond childhood.

Sentinelese

Sentinelese is spoken by a tribe in a remote part of the Andaman Islands, India. This language may well be the most difficult language to learn because no one has been able to live amongst the tribe and record it. The tribe's members never leave the island, preferring to live as their ancestors did thousands of years ago. With only 250 speakers, it is one of the rarest languages in the world.

Where do words come from?

1 Complete the sentences or answer the questions.

1 Something that is *colossal* is very …
   (**a**) big.   **b** loud.   **c** small.

2 If something is *documented*, it is …
   a repeated.   **b** recorded.   **c** forgotten.

3 Something that can be seen or understood is …
   a innovative.   **b** unconventional.   **c** apparent.

4 Something *finite* has …
   a a limit.   **b** no end.   **c** a bad end.

5 What do we call someone's ability to think of clever, inventive ways of doing something?
   a ingenuity   **b** inspiration   **c** innovative

6 If something is *abundant*, it is available in _____ quantities.
   a small   **b** decreasing   **c** large

7 Which verb means to think of a lot of ideas in a group?
   a coin   **b** brainstorm   **c** originate

8 *Inspiration* gives you ideas for doing something …
   a frequently.   **b** new.   **c** again.

9 What do we call a word or expression that refers to a particular subject?
   a function   **b** term   **c** tool

10 Which word is a synonym for *coin*?
   a make   **b** suggest   **c** invent

11 Which verb means *to start or cause to happen*?
   a originate   **b** discover   **c** believe

12 *Unconventional* means something is …
   a unusual.   **b** unique.   **c** useless.

13 If something is *intriguing*, it is …
   a fascinating.   **b** boring.   **c** obvious.

14 Something *innovative* uses _____ methods and ideas.
   a well-known   **b** old-fashioned   **c** new

15 Which word is a synonym for *pass away*?
   a create   **b** invent   **c** die

Collocation

2 Replace the words in bold with the correct form of the words in the box.

care for   ~~coin~~   collect   get   have   search   shut down   switch

1 The word *blog* was **invented** _coined_____ by John Barger in 1997.

2 I'm **exploring** _____ the internet for information about the man who invented the light bulb.

3 We **got** _____ a lot of data from the questionnaires we did with students.

4 Could you **turn** _____ on the light? I can't see.

5 The Americans don't **take** _____ as many holidays as the Europeans.

6 Did you **have** _____ any ideas for a birthday present for Jack when you were shopping?

7 Please **turn off** _____ your computers when you've finished using them.

8 Would you **like** _____ a cup of tea?

Computing words

3 Complete the email with the words in the box.

data-mining   digitally enhanced   malware   phish   podcast   ~~social networking~~   webinar   wiki

Hi Kevin,

I'm doing research into ¹ _social networking_ sites for my project and I've just taken part in a ² _____ on the internet about the dangers of these sites for 'friends'. You can download the ³ _____ of the presentation to your MP3 player. Anyway, a lot of ⁴ _____ takes place on these sites as companies look for the latest trends so they can use them in marketing and advertising. Then there are criminals who ⁵ _____ for people's bank details and things like that by pretending to be trustworthy companies. And of course there is a lot of ⁶ _____ such as viruses that can harm your computer. But apart from all this, you can't even trust some people's photos on these sites because they are sometimes ⁷ _____ to make them look better! If you're interested in learning more there is a ⁸ _____ where you can find and add information on the subject. I'll give you the address when I see you tomorrow.

Best,

Tim

Past tenses for distancing

1 Match the sentences with the people in the box.

airline passengers   car salesman
customers at a travel agent's   employee
hotel receptionist   secretary   shop assistant   ~~waitress~~

1 'Do you want chips with your steak?' _waitress_
2 'I was wondering if we could discuss my salary?'
   _____
3 'We fancy a skiing holiday. What have you got?'
   _____
4 'You can pay for the suit by credit card if you like.'
   _____
5 'How many rooms were you thinking of reserving?'
   _____
6 'I can give you an appointment with Mrs Redman at
   4 pm. Is that OK?' _____
7 'We were hoping to have seats in first class.'
   _____
8 'I was thinking that you might like to take it for a test
   drive.' _____

2 Which sentences from exercise 1 are more formal and
which are more informal? Write *formal* or *informal*.

1 _informal_   4 _____   7 _____
2 _____   5 _____   8 _____
3 _____   6 _____

3 Which sentences use past tenses for distancing and which
use past tenses for talking about the past?

1 'Did you have a good time on the trip?'
   talking about the past
2 'I was wondering if you are applying for any other jobs?'
   _____
3 'We didn't have a reservation so we had to look
   elsewhere.' _____
4 'We wanted to go to that new pizzeria but it was fully
   booked.' _____

5 'Good evening, madam. Did you have a reservation?'
   _____
6 'I wanted to reserve a table for four at 8 pm.'
   _____

4 Read the sentences and organize them into two
conversations: a more formal conversation and a more
informal one.

1 Let me see … yes, we do: smoking or non-smoking?
2 No, I'm sorry. You'll have to hang them on the back of
   your chairs.
3 Yes. Do you have a table for two?
4 Of course, sir. There's a phone by the cloakroom.
5 Certainly, sir. Did you want to leave your coats in the
   cloakroom before sitting?
6 Smoking, please. By the way, is there anywhere to leave
   our shopping bags?
7 Yes, the name's Davidson. We were hoping for a table in
   a non-smoking area.
8 Yes, please. And I was wondering if I can make a phone
   call. I've forgotten my mobile.
9 Good evening. Did you have a reservation?
10 Hello. Can I help you?

Formal conversation: _9_ , ___ , ___ , ___ , ___
Informal conversation: ___ , ___ , ___ , ___ , ___

5 Rewrite the informal sentences using distancing. In some
cases, more than one answer is possible.

1 Have you got a ticket?
   Did you have a ticket?
2 We want to invite you for dinner.
   _____
3 How long do you want to stay?
   _____
4 Is the meeting room available?
   _____
5 Can I see the doctor?
   _____

●●●●● CHALLENGE! ●●●●●

Think of some informal and more formal situations that you
have experienced recently and write what you said.

Excuse me, I was wondering if I could speak to the headmaster.
Mike, can I borrow your notes from yesterday's English class?
_____
_____
_____
_____

Words about words

1 Match the words in the box with the sentences. Use each word twice.

acronym	alliteration	anagram	cliché	simile

1 He's working in Germany, where he teaches EFL.
   acronym

2 William Grossman said, 'the eyes – they see!'
   _____

3 I'm going to leave no stone unturned in my efforts to discover the truth. _____

4 Don't drink the dirty water! _____

5 He's as brave as a lion. _____

6 He's a very down to earth person. _____

7 The NATO headquarters are in New York. _____

8 Astronomers are *moon starers*. _____

9 Dad grumbles like a bear in the mornings. _____

10 Sue's sister is sleeping. _____

2 Match the beginnings (1–8) with the endings (a–h) to form well-known similes.

1 as easy as   a the hills
2 as cold as   b honey
3 as dry as   c the grave
4 as blind as   d a bat
5 as free as   e pie
6 as old as   f ice
7 as silent as   g a bone
8 as sweet as   h a bird

3 Read the text quickly. When was the word *acronym* first used?

4 Are the sentences true or false? Correct the false sentences.

1 Acronyms were used two thousand years ago. _T_

2 Banners with acronyms were easier to carry than banners with full words. ___

3 The word *acronym* dates back to Roman times but wasn't used widely until the 20th century. ___

4 Linguists ignored acronyms even though they were frequently used in everyday conversation. ___

5 A lot of modern acronyms have come about because of scientific advances. ___

6 One reason for the growing popularity of acronyms in society is money. ___

7 Acronyms are still not taken seriously by language experts. ___

8 Some people claim modern acronyms lead to confusion.
   ___

NMAP! (No more acronyms, please!)

Over two thousand years ago, the Romans were led on marches by a soldier carrying a banner that bore the acronym SPQR. These four letters stood for the official Latin name for the Roman Empire, which was Senatus Populus que Romanus. Historians often tell us that the Romans were practical people and on this occasion it would seem that they are right. Carrying a banner that displays four letters across the colossal Roman Empire was obviously a lot easier than carrying one that bore twenty-four.

However, despite this early example of the usage of an acronym, it wasn't until the 20th century that the word acronym was coined. In 1943, David Davies, a scientist in the USA, used acronym to describe a word created from the first letters of a series of words. Apparently, nobody had invented a word to describe this linguistic device until then because it was rarely used and linguists didn't pay any attention to it. However, with the great advances in science and technology of the 20th century, the use of acronyms became more and more frequent. Now, at the beginning of the 21st century, the use of acronyms has reached huge proportions.

Thanks to the advent of communications technology, acronyms have become increasingly popular. The cost of sending text messages can be considerably reduced by using acronyms instead of complete expressions, and the ingenuity of text message users is constantly producing new examples. This in turn has led to the development of a whole new linguistic area where experts debate over whether the abbreviations used on mobile phones are true acronyms or whether they are a mixture of acronyms and other linguistic devices. Whatever conclusion they come to, the proliferation of abbreviated forms in the media has led some people to say it is becoming difficult to understand what is being discussed. And that, as the Romans would no doubt have agreed, is hardly very practical.

●●●●●● CHALLENGE! ●●●●●●

Make a list of five acronyms in English and write out their full meaning.

Acronym	Meaning
1 _____	_____
2 _____	_____
3 _____	_____
4 _____	_____
5 _____	_____

GRAMMAR

Modals for distancing

1 Some of the sentences in these pairs are incorrect. Tick the ones that are correct.

   1 **a** I would think that people use computers too much. ✔

      b I could think that people use computers too much. ☐

   2 **a** Could you tell me what time it is? ☐

      b Could you possibly tell me what time it is? ☐

   3 **a** Would I allowed to interrupt? ☐

      b Might I be allowed to interrupt? ☐

   4 **a** Could you like to see the film? ☐

      b Would you like to see the film? ☐

   5 **a** Could you have time to answer a few questions? ☐

      b Would you have time to answer a few questions? ☐

   6 **a** Would you be interested in coming too? ☐

      b Might you be interested in coming too? ☐

2 Write tentative sentences, questions and requests for the following situations using the words in brackets.

   1 You want to use my mobile phone. (could / use)
      Could I use your mobile phone?

   2 You want to ask me how old I am. (could / possibly / tell)

   3 You want to ask me to stop smoking. (would / ask)

   4 You want to give your opinion that Japanese is very difficult to write. (would / think)

   5 You want to invite me to a conference. (would / come)

   6 You want to ask if I'm interested in going to an art exhibition. (might / be)

   7 You want a cup of coffee. (could / have)

   8 You want to ask me how much I earn. (could / possibly / tell)

3 Complete the sentences with the words in the box.

advise	ask	like	possibly	think	~~would~~

   1 I _would_____ say that communication has many forms.

   2 Might I _____ you to switch off the light?

   3 Could you _____ give me a lift home?

   4 I would _____ that the expression is now a cliché.

   5 Would you _____ to join our chess club?

   6 We would _____ all guests to take their seats as soon as they arrive.

4 Complete the email. Use a different word in each gap.

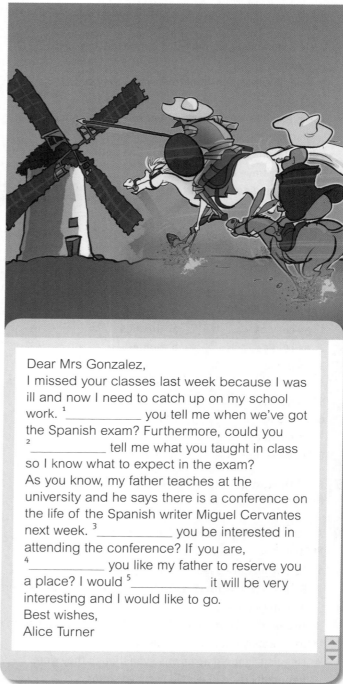

Dear Mrs Gonzalez,

I missed your classes last week because I was ill and now I need to catch up on my school work. ¹_____ you tell me when we've got the Spanish exam? Furthermore, could you ²_____ tell me what you taught in class so I know what to expect in the exam?

As you know, my father teaches at the university and he says there is a conference on the life of the Spanish writer Miguel Cervantes next week. ³_____ you be interested in attending the conference? If you are, ⁴_____ you like my father to reserve you a place? I would ⁵_____ it will be very interesting and I would like to go.

Best wishes,
Alice Turner

●●●●●● **CHALLENGE!** ●●●●●●
Draw three emoticons and explain what they mean.

_____

_____

_____

An opinion essay (1)

Preparation

1 Read the essay. Choose the correct answers.

Learn a foreign language at home before you go abroad

Most people would probably agree that if a person wants to learn a language, the best way to do it is to live in a country where it is spoken. However, although this would seem true, many a young person's linguistic adventure has sadly ended in tears because of bad planning and a lack of patience.

Living abroad can be expensive and ¹**with regard to /** **this means that** anyone who wants to do so for a long enough time to improve their language skills needs money. Most young people in this situation look for work in their new country and this is where problems can begin. ²**Hence / Considering that** most employers will expect their staff to already speak the native language fluently, anybody arriving from abroad with a poor level of the local language has little chance of finding a job. ³**Therefore / Nevertheless**, without the chance of earning any income, the once hopeful language learner has to return home. ⁴**Albeit / Nevertheless**, with careful planning, a trip abroad to learn a language can be a success.

In the first place, it is best to use such a trip to build on the language skills that you've already accumulated rather than to begin a language from scratch. It can be demotivating if you don't understand what is happening around you. However, if you already have a good base, you will soon gain confidence and progress rapidly. ⁵**This means that / Hence** the importance of your language studies at school. By studying the grammar and vocabulary of a language, you are building the foundations that will enable you to become a fluent user. It might be a cliché, but patience is definitely a virtue!

Furthermore, ⁶**with regard to / considering that** financing your trip abroad, try to avoid the need to look for work. All governments offer grants to students who want to study abroad and if you have the chance of obtaining one, ⁷**albeit / therefore** a slim one, apply for it. If that fails, look for organizations that offer exchange trips with students who are interested in learning your language. That way, you'll make friends with people who are interested in your language and culture and that will help you to get know theirs. Where possible, a trip abroad to learn a language should focus on improving language skills and nothing else.

2 Complete the sentences with the words in the box.

> albeit   considering that   ~~hence~~   nevertheless
> therefore   this means that   with regard to

1 I've got some important news to tell you – <u>hence</u> the email.
2 It was a cold, rainy day. _____, more people came than we had expected.
3 He finally agreed to come, _____ unwillingly.
4 _____ the contract, this will be sent to you soon.
5 _____ he's only been studying for a year, he speaks English very well.
6 The new trains have more powerful engines and are _____ faster.
7 I can hear the bell. _____ the lesson has ended.

3 Which linking words in exercise 2 refer to reference, contrast and consequence?

Reference: <u>with regard to</u> , _____
Contrast: _____ , _____
Consequence: _____ , _____ , _____

Writing task

4 Think about the following questions and make notes.

1 Is there a university / language institute that is famous for teaching your language?
2 Is there a city / Are there cities that are popular with people that come to your country to learn your language?
3 Do you know of any good websites for learning your language?
4 Which magazines, newspapers, writers or websites would you recommend to people who want to practise using your language?

5 In your notebook write an opinion essay about the best way to learn your language. Write 200–250 words.

- Explain the method or methods that you think work.
- Say why it's effective. Give examples.
- Describe complementary methods and say why they are effective.
- Write a conclusion.

Check your work

Have you

☐ researched the most popular methods that learners of your language use?
☐ thought of arguments and examples to support your opinion?
☐ organized your material into four paragraphs?

SELF CHECK 2: GRAMMAR

1 Answer the questions.

1 What is the name of the technique that is used to create a polite tone in more formal situations? _____

2 Which two tenses are often used to make questions and requests in more formal situations? _____

3 Which tense is often used with the verb *wonder* to make polite requests? _____

4 Name two other verbs that are often used in the same tense as *wonder*. _____

5 Complete this question so that it has a polite tone: What _____ you want to order, sir?

6 Write three modal verbs that are used to make speech more tentative. _____

7 Write an adverb that is used with *could* to make requests even more polite. _____

8 Which modal verb is used to make statements more tentative and commands less direct? _____

9 Complete the phrase with the modal verb and infinitive that can be used to make the statement *In my opinion*, more tentative: *I* _____

10 Complete this command so that it has a polite tone: We _____ clients not to smoke.

Your score ___ /10

2 Tick the best statement, question or request for each situation. In some cases, both are appropriate.

1 A young person speaking to an elderly person.
  a Excuse me, could you tell me where the bus stop is? ☐
  b Where's the bus stop? ☐

2 A university lecturer talking to her students.
  a Might you be interested in having a coffee break? ☐
  b Do you want to have a coffee break now? ☐

3 A young shop assistant talking to a teenage customer.
  a Do you want to try it on in the changing rooms? ☐
  b Would you like to try it on in the changing rooms? ☐

4 A receptionist talking to a newly arrived client at an expensive hotel.
  a How many days were you thinking of staying for? ☐
  b How long do you want to stay for? ☐

5 A young waiter talking to older clients.
  a Would you like to order? ☐
  b What were you thinking of ordering? ☐

6 A new employee giving their opinion to the head of the department.
  a We should change our marketing strategy. ☐
  b I would think we should change our marketing strategy. ☐

7 Two school friends chatting to each other.
  a What time is it? ☐
  b Could you tell me what time it is? ☐

8 A company secretary speaking to an important visitor.
  a Would you be interested in speaking to the director? ☐
  b Do you want to speak to the director? ☐

9 A mother and father at dinner time.
  a I was hoping you would pass me the salt. ☐
  b Pass me the salt, please. ☐

10 The director of a museum speaking to visitors from a government department.
  a We would ask all visitors to avoid touching the exhibits. ☐
  b Might I request that all visitors avoid touching the exhibits? ☐

Your score ___ /10

3 Use distancing to rewrite the sentences. Use the correct form of the words in brackets.

1 Don't use mobile phones in the cinema. (ask)
_____

2 Is the new book by Jack Thompson available? (hope)
_____

3 Do you want to come shopping with me? (like)
_____

4 Do you have any watches for $30? (wonder)
_____

5 In my opinion, children should wear uniforms to school. (think)
_____

6 Are you interested in seeing the new film? (be)
_____

7 Have you got a ticket for the flight? (did)
_____

8 Can you lend me your bicycle? (possibly)
_____

9 We want to invite you to visit us in Italy. (think)
_____

10 Where's the local hospital? (tell)
_____

Your score ___ /20

Total ___ /40

1 Complete the vocabulary quiz with words from Unit 2.

QUIZ

1 To _____ is a synonym for *to coin*.
2 TEFL is an _____ for Teaching English as a Foreign Language.
3 Which adjective means *more than enough*? _____
4 To _____ is a phrasal verb which means *to die*.
5 Something that has an end is _____.
6 Internet criminals _____ online to try and find people's bank and credit card details.
7 _____ is a synonym for *shut down*.
8 A computer virus is an example of _____.
9 You can often listen to a radio programme again by downloading a _____ of it.
10 A _____ is the use of an expression to compare one thing with another.
11 'Bill buys big bananas' is an example of _____.
12 Something _____ is very interesting because it is unusual or mysterious.
13 A _____ picture has been made to look better with a computer program.
14 Which adjective means *extremely big*? _____
15 _____ is something that gives you ideas to do new things.
16 _____ *on* or *off* has the same meaning as *turn on* or *off*.
17 A phrase or expression that has been used so often that it has lost its effect is called a _____.
18 We decided to _____ some ideas and then looked at a few of them in more detail.
19 There are a lot of computer _____ such as 'file extension' that I don't understand.
20 *Worth* is an _____ of *throw*.

Your score _____ /20

2 Complete the text with the correct form of the words in brackets.

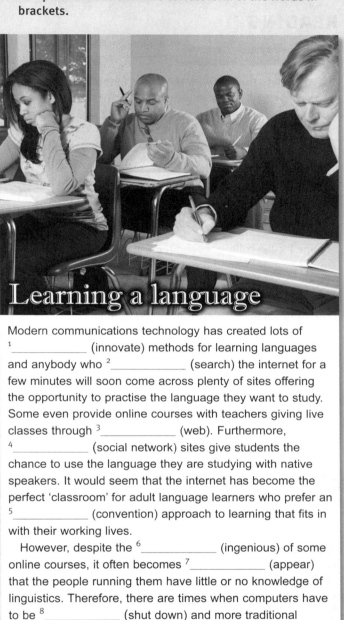

Learning a language

Modern communications technology has created lots of
1 _____ (innovate) methods for learning languages and anybody who 2 _____ (search) the internet for a few minutes will soon come across plenty of sites offering the opportunity to practise the language they want to study. Some even provide online courses with teachers giving live classes through 3 _____ (web). Furthermore, 4 _____ (social network) sites give students the chance to use the language they are studying with native speakers. It would seem that the internet has become the perfect 'classroom' for adult language learners who prefer an 5 _____ (convention) approach to learning that fits in with their working lives.

However, despite the 6 _____ (ingenious) of some online courses, it often becomes 7 _____ (appear) that the people running them have little or no knowledge of linguistics. Therefore, there are times when computers have to be 8 _____ (shut down) and more traditional methods used. Adults who really want to experience the best and most successful language learning methods have to return to the place where they 9 _____ (originate): the classroom. Although they might 10 _____ (not care) for going to class after a long day at the office, technology has yet to find a replacement for one of the most important elements of any successful language course: a good teacher.

Your score _____ /10

Total _____ /30

3 Eureka!

READING

1 Complete the text with the words in the box.

~~device~~ diagram engineer modify patent
potential prototype

In the 1960s, Martin Cooper was watching the science fiction TV series *Star Trek*, when he had a 'Eureka!' moment. One of the TV characters was speaking into a small communication [1] _device_____. Cooper realized the idea had [2] _____, a tiny portable telephone could be a success. The next day he drew a [3] _____ of a mini phone for his colleagues and then they thought about how to [4] _____ and build the small parts it would need. The [5] _____ they made was much bigger than the one on TV and they had to [6] _____ the electronic components because the world's first mobile phone didn't work properly. Finally, Cooper made the first mobile phonecall on 3 April 1973 and a [7] _____ was printed showing that Cooper was the inventor of the mobile phone.

2 Read the text quickly. What two problems does the Aquaduct bicycle solve?

3 Answer the questions.

Which paragraph talks about …
1 an organization taking on a difficult task? _B_
2 the results of a competition? ____
3 the process involved in creating a new device? ____
4 electrically powered devices? ____
5 the ways that water is cleaned? ____
6 finding time to do other things? ____

4 Are the sentences true or false? Correct the false sentences.

1 Most people think devices like the mobile phone and computers have changed our lives. _T_
2 Only 1.1 billion people on the planet have access to clean drinking water. ____
3 The Aquaduct was invented by a company involved in issues that affect the whole planet. ____
4 Collecting and cleaning water has been a time-consuming task until now. ____
5 The water is cleaned when the rider arrives home. ____
6 The Aquaduct won first prize in a race for all types of pedal-powered vehicles. ____

pedal power

A When asked to think about the inventions that have changed our lives the most in the past few years, many people think of inventions related to communications technology, for example, the internet, mobile phones or satellite navigation systems. However, there is one recent invention that has the potential to change the lives of more than a billion people around the world. And it can do this without the aid of a computer, or even electricity.

B Clean and safe drinking water is something most of us take for granted, but for 1.1 billion people living in developing countries, this just isn't the case. An international design company that works to address global issues accepted the challenge to invent a device that would help to end this problem. They came up with Aquaduct – a special bicycle that was engineered to solve two huge water problems in the developing world: transportation and sanitation.

C In some countries, women and children must walk up to seven kilometres a day to collect water. And once they get it home, the water must be boiled. The Aquaduct bicycle solves both of these problems. The bicycle has been designed to carry water, and, as the rider pedals home, the water is cleaned by a special pump that is connected to the bicycle's pedals and wheels. As well as providing clean water, the bicycle also saves time, so more time can be spent on other household chores or schoolwork.

D The Aquaduct was engineered in only three weeks. First, diagrams of the important parts of the device, for example, the pump, water filter and containers were created. Then the designers built a prototype of Aquaduct using an ordinary bicycle, cardboard and tape. After modifying certain aspects of the design based on this prototype, a completed Aquaduct was built.

E The Aquaduct went on to win first prize in a design competition. The competition was open to all pedal-powered vehicles, with the first prize going to an invention that really can change lives.

The origin of inspiration

1 **Complete the sentences or answer the questions.**

1 Something that is *irrelevant* is ...
   (a) unimportant.   **b** significant.   **c** important.

2 If you *take a break*, you ...
   a relax.   **b** work hard.   **c** are ill.

3 Which noun means having a high knowledge of something?
   a density   **b** volume   **c** expertise

4 When something is moved from its original position, it is ...
   a submerged.   **b** displaced.   **c** emerged.

5 If something is *considerably* bigger, it is _____ bigger.
   a a little   **b** hardly any   **c** a lot

6 *Volume* refers to the _____ contained in an object or solid shape.
   a material   **b** space   **c** liquid

7 Which noun refers to a written or spoken report of an event?
   a account   **b** tale   **c** announcement

8 When you are *commissioned* to do something, you are _____ to do it.
   a begged   **b** forced   **c** asked

9 *To craft* something means to make it in a _____ way.
   a bad   **b** skilled   **c** very fast

10 When you are *suspicious* about something, you think something might be ...
   a wrong.   **b** expensive.   **c** fun.

11 Which verb means *to appear by coming out of something*?
   a emerge   **b** exacerbate   **c** submerge

12 The adjective *monumental* is used to say something is ...
   a irrelevant.   **b** important.   **c** creative.

13 _____ refers to the relationship between the mass and size of a substance.
   a Height   **b** Width   **c** Density

14 If you *exacerbate* something, you make it ...
   a worse.   **b** bigger.   **c** better.

15 *To submerge* means to make something go _____ water.
   a through   **b** on   **c** under

Prefixes

2 **Replace the words in bold with the prefixes in the box.**

| anti   auto   mal   semi   ultra |

1 I'm afraid your mobile phone is functioning **incorrectly**. _malfunctioning_

2 He's **against** marriage and he wants to stay single. _____

3 That's a **very** short haircut. You're almost bald! _____

4 No, you don't need to press any buttons to record the programmes. It records them **itself**. _____

5 We're not giving you a permanent contract but it's **nearly** permanent: it's for twenty years. _____

6 He wrote his **own** biography last year and it was a success when it was published. _____

7 It's a great computer but it's **really** expensive. _____

8 It's **not 100%** synthetic. There are some natural materials in it. _____

9 This newspaper is **against** nuclear power and I don't agree with it. _____

10 He was ill so long because of the **bad** treatment he received. _____

Phrasal verbs: *break*

3 **Choose the correct answers.**

1 The burglars broke (into) / **away** the shop through an office window.

2 An epidemic broke **up** / **out** because of the bad quality of the drinking water.

3 He broke **into** / **off** a branch from a tree and used it as a walking stick.

4 His art collection has been broken **down** / **up** and sold off to different buyers.

5 Andy broke **away** / **out** from the main group of runners and led the race to the finish.

6 The train broke **off** / **down** just outside the station.

4 **Complete the sentences with the correct prepositions from exercise 3.**

1 Joe broke _off_ a piece of chocolate for me.

2 The Second World War broke _____ in 1939.

3 Someone broke _____ my car last night and stole an MP3 player I'd left on the back seat.

4 The thief grabbed her bag but she managed to break _____ and look for help.

5 We broke _____ an old wardrobe and used the wood to make a fire.

6 My scooter broke _____ and I had to push it home.

Conditionals without *if*

1 Choose the correct answers.

1 The car can be easily fixed (provided that) / **suppose** you buy the necessary spare parts.

2 **Provided / Supposing** that Mike hadn't brought his map. We would never have found the hotel!

3 **As long as / Imagine that** you add salt, it will taste fine.

4 **On condition that / Imagine that** the battery had run out. We wouldn't have been able to call mountain rescue.

5 You can lend him some money **supposing / on condition** that he pays you back soon.

6 **So long as / Imagine that** the weather stays good, we should have a good day's sailing.

2 Match the beginnings (1–8) with the endings (a–h).

1 Imagine you lost your job. f
2 Provided that it doesn't rain, ___
3 Suppose you decided to sell your bike. ___
4 The money will be returned ___
5 Supposing we hadn't booked the tickets early. ___
6 As long as you've successfully completed the course, ___
7 You'll be able to take part in the marathon ___
8 We'll arrive on time ___

a provided that you are physically fit.
b on condition that you have the receipt.
c We wouldn't have got good seats.
d as long as there are no problems with the trains.
e you'll get a certificate.
f Would you be able to find another one quickly?
g How much would you want for it?
h we'll play tennis.

3 Each sentence contains an extra unnecessary word. Find the words and cross them out.

1 So long as you've ~~been~~ passed your first degree, you can do a master's.
2 Supposing that the wheel hadn't been invented. The world would have be very different now.
3 Imagine that you hadn't passed the course. You wouldn't not be at university now.
4 We'll have the meeting here, so long as that you can reserve the room.
5 Suppose you had been born a hundred years ago. Your life would have to been much harder.
6 Imagine as he hadn't come. We would have been upset.
7 As long as you will leave home on time, you'll catch the train at 6 o'clock.
8 Provided that my teacher doesn't mind, I'll have hand in the project next week.

4 Complete the text with one word or with the correct form of the verbs in brackets. In some cases, more than one answer is possible.

¹Imagine that inventors from Al-Jazari to Karl Benz ²_____ (not develop) the motor engine. The world ³_____ (be) a very different place today. ⁴_____ air, rail or road travel did not exist. If we ⁵_____ (not able) to travel and transport products so easily, the world's economy ⁶_____ (not function) in the way it does. However, in reality, ⁷_____ that you ⁸_____ (live) in a town or city, travelling isn't a problem because of public transport. And as long ⁹_____ a person ¹⁰_____ (have) a driving licence, they can go wherever they want. The motor engine has made the whole world mobile.

●●●●● CHALLENGE! ●●●●●

Think of some imaginary conditions and the effects they would have had on your life. Write three sentences.

Supposing my sister hadn't been born. I wouldn't have had anyone to play with when I was a child.

1 _____
2 _____
3 _____

Think of some necessary conditions and the effects they might have on your life now or in the future. Write three sentences.

Provided that I study hard, I'll be able to do the degree that I want to at university.

4 _____
5 _____
6 _____

Success versus failure

1 Match the words in the box with the definitions.

> aggravate   breakthrough   enable   frustrate   ~~overcome~~
> persevere   setback   struggle

1 to manage to control or defeat something _overcome_
2 to make it possible to do something _____
3 to continue to do something in a determined way, despite continual problems and difficulties _____
4 to try very hard to do something difficult _____
5 to make something worse or more serious _____
6 to cause a person to feel annoyed or impatient because they cannot do or achieve what they want _____
7 an important discovery or development _____
8 a difficulty or problem that stops you progressing as fast as you would like _____

2 Complete the sentences with the correct form of the words from exercise 1.

1 Jack is _struggling_ with his maths homework as usual.
2 The new underground will _____ thousands of people to get to work much more quickly.
3 I've failed a few times but I'm not going to give up. I shall _____ until my dream comes true.
4 The bank's attitude really _____ me. They won't lend me the money I need to expand the business.
5 Doctors are expecting a _____ in the treatment of the illness that will save lots of lives.
6 Ann suffered a _____ when she failed her exams.
7 If you tell him what you really think, you'll just _____ the situation and make things worse.
8 She was frightened of heights but she managed to _____ her fear and became a mountaineer.

3 Read the text quickly. When did the two original inventors carry out their experiments?

4 Match the sentences with the names of the inventors.

1 He decided to reduce something in his invention to make it work better. _Ibn al-Haitham_
2 He risked his life to make experiments. _____
3 He discovered one thing whilst hiding from another. _____
4 He became world famous because of an official document. _____
5 He decided to add something to his invention to make it work better. _____
6 He created something as a result of his work and the work of others. _____

Back to the future

Ask most people who invented the telephone and they'll reply, 'Alexander Graham Bell.' However, investigate a little closer and you'll see that the Scottish inventor was simply the first person to take out a patent for the telephone. There were many other people involved in developing the telephone and they all deserve credit for their contributions. And that is the story of nearly every invention. Here, we look at the origins of just two examples of our 'modern' technology.

The airplane
Although the Wright brothers got all the credit for inventing the airplane after their inaugural flight in 1903, the first recorded flight in history had been made about a thousand years earlier by Abbas ibn Firnas. Abbas ibn Firnas was a poet, astronomer and engineer who designed and built two light wings. He then jumped off a mountain and managed to stay in the air for ten minutes before surviving a crash. After studying his own flight, he realized that a successful flying machine would need a tail as well as wings for it to land properly.

The camera
A thousand years ago mathematician, astronomer and physicist Ibn al-Haitham was sheltering from the hot sun at home in Cairo when he noticed that sunlight was entering his darkened room through a small hole in the window shutters. Ibn al-Haitham suddenly realized that the light passing through the small hole produced an image on the wall of the room. Through experiments, he discovered that the smaller the hole that the light passed through, the better the image and he went on to invent the world's first simple camera.

CHALLENGE!

Think of an invention that you think is useful. Do some research on it and write a brief description of it. Say who is given the credit for inventing it and say if other people also claim to have invented it.

_____
_____
_____
_____
_____

If only...

1 **Complete the rules with the correct tenses or expressions.**

We can use *If only* to talk about situations in the present, past or future.

1 *If only* + _____ talks about the present.

2 *If only* + _____ talks about the past.

3 *If only* + _____ + infinitive talks about the future.

4 When *If only* is used in the first person singular with the verb *be*, we can use _____ instead of _____.

2 **Tick (✓) the two endings which are correct.**

1 If only he …

a is never late. ☐

b would arrive soon. ✓

c had taken his mobile phone. ✓

2 If only my mum and dad …

a hadn't gone on holiday. ☐

b were here. ☐

c like football. ☐

3 If only you …

a will bring my book tomorrow. ☐

b hadn't told everyone my secret. ☐

c studied more. ☐

4 If only Japanese …

a has been taught at school. ☐

b were easier. ☐

c was written differently. ☐

5 If only I …

a were in the school chess team. ☐

b will pass the exam. ☐

c could swim. ☐

3 **Complete the sentences by putting the verbs in brackets in the correct tense.**

1 If only I <u>had remembered</u> (remember) to switch off my computer last night.

2 If only they _____ (be) here now.

3 If only our grandparents _____ (arrive) before the meal starts.

4 If only we _____ (see) his last film.

5 If only the parcel _____ (come) tomorrow morning.

6 If only he _____ (have) the answers with him at this moment.

7 If only he _____ (visit) the doctor earlier.

8 If only Mark _____ (phone) this evening.

4 **Rewrite the sentences using *if only* and the correct tenses.**

1 I haven't got a mobile phone so you can't contact me.
<u>If only I had a mobile phone, you could contact me.</u>

2 I didn't know you were ill so I booked the tickets.
_____

3 He drove very fast so he had an accident.
_____

4 We haven't got any money so we can't go on holiday.
_____

5 I don't live on the coast so I can't go to the beach.
_____

6 They were late so they didn't have anything to eat.
_____

7 I didn't go to the police so I didn't know what to do.
_____

8 I'm frightened of heights so I won't go climbing.
_____

● ● ● ● ● **CHALLENGE!** ● ● ● ● ●

Write three sentences with *if only* about things that you wish were different at the moment.

I wish I had more free time.

1 _____

2 _____

3 _____

Write three sentences with *if only* about things that you wish had been different in the past.

I wish we had won last week's match.

4 _____

5 _____

6 _____

An opinion essay (2)

Preparation

1 Read the essay. What is the writer's main point?

Ahead of their time

¹_____ Perseverance, great intelligence and an incredible desire to experiment are just a few of them. However, the inventors that the world remembers for the wonderful devices that they created also had another thing in common: they were fortunate enough to be in the right place at the right time.

If an inventor is to be successful, ²_____. Apart from possessing the qualities mentioned above, they also need to be living and working in an environment that allows them to develop and practise their skills. Educational opportunities, financial support and the chance to experiment and turn abstract ideas into real devices and machines are essential. Above all, ³_____ if they are born at a moment in history when great changes are taking place in society as a whole.

Thomas Edison, Karl Benz and other well-known inventors of the 19th and 20th centuries all had the good fortune to be born at a time when the industrial revolution was dramatically changing how we created and manufactured technology. ⁴_____. At the end of the 20th and the beginning of the 21st centuries, incredible developments in communications technology have given inventors like Tim Berners-Lee and Martin Cooper the chance to see their ideas become reality. Imagine that they had been born a hundred years earlier. What would have happened to them?

Perhaps they would have committed their ideas to paper in the hope that future generations would one day recognize their genius. That is what happened to two of the greatest minds that the world has ever seen: Al-Jazari and Michelangelo. ⁵_____, but they were still not advanced enough to allow them to put their incredible ideas into practice. They were two of the greatest talents that the world has ever produced, ⁶_____.

2 Complete the article with the clauses and sentences.

a It was a great to time to be alive for an inventor.

b Both of them lived in societies that were socially and technologically advanced

c a lot of factors have to coincide

d Successful inventors share many qualities.

e it helps

f but they were born ahead of their time

3 Look at the clauses and sentences in exercise 2. Decide if they are examples of simple sentences or form part of compound or complex sentences in the exercise 1 text.

Simple sentences: d , ___

Compound sentences: ___ , ___

Complex sentences: ___ , ___

Writing task

4 Do some research on an invention that you think has been very important.

• Find out who invented it and when.

• Find out which inventors helped develop the invention.

• Find some examples of the benefits that this invention has produced.

• Find some examples of the negative effects of not being able to use this invention.

5 In your notebook write an opinion essay about what you think is the best invention ever. Write 200–250 words.

• Explain which invention you think has been the best and why.

• Give examples of how it has been beneficial.

• Give examples of what the situation would be like without this invention.

• Write a conclusion.

Check your work

Have you

☐ done detailed research on an invention?

☐ thought of arguments and examples to show how useful the invention is?

☐ thought of what the world would be like without the invention?

☐ used a variety of simple, compound and complex sentences?

1 **Answer the questions.**

1 Which modal do we use after *if only* to refer to the future? _____

2 *Suppose, supposing (that)* and _____ can replace *if* in sentences that express unreal conditions.

3 *As long as, provided (that)* and _____ can replace *if* in sentences that express conditions.

4 How many sentences do conditionals that begin with *Supposing (that)* require? _____

5 Which tense do we use after *if only* to refer to the past? _____

6 *If only* is often used in independent clauses and what other type of clause? _____

7 Which form of the verb *to be* is used after *if only* to refer to the third person in the present? _____

8 Which word can replace the first *as* in the phrase *as long as*? _____

9 Which tense do we use after *if only* to refer to the present? _____

10 Where in a sentence does a conditional clause beginning with *supposing (that)* appear? _____

Your score ___ **/10**

2 **Tick the best continuation for each sentence. In some cases, both are correct.**

1 If only he had taken the train instead of the bus,
   a he would have arrived in Manchester much earlier. ☐
   b he would arrive in Manchester much earlier. ☐

2 If only I knew Mary's phone number,
   a I would phone her. ☐
   b I phoned her. ☐

3 Imagine that it hadn't rained.
   a We could have gone on the picnic. ☐
   b The festival wouldn't have been cancelled. ☐

4 Suppose he hadn't told you the truth.
   a What would you have said? ☐
   b What would you say? ☐

5 You can take my camera on holiday,
   a supposing that you give it back to me next week. ☐
   b on condition that you give it back to me next week. ☐

6 So long as I work hard,
   a I'll have a chance of passing the exams. ☐
   b I have a chance of passing the exams. ☐

Your score ___ **/6**

3 **There are mistakes in four of the sentences. Find the mistakes and correct them.**

1 Imagine that you hadn't sold your car, we could have gone on a driving holiday.

_____

2 If only that he would to bring the children back soon. It's their bed time!

_____

3 Provided you tell your parents, you'll be welcome to visit us.

_____

4 If only they hadn't gone away, they could come on the trip with us.

_____

5 We'll let you use our flat supposing that you agree to pay all the bills.

_____

6 If only John would let us know when he is arriving.

_____

Your score ___ **/6**

4 **Rewrite the sentences using the prompts.**

1 I'm lonely.
   If only _____

2 If you pick me up, I'll help you to fix your bicycle.
   Provided that _____

3 If Tim Berners-Lee hadn't invented the World Wide Web, the internet wouldn't be so good.
   Imagine that _____

4 If we had caught the bus on time, we wouldn't have bumped into Mike.
   Suppose that _____

5 I left my school bag on the bus.
   If only _____

6 I want my best friend to phone.
   If only _____

7 If I have the receipt, they'll give me a new computer.
   On condition that _____

8 If you don't come to training, you won't be picked for the team.
   So long as _____

Your score ___ **/8**

Total ___ **/40**

SELF CHECK 3: VOCABULARY

1 Complete the vocabulary quiz with words from Unit 3.

QUIZ

1 To *break* _____ a building is to enter by force with the intention of stealing.
2 To _____ means to experience difficulty but to make a great effort to succeed in something.
3 The prefix _____ is used to say that someone does something to or for themselves.
4 If you _____ something, you make it in a skilled way.
5 If you have a _____ task, you have a big job to do.
6 To _____ something means to force it to go under the water.
7 _____ refers to the amount of space in a place or object.
8 When a machine or vehicle stops working, we say it *breaks* _____.
9 The diver _____ from the sea with the treasure in his hands.
10 To _____ something means to move it from its original position.
11 _____ is a synonym for *exacerbate*.
12 He was _____ to paint the king's portrait.
13 The phrasal verb _____ means to break something into smaller pieces.
14 If you have doubts about someone, you are _____ of them.
15 We use *break* _____ to say that something unpleasant starts.
16 The phrasal verb _____ means to escape from the person holding you.
17 When you can't achieve what you want, the situation _____ you.
18 _____ refers to the relationship between a material and its size.
19 The prefix _____ is used to say something is bad or unpleasant.
20 Something _____ is not considered important.

Your score ___ /20

2 Complete the article with the correct words (a–d).

When the American inventor Thomas Edison was asked to explain the reasons for his numerous scientific [1]_____, he replied that it was due to 99% perspiration and 1% inspiration. In other words, he [2]_____ with his investigations until he had [3]_____ all the obstacles and [4]_____ that stood between him and the creation of a new invention. However, although the [5]_____-intelligent inventor obviously knew what he was talking about, there is another quality that has [6]_____ great scientific advances to be made over the centuries: serendipity.

Serendipity refers to lucky chance and without it the world would be a [7]_____ worse place. Just one example shows how useful serendipity can be. According to his own [8]_____, scientist Alexander Fleming left his laboratory without cleaning all his material so he could [9]_____ a well-deserved break. On returning to his lab some days later, he found a strange substance growing in a glass dish which he decided to name penicillin. Penicillin is the basic element of one of the greatest advances in medicine: antibiotics. While nobody doubted Fleming's scientific [10]_____, he hadn't expected to create a medicine that would save millions of lives while he was on holiday. He had come across it by chance!

	a	b	c	d
1	breakouts	breakaways	breakthroughs	breakdowns
2	persevered	submerged	crafted	exacerbated
3	overdone	overgrown	overloaded	overcome
4	left back	setbacks	settings	instructions
5	auto-	ultra-	anti-	semi-
6	enabled	abled	could	been
7	suspiciously	lately	considerably	very
8	announcement	account	history	biography
9	make	give	take	leave
10	expertise	expert	advice	thinking

Your score ___ /10

Total ___ /30

Unit 3 • Eureka! 27

4 It's a must-have!

READING

Before reading: The retail trade

1 Complete the sentences with the correct form of the verbs in the box.

> acquire   ask for   boost   ~~generate~~   maximize
> protect

1 The government _generated_ more revenue last year by increasing taxes on luxury goods.
2 I _____ various electronic products in the sales, including this HD recorder.
3 The TV didn't work so we took back to the shop and _____ a refund.
4 We try to _____ our margins by making more profit on expensive items.
5 In an effort to _____ profits, airlines have started charging passengers for meals and drinks.
6 Supermarkets often make special offers to try and _____ sales and increase profits.

2 Read the text quickly. Why are expensive products placed at eye-level?

3 Choose the correct answers.

1 Why do we enjoy shopping?
   a Because we can meet people of all ages.
   b There are various theories.
   c Because we can't control our behaviour.
2 How do retailers try to influence consumers?
   a They make consumers believe they desperately want things they don't need.
   b They build shopping malls that only have expensive boutiques.
   c They attract consumers to other shops by having a well-known store in the shopping mall.
3 What is the point of labelling products 99p?
   a To make consumers believe they are spending less.
   b To make it easier for shop assistants to calculate prices.
   c To encourage consumers to shop economically.
4 How do shops protect their margins?
   a By placing the most popular goods with customers at eye-level.
   b By placing the goods that make most profit at eye-level.
   c By placing the special offers at eye-level.

THE PSYCHOLOGY OF SHOPPING

Why do people of all ages find a trip to the local shopping mall to be such a favourite pastime? What do we get out of the shopping experience? Is it all about the psychological benefit of acquiring a product or service that we desperately want? Or is it an enjoyable way of killing time? And do the actions of retailers influence consumers' behaviour?

Undoubtedly, the actions of retailers have an impact on consumer behaviour. Almost everyone has experienced buying something that they hadn't planned on buying, or didn't even need. What are the techniques used to influence consumer behaviour?

It is common to locate at least one large popular store in a shopping mall. This store will attract people to the mall, which in turn can boost sales throughout the mall by increasing the number of people who visit other stores, such as expensive boutiques. Many consumers may not intend to buy from a boutique, but if they happen to see something appealing whilst on their way to the larger store, they may buy on impulse.

Once inside a shop, the consumer is exposed to even more techniques that encourage them to buy. First of all is the price. Products are priced at psychologically-sensitive points, for example £29.99 instead of £30. Although the 99p pricing is more demanding for shop staff, retailers prefer to price at just under a significant amount, in this case £30.00. Psychologically speaking, consumers feel that they are spending less, so they are more likely to buy – even though 1p is not much of a saving! Secondly, products with the highest margins are placed at eye-level since it has been documented that consumers are more likely to buy products in their line of sight. This strategic placing helps to maximize the retailer's profit on certain products and protect their profit margin in general.

Although these techniques seem simple, they are powerful. Many retailers rely on them to generate their revenue. Look out for them the next time you visit the shopping mall.

VOCABULARY

Targeting teenagers

1 Complete the sentences or answer the questions.

1 Which adjective means to behave in an embarrassed, uncomfortable way?

   a awkward   **b** persistent   **c** potential

2 An advertisement that uses a famous person is called a / an ...

   a commercial.   **b** technique.   **c** endorsement.

3 *Disposable income* is money that you spend on ...

   a bills.   **b** taxes.

   c what you want.

4 If you *set something* _____, you keep it to use later.

   a aside   **b** up   **c** down

5 If someone is *well off*, they are ...

   a poor.   **b** wealthy.   **c** consumers.

6 Your salary and other income can be referred to as your *earning* ...

   a money.   **b** power.   **c** cash.

7 The adjective _____ describes something that lasts for a long time or happens often.

   a potential   **b** unprecedented   **c** persistent

8 To _____ a product means to promote and plan the way you're going to make it available.

   a quarrel   **b** market   **c** target

9 The adjective _____ talks about the possibilities of the development of something.

   a potential   **b** skilled   **c** very fast

10 Something *unprecedented* has _____ existed in the past.

   a sometimes   **b** always   **c** never

11 When you have a *preference* for something, it means you _____ it more than other things.

   a hate   **b** like   **c** dislike

12 Products are _____ different groups of consumers by shops.

   a given to   **b** targeted at   **c** purchased for

13 *To quarrel* is a synonym for *have a* ...

   a laugh.   **b** chat.   **c** row.

14 If you *have a* _____, you exercise your right to give your opinion on something.

   a say   **b** shout   **c** chat

15 The phrasal verb *leave* _____ means not to include someone or something.

   a off   **b** out   **c** on

Advertising vocabulary

2 Complete the text with the words in the box.

> billboards   hype   jingle   logo   product placement   ~~slogan~~

A good marketing campaign is important for a new product. TV adverts use a catchy [1] slogan that people will remember easily, and the short phrase might be sung to music to create a [2] _____. Furthermore, big street [3] _____ are covered in pictures of the new product. Adverts help people associate the product with the company [4] _____, a symbol which will already be well-known. Multi-national companies also buy space on TV series or films so that through [5] _____ viewers can see the new product in use. There are also unconventional techniques. One low-cost airline said they would charge passengers to use the toilet during flights. It wasn't true but the media [6] _____ that surrounded the story gave the airline a lot of free publicity.

Idioms: marketing

3 Match the words (1–6) and (a–f) to form idioms.

1 to corner   **a** business
2 to drum up   **b** something on the line
3 to think   **c** to scratch
4 not up   **d** pipeline
5 in the   **e** outside the box
6 to put   **f** the market

4 Complete the sentences with the correct idioms from exercise 3.

1 The internet advertising campaign needs to drum up business from teenagers. They are the target market.

2 The last TV commercial was _____ and we need to raise standards.

3 The advertising agency has several new ideas _____ for our designs for next season.

4 They are going _____ fast-food _____ easily as they have very few competitors in this city.

5 Our company is about _____ its reputation _____ with this new model. If it fails, we'll lose a lot of credibility.

6 We need _____ and come up with an unconventional advertising campaign.

GRAMMAR

The passive with preparatory *there*

1 Choose the correct answers.

1 There **are** / **is** thought to be over three thousand shoppers at the mall at this moment.

2 There **was** / **were** believed to be a robbery at the school last night.

3 There **are** / **were** said to be too many people at last week's concert.

4 There **are** / **is** presumed to be more ecological ways of manufacturing products these days.

5 There **are** / **were** felt to be too many unsuitable candidates for the job when they came for the interview.

6 There **is** / **were** reported to be a storm heading in this direction.

7 There **were** / **was** believed to be no need for formal dress at last week's leaving dinner for Jack.

8 There **is** / **are** said to be lots of people interested in the launch of the product.

2 Use the verbs and the words to write sentences in the past simple passive with preparatory *there*.

1 estimate / 24,000 people at the football match
   There were estimated to be 24,000 people at the football match.

2 say / a link between good hotels and an increase in tourism

3 report / thousands of readers waiting for the new book to go on sale

4 say / a disruptive group of students in the school

5 believe / an error in the computer program

6 estimate / a market for the new product

7 think / not enough shop assistants in the store

8 feel / too many inappropriate TV commercials for that time of the evening

3 Complete the news report with the correct present simple and past simple passive forms of the verbs in brackets and preparatory *there*.

… and here is the latest report from the fire at Broadhouse shopping mall. At present, [1] there are thought to be (think) no serious injuries to shoppers or staff at the centre. However, [2]_____ (believe) considerable damage to shops. The fire brigade said the fire started in a restaurant kitchen. [3]_____ (say) an escape of gas in the kitchen. [4]_____ (estimate) about 500 shoppers in the shopping mall at the time the fire started but they were all evacuated quickly. [5]_____ (report) over a hundred firefighters fighting the fire at one stage. [6]_____ (say) a safety investigation team that is deciding at this moment if the mall can be reopened.

4 There are mistakes in five of the sentences. Find the mistakes and correct them.

1 There ~~is~~ believed to be a lot of problems with the marketing campaign. are

2 There were reported to be an accident in the city centre yesterday evening. _____

3 There are believed to be too many questions in last week's exam. _____

4 There is said a better offer at the new computer store. _____

5 There are felt to be a few areas that need working on this week. _____

6 There are estimated to be a world market worth $5 million for these phones. _____

●●●●● CHALLENGE! ●●●●●

Use the passive with preparatory *there* to write a few sentences about some local, national and international news items that you have heard recently.

There was reported to have been a big accident on the motorway last weekend.

_____

_____

_____

Shopping habits

1 Match the words (1–8) and (a–h) to make expressions related to shopping.

1	a good	a	money
2	must-have	b	list
3	cheap	c	item
4	price	d	offers
5	shopping	e	buy
6	shopping	f	spree
7	terrific	g	tag
8	wasteful with	h	deals

2 Complete the sentences with the expressions from exercise 1.

1 The _price tag_ says it costs £9.99.

2 The iPad has become a _____ and everybody wants one.

3 You should always write a _____ before you go to the supermarket.

4 He's so _____. He never saves anything.

5 I went on a _____ on Saturday and bought a suit, shoes and three shirts.

6 There are some _____ at the bookshop. Buy two novels, get one free!

7 There were some _____ at the travel agent's. A week in Italy for only £300 per person.

8 This computer is a really _____ at £350. It comes with loads of programs installed.

3 Read the quiz questions and answer them.

> **Answer the questions to our fun quiz and find out if you're an experienced consumer or just a window shopper.**
>
> 1 Where is your favourite place to meet friends?
>   a The shopping mall   b A café   c The gym
> 2 When you walk into a store, do you …
>   a know the shop assistants' names and never walk out empty-handed?
>   b spend as little time as possible, buying what you need and then leaving?
>   c enjoy browsing even if you don't buy anything?
> 3 Have you ever bought anything that you couldn't afford?
>   a Regularly.   b Once, but you felt guilty about it.
>   c You never buy anything you can't afford.
> 4 What do you buy when you go shopping?
>   a Things that you want.   b Things that you really need.
>   c You just look and rarely buy.
> 5 When you get your pocket money or allowance, how long is it before you spend it all?
>   a A day.   b A few weeks.   c A month.
> 6 How do you feel when you come back empty-handed from a shopping trip?
>   a You've got no idea because it's never happened.
>   b Disappointed if you really needed something but couldn't find it.
>   c Happy, because you've saved your money.

4 Now read what your answers mean.

Mostly a answers
You are definitely a shopping fanatic! Most people enjoy shopping but you should make sure that it doesn't become your only leisure activity. Material things don't actually make us happy. The best things in life, family and friendship, are free!

Mostly b answers
You have a balanced approach to shopping and are a very practical shopper. You know shopping can be fun, especially if you go with friends, but you don't waste your time or money in shops if it isn't necessary.

Mostly c answers
More than a window shopper, you are anti-spending! However, make sure that your dislike of shopping doesn't mean that you always have to be borrowing things from friends; you don't want to be seen as a nuisance!

●●●●● **CHALLENGE!** ●●●●●
Think of two more questions about shopping for the quiz.

_____

_____

Gerunds: perfect, passive and negative

1 Match the beginnings (1–3) with the endings (a–c) to complete the rules.

1	A perfect gerund contains	a	*not* before the present participle.
2	A negative gerund contains	b	the present participle of the verb *be* and the past participle.
3	A passive gerund contains	c	the present participle of the verb *have* and the past participle.

2 Rewrite the sentences using passive gerunds.

1 Kate was shocked at the coach excluding her from the team.
  Kate was shocked at being excluded from the team.

2 The workers are angry about the company sacking them.
  _____

3 My mum and dad were unhappy about the gas company sending them the wrong bill.
  _____

4 We were thrilled about the TV company inviting us to appear on the quiz show.
  _____

5 Andy felt bad about the teacher sending him home for bad behaviour.
  _____

6 He insists on the company paying more for his work.
  _____

7 They were interested in the manufacturer consulting them about their opinions.
  _____

8 Clients are annoyed about staff treating them badly.
  _____

3 Use the perfect gerund form to join the sentences. Use the preposition *about* after all of the adjectives.

1 I was unhappy. I had failed the exam.
  I was unhappy about having failed the exam.

2 We were embarrassed. We had missed the plane.
  _____

3 Alice felt good. She had helped her elderly neighbour.
  _____

4 He was thrilled. He had received a pay increase.
  _____

5 They were angry. They had lost their suitcases.
  _____

6 Mark was disappointed. He had missed the beginning of the film.
  _____

7 They were annoyed. They had made a mistake.
  _____

8 We were pleased. We had won the competition.
  _____

4 Complete the text with the correct gerund forms of the verbs in brackets.

I was happy about [1]*having finished* (finish) my trip to the new shopping mall. It was so full. There were lots of people who were annoyed about [2]_____ (not / allow) to enter some shops. They were packed! Other people were disappointed about [3]_____ (not / give) a table in the mall restaurants because they had too many customers. I was only interested in [4]_____ (show) a new computer at the Techno store. The Techno shop assistants were pleased about [5]_____ (ask) so they could show off their computer skills. However, although I liked their computers, I was sorry for [6]_____ (not / bring) enough money to buy one. I'll have to go back again next week!

●●●●● **CHALLENGE!** ●●●●●

Write five sentences about three things that you have recently done. How do you feel about them?

I was angry about having lost my mobile phone.

1 _____
2 _____
3 _____
4 _____
5 _____

A product description

Preparation

1 Read the essay. What is the practical advantage of a transparent phone?

Invisible phones

Mobile phones, ¹_____, have continued to get smaller and smaller since then. Furthermore, they have developed into wide-ranging communications tools which offer users internet connection, MP3, TV, radio, GPS and the possibility of taking photos and filming and of being photographed and filmed. Mobile phones, ²_____, have become must-have items and if one American manufacturer has its way, they will continue to be so.

Designer Seunghan Song, ³_____, has come up with a prototype for a mobile phone that he hopes will become reality within five to ten years' time. His new phone will be about the size of current phones but a lot thinner. However, that is not the feature that will catch people's attention. What makes Song's phone special is that it is a thin piece of transparent glass that you can see through. Furthermore, the glass changes with the weather. When it's sunny, the glass is clear and when it rains, rain drops appear on it.

However, the design, ⁴_____, also has a practical side. By being made entirely of glass, the whole surface area will be used as a screen and reading emails and looking at photos and videos will put less of a strain on the eyes. Of course, there is one potential problem with a transparent phone. When the battery runs out, will you be able to find it?

2 Rewrite the relative clauses as appositive phrases and then match them with the spaces (1–4) in exercise 1.

  a who is from Japan

  b which are owned by 68% of the world's population

  c which is being tested at the moment

  d which were first available in 1973

3 Choose the correct answers. In some cases, both options are correct.

  1 Martin Cooper, **who a telecommunications engineer, / a telecommunications engineer,** invented the mobile phone.

  2 Information Technology, **which has changed the way we work / the way we work,** doesn't always function well.

  3 The advertising campaign, **which will include product placement / product placement,** will be extremely expensive.

  4 The shopping mall, **open next week / which will be open next week,** will have car parking space for 2,000 vehicles.

  5 Andy, **who studies electronic engineering / electronic engineering,** loves shopping.

  6 This new camera, **which is the latest model / the latest model,** chooses the best image for you.

Writing task

4 Think of a product that you often use and make notes on the following:

- the things it is used for.
- how popular it is.
- how it has changed over time: the design, the size, the features it offers, etc.
- how it might change in the future.

5 In your notebook write a product description. Write 200–250 words.

- Explain how it is used and how popular it is.
- Describe its features and mention how they have improved over time.
- Describe possible future developments of the product.

Check your work

Have you

☐ done some research on the product?

☐ covered all the points in the plan?

☐ used a variety of longer sentences with relative clauses and shorter sentences with appositive phrases?

SELF CHECK 4: GRAMMAR

1 Answer the questions.

1 Write three verbs that are often used with the passive with preparatory *there*. _____

2 Which gerund form contains the present participle of the verb *have* and the past participle? _____

3 What is the passive with preparatory *there* used to make? _____

4 What are gerunds often used after? _____

5 What does the word *there* act as in a sentence formed by the passive and preparatory *there*? _____

6 Which gerund form contains the present participle of the verb *be* and the past participle? _____

7 What must the passive verb agree with in a sentence with the passive with preparatory *there*? _____

8 What is it not possible to use in a negative gerund? _____

9 Which gerund form contains *not* before the present participle? _____

10 What structures come after the past participle in a sentence formed by the passive and preparatory *there*? _____

Your score ___ /10

2 Rewrite the sentences using the passive with preparatory *there*.

1 It is thought that there are too many advertisements aimed at children.
_____

2 It was said that there were more than a thousand students at the school last year.
_____

3 It was reported that there was an increase in tourism in the city.
_____

4 It is felt that there is too much pollution from cars in the city centre.
_____

5 It is estimated that there are millions of online shoppers around the world.
_____

Your score ___ /10

3 Complete the text with the correct passive with preparatory *there* and gerund forms of the verbs in brackets.

¹_____ (report) about five hundred local people at yesterday's meeting. The leader of the local residents, Ray Smith, said he was pleased about ²_____ (have) the chance to explain why his organization is against plans for a new shopping mall. At present, ³_____ (say) plans to build the mall on the local park. However, Smith said he was annoyed at ⁴_____ (not / give) a copy of these plans before the meeting but he was happy about ⁵_____ (meet) local councillor Mary Townsend. Townsend, speaking afterwards, said ⁶_____ (believe) an opportunity to maintain the park and build a shopping mall as well. Townsend also said ⁷_____ (think) many residents who would welcome new shopping facilities in the area. Smith said he was disappointed about ⁸_____ (not / tell) about Townsend's views before meeting her. Smith says he isn't aware of ⁹_____ (be) in contact with any local residents who want the mall. However, ¹⁰_____ (think) a majority of councillors who are now in favour of the mall and Mr Smith's group will have a hard time stopping it.

Your score ___ /10

4 Choose the best continuation for each sentence. In some cases, both are correct.

1 There were thought to be
   a a possibility of selling the computer at a discount price. ☐
   b various ideas for a new type of computer. ☐
2 We were angry about
   a having had to wait for a table for so long. ☐
   b being given a parking fine. ☐
3 They said the film was terrible and Sara was pleased about
   a not being invited to see it. ☐
   b having not seen it. ☐
4 There are said to be
   a a large amount of treasure at the bottom of the ocean. ☐
   b lots of artefacts and jewels on board the ship. ☐
5 There was reported to be
   a a group of soldiers moving towards the capital. ☐
   b a lot of fighting around the royal palace. ☐

Your score ___ /10

Total ___ /40

1 Complete the vocabulary quiz with words from Unit 4.

QUIZ

1 The phrasal verb *leave* _____ means not to include something.

2 If you are _____ *off* you have plenty of money.

3 Somebody who walks in an _____ way has an unattractive style of moving.

4 If you _____ *the market*, you have few or no competitors.

5 A _____ is a big advertisement that is put up on the sides of buildings and alongside roads.

6 A _____ is a symbol used by a company on its products.

7 *Price* _____ are the labels that are put on items for sale in a shop.

8 A _____ item is something that you really want, although you might not need it.

9 A _____ is something everyone should write before they go shopping.

10 To _____ *something aside* means to leave it to be used later, perhaps for a special purpose.

11 The adjective _____ refers to something that lasts a long time and doesn't go away.

12 Shops use advertising to _____ *up business*.

13 If something is planned to happen soon, you can say it's *in the* _____.

14 Your _____ *income* is the money you have left over after paying for food, bills, etc.

15 If something *is not up to* _____, it isn't at an acceptable level.

16 If you go on a *shopping* _____, you spend some time visiting and buying from shops.

17 A _____ is a short, easily remembered phrase that is used in an advertisement.

18 Someone who is _____ *with money* doesn't use their money carefully.

19 *Product* _____ involves putting products in TV programmes and films.

20 *Arguing* is a synonym for _____.

Your score ___ /20

2 Complete the article with the correct words (a–d).

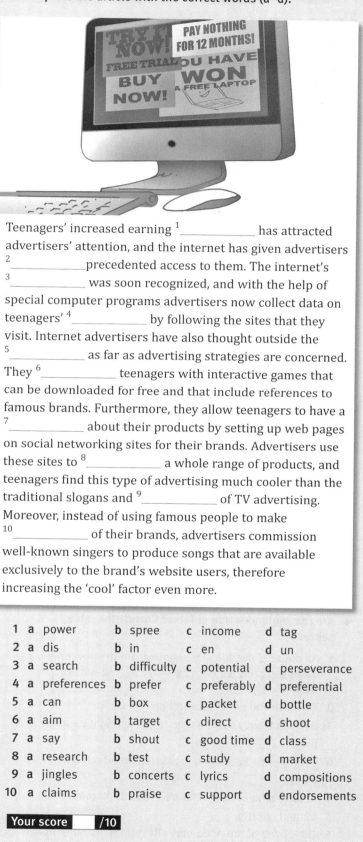

Teenagers' increased earning [1]_____ has attracted advertisers' attention, and the internet has given advertisers [2]_____precedented access to them. The internet's [3]_____ was soon recognized, and with the help of special computer programs advertisers now collect data on teenagers' [4]_____ by following the sites that they visit. Internet advertisers have also thought outside the [5]_____ as far as advertising strategies are concerned. They [6]_____ teenagers with interactive games that can be downloaded for free and that include references to famous brands. Furthermore, they allow teenagers to have a [7]_____ about their products by setting up web pages on social networking sites for their brands. Advertisers use these sites to [8]_____ a whole range of products, and teenagers find this type of advertising much cooler than the traditional slogans and [9]_____ of TV advertising. Moreover, instead of using famous people to make [10]_____ of their brands, advertisers commission well-known singers to produce songs that are available exclusively to the brand's website users, therefore increasing the 'cool' factor even more.

1 a power b spree c income d tag
2 a dis b in c en d un
3 a search b difficulty c potential d perseverance
4 a preferences b prefer c preferably d preferential
5 a can b box c packet d bottle
6 a aim b target c direct d shoot
7 a say b shout c good time d class
8 a research b test c study d market
9 a jingles b concerts c lyrics d compositions
10 a claims b praise c support d endorsements

Your score ___ /10

Total ___ /30

5 You're cured!

READING

Before reading: Medicine

1 Complete the sentences with the correct noun form of the verbs in the box.

> affect   medicate   prescribe   proceed   ~~recover~~
> research   try

1 He made a very quick _recovery_ from the operation and was soon back at work.
2 They're doing clinical _____ of the drug on animals before they use it on patients.
3 She has responded well to the _____ and it seems that she's finally getting better.
4 When we left the doctor's we immediately took the _____ to the chemist's to get the tablets.
5 Medical _____ and tests have shown that the state of our minds can have an influence on our health.
6 I took a tablet for my headache but it hasn't had any _____. In fact, it's worse.
7 He was disciplined because he didn't follow the standard safety _____.

2 Read the text quickly. What medical problem did Belinda Dewey have?

3 Choose the best title for the text.

a The end of drugs
b It's just your imagination
c Mind over matter
d Changing the way patients think

4 Are the sentences true or false? Correct the false sentences.

1 All patients in clinical trials are given the new drugs. _F_
   Half the patients are given the new drugs and half are given a
   placebo.
2 The 'placebo effect' doesn't always work. ____
3 Belinda Dewey had no idea that she might be given a placebo. ____
4 Belinda Dewey's blood pressure was affected by the placebo. ____
5 Research has shown that placebos don't really make patients better. ____
6 The power of the mind may affect patients more than was originally thought. ____

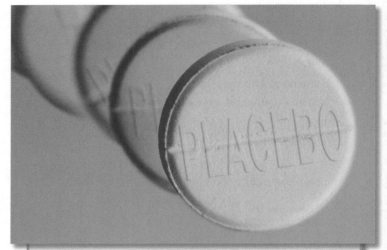

All new drugs and medicines brought out by pharmaceutical companies have to undergo very rigorous testing procedures before they are available at the chemist's. Part of the procedure includes clinical trials where new drugs are tested on patients to find out if they are effective or not. During these trials, half the patients are given the actual medicine and the other half are given a placebo – in other words, a pill that doesn't contain any medicine at all. What is interesting is the fact that placebos can have the same effect as a normal drug in curing a patient. This phenomenon is called the 'placebo effect'.

Belinda Dewey took part in a clinical trial for a new drug to control blood pressure. Although she was told that she might be getting a placebo, the 30-year-old firmly believed that she was getting the real medicine. Just a few weeks into the clinical trial, Dewey's blood pressure began to drop, and her headaches related to her blood pressure got better.

So when Dewey learnt she had in fact been taking a placebo all along, it was a surprise. She knew that she may have been given a placebo, but she thought that there was a greater chance that she'd be given the real drug. At the end of the trial, she felt confused. She felt that the pill had worked, but it shouldn't have.

Belinda Dewey is not unusual. For years, scientists have observed that some patients did respond to placebos in place of real medicine, and they thought this placebo effect was just the result of the patients' imaginations. Although a patient's blood pressure was better, this patient wasn't actually better. Or so scientists thought.

Now, using medical scanners to look into the brains of patients who respond to placebos, researchers have discovered that the placebo effect is not just in patients' imaginations. New research shows that belief in a placebo treatment actually leads to changes in brain chemistry. Now researchers are taking more seriously the power of the mind and thought to affect the brain in a chemical way.

The healing power of plants

1 Complete the sentences or answer the questions.

1 Something that can cause death is …
   a lethal. **b** effective. **c** wild.

2 A measured amount of medicine is called a …
   a patent. **b** crush. **c** dose.

3 A *patent* gives you the exclusive right to sell a new _____ or product.
   a plant **b** invention **c** substance

4 If a substance *relieves* an unpleasant feeling, you feel …
   a sick. **b** worse. **c** better.

5 *Trial and* _____ is when you do different tests until you find the right way of doing something.
   a error **b** mistake **c** upset

6 When something *abates*, it becomes less …
   a important. **b** strong. **c** loud.

7 When something is poisoned, it is …
   a tolerated. **b** neutralized. **c** contaminated.

8 To _____ means to reduce something in size or in importance.
   a extract **b** diminish **c** remedy

9 A noblewoman is a member of the …
   a upper class. **b** working class. **c** military.

10 If you have a *swelling*, a part of your body becomes …
   a bigger. **b** smaller. **c** hot.

11 A _____ is a successful way of curing an illness or disease.
   a bark **b** remedy **c** legend

12 An *extract* is a _____ taken from a plant, flower, etc.
   a fruit **b** leaf **c** substance

13 When you *crush* something, you _____ it very hard.
   a stroke **b** press **c** massage

14 If you *neutralize* something, you _____ its effect.
   a permit **b** stop **c** increase

15 If your body _____ a drug, it is not affected badly by it.
   a tolerates **b** rejects **c** refuses

Word formation

2 Write the noun forms of the following verbs.

1 contaminate   contamination
2 cure   _____
3 extract   _____
4 neutralize   _____
5 patent   _____
6 relieve   _____
7 tolerate   _____
8 treat   _____

The body and medical conditions

3 Are the sentences true or false? Correct the false sentences.

1 The ~~brain~~ is a small tube-shaped part near your stomach. In humans, it has no real function. F
   (the appendix)

2 The pancreas is near the stomach and produces insulin in addition to helping your body deal with the food you eat. ____

3 A lung is one of the two parts of your body that separate waste liquid from your blood. ____

4 The spleen is a small organ near your stomach that controls the quality of the blood in your body. ____

5 The liver is the organ inside your chest that sends blood round your body. ____

6 A kidney is one of a pair of organs in your body that are inside your chest and are used for breathing. ____

7 The appendix is the part of your body that cleans your blood. ____

8 The stomach is where food goes after you have eaten it. ____

9 The heart controls your thoughts, feelings, memories and movements. ____

4 Complete the table with some of the parts of the body from exercise 3.

Name of illness	Part of the body affected
1 amnesisa	_____
2 asthma	_____
3 cramps	_____
4 diabetes	_____
5 stroke	_____
6 tuberculosis	_____
7 ulcer	_____

GRAMMAR

Preparatory *it* as subject

1 Complete the sentences with *how*, *that*, *where*, *who* and *to*. In some cases, more than one word is possible.

1 It was great <u>to</u> meet them last night.
2 It's a pity _____ miss the match.
3 It's amazing _____ many people have caught the flu.
4 It's interesting _____ none of the other patients suffered side effects.
5 It's clear _____ he gets his intelligence from.
6 It isn't surprising _____ they didn't arrive on time.
7 It is not known _____ the disease originated.
8 It's sad _____ hear that Jack isn't feeling well.

2 Match the sentence beginnings (1–8) with the endings (a–h) to make sentences.

1 If you don't want to get lost, it's important ___
2 Mr Houchen? I'm Dave Bennett. It's nice ___
3 If you haven't got a ticket, it's advisable ___
4 When we've got exams, it's essential ___
5 Kate really likes French and it's incredible ___
6 The team has been playing really well so it's amazing ___
7 Before you go to the airport it's important ___
8 Looking at the GPS it isn't clear ___

a where the hotel is.
b that they lost 5–0.
c that we have enough time to study.
d to book a seat quickly.
e to meet you!
f that you follow the route that I've marked on the map.
g to see how quickly she has learnt to speak it.
h to check that you've got your passport.

3 Complete the text with preparatory *it* followed by the adjective in brackets and a clause or infinitive form.

¹<u>It's clear that</u> (clear) today's young people like to play electronic games, but ²_____ (obvious) they don't help you burn calories. Actually, ³_____ (important) realize that you put on weight when you watch TV and play computer games. How? Well, studies have shown that ⁴_____ (common) eat snacks while you do these things. When you don't move much ⁵_____ (normal) your body feels bored and wants to do something and eating is better than nothing! So ⁶_____ (essential) switch off your TVs and computers and do some exercise for a least an hour a day. After a few weeks you'll think that ⁷_____ (amazing) you never did any sport before. Furthermore, for many people ⁸_____ (surprising) discover that being in good physical shape also makes them mentally fitter and they're able to play electronic games even better!

4 Rewrite the sentences beginning with preparatory *it*.

1 That Dr Smith is going to do the operation is good news.
   <u>It's good news that Dr Smith is going to do the operation.</u>
2 To be in hospital for a long time is very stressful.
   _____
3 That she has been accepted at university is fantastic.
   _____
4 Where the accident happened wasn't very clear.
   _____
5 That he doesn't feel well after taking the tablet is surprising.
   _____
6 That she didn't break a leg when she fell was very lucky.
   _____
7 To be waiting so long is really annoying.
   _____
8 Where he left his briefcase is a mystery.
   _____

● ● ● ● ● **CHALLENGE!** ● ● ● ● ●

Write some advice for people that are about to take up a fitness programme or a sports activity.

It's essential to receive proper training if you're going to start an activity that you've never done before.

_____
_____
_____

Sensations

1 Complete the sentences with the words in the box.

> aromatic bitter clammy ~~deafening~~ mouth-watering
> scorching slimy

1 Could you turn down the radio? It's _deafening_ !
2 My grandmother always prepares us _____ meals.
3 You should use _____ oils on your face. They rehydrate your skin and make you smell nice.
4 There was just a little water in the swimming pool and the sides were covered in a _____ substance that smelt disgusting.
5 It was so _____ on the beach that we had to spend all the time in the water.
6 This coffee is _____. Could you pass me the sugar?
7 I had to dry my hand after greeting the boss. His hands were really _____.

2 Complete the text with the words in the box.

> butterflies lightheaded queasy sniffles ~~weather~~

My brother Mark says he feels a bit under the ¹_weather_ but I don't think he's ill. I'm sure he's got ²_____ in his stomach because he's nervous about tomorrow's exam. He said he was feeling ³_____ after lunch but I was with him and he ate far too much – that's why he felt sick! Admittedly, he has got the ⁴_____, but everybody gets a cold at this time of year. No, I know my brother. When he had his last exam he said the same things; he even felt ⁵_____ and nearly fell over as he walked into the classroom! But I don't know why he worries so much, because he always passes!

3 Read the article and match the headings (1–4) with the paragraphs (A–D).

1 I eat therefore I think
2 Real brain training
3 Jog to exam success
4 Don't bottle it up

4 Are the sentences true or false? Correct the false ones.

1 Students who do physical exercise can increase their learning capacity. T
2 Fatty foods improve our levels of concentration. ___
3 Missing out meals can affect your ability to retain information. ___
4 People's ability to learn and remember suffers at some stage in their lives. ___
5 Sport is as good as chatting to people when trying to overcome stress. ___
6 Studying foreign languages and musical instruments is a real challenge for our brains. ___

If you haven't got the time or the money to spend on expensive therapies and spas, we've got some tips that will help you get the most important part of your body fit easily and cheaply: your brain. To find out how, read on!

A ___
When the Roman poet Juvenal wrote of the benefits of a healthy mind in a healthy body, he identified one of the secrets of improving mental health: physical exercise is just as beneficial for the brain as it is for the body. Medical research has shown that walking fast for thirty minutes three times a week improves a person's learning abilities by 15%! What's more, students who exercise three or four times a week frequently achieve better exam results.

B ___
For the brain to function well it needs to be fed regularly, but it's very fussy about what it eats. Given that 60% of the brain is already made of fat, that's not surprising! Studies have demonstrated that students who regularly eat fatty food products have the same levels of concentration and creativity as a 70-year-old person! However, that doesn't mean you should cut out meals; students who don't eat breakfast forget information much more quickly than students who do. A balanced diet that includes salads, fruit, eggs and fish is what the brain craves most of all.

C ___
Everybody suffers stress at different periods of their lives and when they do, their learning and memory suffers. Stress affects the hippocampus, the part of the brain that controls the ability to study things and remember them. Although physical exercise can help, the best cure against stress is confiding in family and friends. As the saying goes, a problem shared is a problem halved!

D ___
Electronic gadgets that promise to improve the capacity and skills of the brain have been fashionable for a number of years now, but they are no substitute for real brain work. Without doubt, the two activities that most activate the brain are language learning and learning to play a musical instrument. Scientists have discovered that your brain physically grows when it works in two languages and that children who learn to play a musical instrument do much better in their studies. So what are you waiting for? Pick up a guitar and start singing in English!

> ●●●●●● **CHALLENGE!** ●●●●●●
>
> **Think of three more things that you can do to improve the performance of your brain.**
>
> A good night's sleep is essential for the brain to work properly the next day.
> 1 _____
> 2 _____
> 3 _____

Preparatory *it* as object

1 Decide which sentence in each pair is correct.

1 **a** We felt that obvious that he was not interested. ☐
   b We felt it obvious that he was not interested. ☐
2 **a** His illness made it a problem for him to take part. ☐
   b His illness made a problem for him to take part. ☐
3 **a** We found that unnecessary to phone in advance. ☐
   b We found it unnecessary to phone in advance. ☐
4 **a** She considered it strange to he had never heard of the technique. ☐
   b She considered it strange that he had never heard of the technique. ☐
5 **a** They believe it unlikely that he will be accepted. ☐
   b They believe it unlikely he will be accepted. ☐

2 Complete the sentences with the words in the box.

> clear   a compliment   difficult   ~~a pleasure~~   a problem
> sad   to the reader   a waste of time

1 My mum considers it _a pleasure_ to cook. She loves it.
2 They didn't consider it _____ that I can't drive and they gave me the job.
3 As they always lose, some players think it _____ to go to training.
4 I found it _____ to concentrate with all the noise, and I took a break until it stopped.
5 We leave it _____ to decide how the story should end.
6 I consider it _____ that I've been offered a pay rise. My boss must be happy with my work.
7 He made it _____ that you had to take the medicine three times a day.
8 She thought it _____ that he didn't have any friends and said he'd be happier if he joined a club.

3 Answer the questions. Use *that* or *to* and the words in brackets.

1 What did you consider interesting? (hear what he had to say)
   I considered it interesting to hear what he had to say.
2 What does Andy find hard? (sit down and study)
   _____
3 What did the bad instructions make difficult? (understand how to use the new computer)
   _____
4 What did the doctor make clear? (Dad would have to stop smoking)
   _____

5 What do his parents find hard to understand? (he could have behaved like that)
   _____
6 What did we think strange? (he hadn't replied to our email)
   _____
7 What did the doctor consider essential? (he was operated on)
   _____
8 What does he consider an honour? (receive the prize on behalf of the whole team)
   _____

4 Complete the text with the correct preparatory *it* as object structures using the words in brackets.

When I went to see the doctor yesterday, he [1] _thought it necessary for me to see_ (think / necessary / for me / see) a specialist about my leg. He had [2] _____ (make / clear / I) shouldn't do any exercise for six months after breaking it, but I always [3] _____ (find / hard / not play) football with my friends at school. However, the doctor [4] _____ (feel / probable / I) 've damaged the bone by returning to sport too soon. Now my parents [5] _____ (find / incredible / I) didn't listen to the doctor's advice; they [6] _____ (consider / necessary / punish) me by not letting me see my friends. I wish I had been able to resist kicking the ball around!

●●●●● **CHALLENGE!** ●●●●●

Write five pieces of advice that doctors give patients when they are recovering from an illness. Make sure that you write sentences with *to* and *that*.

It's essential that you drink plenty of liquids.

1 _____
2 _____
3 _____
4 _____
5 _____

A blog

Preparation

1 Read the blog. What effects did the thermal baths have on the writer?

Relaxing in Budapest – a pleasant surprise!

by Brian West

23 October 2010

We're just finishing another part of our tour of European capitals and we're heading for Vienna in Austria tomorrow. Until now, we've been in the capital of Hungary, Budapest. We arrived there after a tiring journey and although Budapest is one of Europe's ¹jewels_____, we were as dead as ²_____ and didn't feel like sightseeing at all. However, we discovered that the hotel we were staying at for four days had the perfect cure for our tired bodies: thermal baths.

Actually, my dad had intentionally booked this hotel because he knew our bodies would be in ³_____ at this stage of the journey. And he couldn't have chosen better! The Gellért Hotel is next to some thermal baths and after a morning session there we headed off to see the city feeling as right as ⁴_____! In fact my mum and sister would have been happy to stay there all day! There were different baths for men and women but all of them were ⁵_____. The walls were decorated beautifully and the whole building had been recently renovated. The water in the pools was boiling hot and I loved just floating, half asleep. However, my dad wouldn't let me do that for very long and he made me jump into a pool, appropriately called the Finnish pool, which was as cold as ⁶_____! That certainly freshened me up! Anyway, we did the same every morning and we were ready for hours of sightseeing after that.

Now on to Vienna: famous for hot chocolate and cakes, which I'm looking forward to although it won't be so healthy for the body! Having said that, if anybody knows of a good café to recommend, leave a comment!

2 Complete the text with the words in the box.

> works of art   doornails   ice   ~~jewels~~   need of repair
> rain

3 Which words in exercise 2 are used to form metaphors and which are used to form similes?

similes: _doornails_____, _____, _____

metaphors: _____, _____, _____

4 Match the similes (1–6) and metaphors (a–f) that have similar meanings.

1 He was as silent as the grave.
2 I'm as happy as a lark.
3 We are as mad as hatters to go out in this weather.
4 The children were as hungry as bears.
5 The meeting was as dull as ditchwater.
6 The exam was as easy as pie.

a He wolfed his food down in five minutes.
b The match was a walkover.
c The film was a big yawn.
d She's a ray of sunshine.
e I asked his opinion but the silence was deafening.
f They were off their heads to drive at that time of night.

Writing task

5 Think of a place where visitors to your city could relax.

- Is it a public or private place?
- What services does it offer?
- Where is it?
- How long do people usually stay there for?

6 Imagine you are a visitor to your own town. In your notebook describe your experience there in a blog. Describe a place where visitors could relax and take time off from visiting the town. Write 200–250 words.

- Describe the place.
- Describe what you do there.
- Talk about how it makes you feel.
- Write a conclusion.

Check your work

Have you

☐ thought about where visitors usually stay in your town?

☐ thought about places where people go to relax in your town?

☐ covered all the points in the plan?

☐ used a number of similes and metaphors to make your descriptions more interesting?

SELF CHECK 5: GRAMMAR

1 Answer the questions.

1 Where do we normally put longer and more complex structures in a sentence? _____

2 What directly follows preparatory *it* as subject and the verb *be*? _____

3 What type of preparatory *it* is not followed by the verb *be*: object or subject? _____

4 Which adjectives are frequently used with *make* in sentences with preparatory *it* as object: *easier* and _____ ?

5 Complete the sentence: It was interesting _____ he wanted to explain his ideas.

6 What type of preparatory *it* is not used when the subject is a noun phrase: object or subject? _____

7 We can use clauses or _____ with preparatory *it*.

8 Which adjectives are frequently used with *find* in sentences with preparatory *it* as object: *hard*, *unnecessary* and _____ ?

9 Complete the sentence: She found it hard _____ forgive him.

10 An adjective or a _____ directly follow preparatory *it* as object.

`Your score` ☐ `/10`

2 Choose the correct alternative for each sentence. In some cases, both are correct.

1 Our teacher made it clear **that we have to work harder / to work harder**.

2 It's advisable **to get up early / that we get up early**.

3 It was unusual **that the bus arrived so late / to arrive late the bus**.

4 The clear instructions made it easy **to use the digital camera / that the digital camera**.

5 We considered it interesting **to hear what they had to say / he explained the situation**.

6 Jane finds it hard **when she has exams / to study for exams**.

7 It is necessary **leaves the bandage on / to leave the bandage on**.

8 I find it difficult **to believe the results / that believe the results**.

9 It's amazing **that feels so well again / that she feels so well again**.

10 He made it clear **that to take your exam results with you / that you had to take your exam results with you**.

`Your score` ☐ `/10`

3 There are mistakes in eight of the sentences. Find the mistakes and correct them.

1 He made it clear to he was annoyed.

_____

2 It surprising that they shouldn't have received your message.

_____

3 He found it a problem that speak in German at the meeting.

_____

4 It is easy to learn Italian if you already speak Spanish.

_____

5 Many experts it find difficult to accept when they make a mistake.

_____

6 Is essential to tell the truth at all times.

_____

7 The doctor thought his business to ask the patients about their exercise habits.

_____

8 It will be good idea to get there early.

_____

9 He considers it a pity not to visit all the museums in the city.

_____

10 My friends considered me strange that I don't want a mobile phone.

_____

`Your score` ☐ `/10`

4 Write sentences with preparatory *it* as subject and preparatory *it* as object.

1 very unusual / be / at school / at this time

_____

2 not / very clear / we had to arrive before 4 o'clock

_____

3 the doctor / believe / necessary / I go on a diet from tomorrow

_____

4 the nurse / make / clear / Mum had to work less

_____

5 I think / surprising / Mike hasn't called back

_____

`Your score` ☐ `/10`

`Total` ☐ `/40`

1 Complete the quiz questions with words from Unit 5.

QUIZ

1 If you feel _____, it means you feel dizzy.

2 The _____ pumps blood around your body.

3 If something is _____, you can't hear anything.

4 A _____ is a female member of a high social rank.

5 To _____ means to make something poisonous.

6 The noun of the verb *to patent* is _____.

7 A nervous person says they have got _____ in their stomach.

8 A _____ is a measure of medicine.

9 If a part of your body gets bigger, we say you've got a _____.

10 When your body doesn't produce enough insulin, you've got _____.

11 The adjective *aromatic* means something _____ nice.

12 Your spleen produces and cleans your _____.

13 If someone's hands are sweaty and cold, we say they are _____.

14 If something is *mouth-watering*, you want to _____ it.

15 The opposite of sweet is _____.

16 The adjective *scorching* means something is very _____.

17 Your _____ take away waste liquid from your blood.

18 To _____ something means to take it out.

19 Without your _____ you couldn't breathe.

20 You think with your _____.

Your score [ ] /20

2 Complete the article with the correct words (a–d).

Natural healing

Before the arrival of the modern medical service, people often relied on 'old wives' tales'. These were ancient [1]_____ that modern science has demonstrated to be mostly false. This wasn't really important if you were just feeling [2]_____ the weather, but if you were really ill, the [3]_____ suggested by a neighbour to [4]_____ pain could be [5]_____.

People today are wary of old wives' tales but they are attracted to another form of medicine that some doctors think is almost as bad: alternative medicine. Alternative medicine [6]_____ the 'whole person', not just the illness. So if somebody has [7]_____ in the stomach, alternative medicine looks at a person's body, mind and lifestyle in an attempt to [8]_____ the cause of the problem. However, alternative solutions are mostly theory and haven't gone through the [9]_____ and error process like conventional medicine and this is why some doctors don't trust it. But this opposition is gradually [10]_____ as alternative theories are put into practice and the positive results convince the sceptics that alternative medicine has nothing to do with old wives' tales.

1	a results	b predictions	c songs	d remedies
2	a under	b over	c on	d through
3	a recipes	b prescriptions	c directions	d cures
4	a relive	b relapse	c relieve	d redo
5	a lively	b lethal	c safe	d strong
6	a deals	b treats	c looks	d investigates
7	a stroke	b asthma	c amnesia	d cramps
8	a neutralize	b poison	c sweep	d break
9	a test	b examine	c trial	d judge
10	a increasing	b worrying	c residing	d diminishing

Your score [ ] /10

Total [ ] /30

READING

1 Complete the sentences with the correct form of the words in the box.

> analysis   conform   convention   graphology
> pressure   ~~slant~~

1 The books fell off the shelf because it's at a
  slant and not straight.
2 _____ of the statistics from the survey has shown that personality can be affected by diet.
3 _____ is used in some countries to study the personalities of dangerous criminals through their handwriting.
4 All students are expected to _____ to the school rules on clothing. Nobody is allowed to wear clothes that are not part of the uniform.
5 _____ from flood water caused the bridge to collapse.
6 In many countries, it is the _____ for the bride to wear a white dress at the wedding ceremony.

2 Read the text quickly. Which three characteristics of a person's handwriting do graphologists study?

3 Choose the correct answers.

1 Everybody has
  a similar handwriting.
  b their own way of writing.
  c learnt to write in the same way.
2 Some people believe graphology can tell us
  a what a person is like.
  b how a person can be influenced.
  c what a person is thinking.
3 The pressure that a person uses when writing shows
  a whether they are lying.
  b their attention to detail.
  c their feelings and energy levels.
4 The handwriting of a person who isn't very interested in someone or something
  a is very straight.
  b slopes to the left.
  c slopes to the right.
5 Einstein and Picasso both had
  a tiny handwriting.
  b incredible skills.
  c very similar personalities.

More than words

Each person has a unique character and personality. And each person's handwriting is also unique. Although a single teacher may teach hundreds or even thousands of students to write, each student inevitably develops his or her own handwriting style. Does a person's personality influence the style that he or she eventually develops? Those who believe in the art of handwriting analysis, also known as graphology, think it does. This belief is based on the fact that because your brain guides the muscles in your hand, aspects of your inner psyche can be transferred onto paper.

One of the first things a graphologist notices is the amount of pressure used when writing. It is thought that a person's emotional and physical energy is linked to the pressure of their handwriting, so heavy, dark handwriting indicates a highly emotional person, whereas handwriting with a lighter touch shows a person who prefers to avoid situations that require a lot of energy.

The slant of the writing is also important. Handwriting that slants to the right characterizes warm and caring people, whose hearts often control their heads. In contrast, people with vertical handwriting are in control of their emotions, while handwriting which slants to the left is typical of someone who is more indifferent and who could appear to be thick-skinned.

Graphologists also examine the size of the handwriting. Small handwriting indicates dedication and concentration, whereas larger handwriting reveals an individualistic personality that values being different. Analysing the handwriting of Einstein and Picasso clearly confirms that, though they were both geniuses in their fields, their personalities were like chalk and cheese. Einstein's writing is very small, but every letter is carefully constructed, showing his meticulous attention to detail. Picasso, on the other hand, has a more chaotic style which shows not only his creativity, but also his extreme sense of independence. He was obviously someone who didn't want to conform to the usual conventions of neat handwriting!

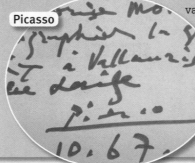

Einstein   Picasso

Birth order and success

1 Complete the sentences or answer the questions.

1 A brother or sister is a ...
   a sibling.   **b** substitute.   **c** second-born.

2 What type of *wisdom* is generally accepted to be true?
   a manipulative   **b** alternative   **c** conventional

3 Which verb means *to mention as proof of a theory*?
   a overlook   **b** cite   **c** gravitate

4 If people pay attention to you, you are in the ...
   a moonlight.   **b** sunlight.   **c** limelight.

5 If you *look up to* someone, you _____ them.
   a ignore   **b** admire   **c** dislike

6 If you don't accept another person's decisions, you can _____ them.
   a override   **b** overcome   **c** overtake

7 An *accommodating* person _____ to help other people.
   a has   **b** refuses   **c** agrees

8 If you do things that other people would be punished for, you *get away with* ...
   a death.   **b** murder.   **c** injury.

9 A _____ person listens to other people's ideas.
   a receptive   **b** receptionist   **c** rebel

10 If you *overlook* something, you _____ to notice it.
   a have   **b** fail   **c** hope

11 If you watch someone or something carefully, you _____ *tabs on them*.
   a leave   **b** make   **c** keep

12 *Sole* can be a synonym for ...
   a always.   **b** only.   **c** a few.

13 When you *gravitate* towards something, you _____ in the direction of something.
   a stroke   **b** fly   **c** move

14 You *advocate* something that you ...
   a disapprove of.   **b** support.   **c** reject.

15 _____ people control other people to their own advantage.
   a Manipulative   **b** Tolerant   **c** Peacemaking

Personality synonyms

2 Match the synonyms (1–7) and (a–g).

1 aloof   **a** dogmatic
2 confident   **b** resolute
3 determined   **c** capricious
4 opinionated   **d** stand-offish
5 reliable   **e** uncompromising
6 stubborn   **f** trustworthy
7 unpredictable   **g** self-assured

3 Choose the correct answers.

1 He's very **capricious** / **dogmatic** and he isn't willing to accept that someone else might be right.

2 You can never be sure how she's going to react. She's so **unpredictable** / **determined**.

3 Mary's very **confident** / **reliable** and if she promises to do something, you can be certain that she'll do it.

4 Tom's very **resolute** / **opinionated** and I'm sure he'll find a way to achieve his objectives.

5 Andy is so shy that he sometimes seems **uncompromising** / **aloof**, but he's friendly when you get to know him.

6 They want someone who is sure of themselves and she came over as **trustworthy** / **self-assured** in the interview so she's got a good chance.

7 Alice can be quite **stubborn** / **stand-offish** and don't think she's going to change her mind about this.

Personality idioms

4 Complete the sentences with the words in the box.

> blanket cheese fuse pie soul shoulders skinned violet

1 Mike was a real wet _blanket_ and refused to take part in any of the games.

2 I can't understand this exercise at all. I'll ask Frank to help me; he's got a good head on his _____ for maths.

3 We're twins but we're like chalk and _____. We've got nothing in common at all!

4 She loves letting everyone know what she thinks and is no shrinking _____ when it comes to expressing her views.

5 It was really boring until Kate arrived and told a few jokes. She was the life and _____ of the party!

6 They were as nice as _____ in the shop and did everything they could to help me.

7 A public figure needs to accept criticism and to be thick-_____.

8 Be careful what you say to the boss because he's got a short _____ and explodes when anyone makes the slightest mistake.

Ellipsis with *either* / *too*

1 Match the sentences (1–8) with the responses (a–h).

1 Sandra has got a new mobile phone. _e_
2 Andy hadn't heard the news. ___
3 We can't stand that TV programme. ___
4 My parents have spoken to the headmaster. ___
5 Jenny is going to study medicine at university. ___
6 I won't be at school tomorrow. ___
7 Vicky didn't send Celia an email. ___
8 Sam went to Paris last year. ___

a I didn't, either.
b Steve did, too.
c Jane won't, either.
d I hadn't, either.
e I have, too.
f We can't, either.
g Mine have, too.
h Kate is, too.

2 Where possible, replace the second sentence with an auxiliary verb and *either* or *too*. In two questions the second sentence cannot be replaced.

1 I didn't go to the interview. Jack didn't go to the interview.
 Jack didn't, either.

2 I think handwriting tests are a good idea. Kevin thinks handwriting tests are a good idea.

_____

3 Mike likes the new touchscreen computers. David doesn't like them at all.

_____

4 We haven't prepared for the play. Alice hasn't prepared for the play.

_____

5 They didn't enjoy the talk on birth order. We really enjoyed the talk.

_____

6 Fiona can't speak German fluently. I can't speak German fluently.

_____

7 Frank spoke to the career guidance officer. Tom spoke to the career guidance officer.

_____

8 Our parents don't approve of that computer game. Our teachers don't approve of that computer game.

_____

3 Write responses to the sentences with an auxiliary verb and *either* or *too* to show that you agree with the speaker.

1 Andy is happy about the exam results. _I am, too._
2 We won't go on the school trip. _____
3 Danny has bought some new trainers. _____
4 Jane loves cooking. _____
5 They didn't see the film. _____
6 Frank hasn't sent Mike a birthday card. _____
7 Ann is studying graphology. _____
8 We've finished the homework. _____

4 Complete the dialogue with an auxiliary verb and *either* or *too*, where necessary. You can't use *either* or *too* in two questions.

Kate I have decided to go on the school skiing trip.
Diana Great! ¹_I have, too_. It should be fun, although I'm a bit worried because I've never skied before.
Kate ²_____, but I'm going to be in the beginner's group because I've forgotten how to do it!
Diana ³_____. We can fall over together! I've bought a ski suit but I haven't bought any boots or skis.
Kate ⁴_____. I'll rent them at the ski resort.
Diana ⁵_____. But my sister's lending me her ski helmet, so I don't have to buy one of those.
Kate ⁶_____. My old ski helmet is too small for me now and I can't wear it.

●●●●●● **CHALLENGE!** ●●●●●●

Write a list of four activities that your friends have talked about today and use ellipsis with *either* / *too* to talk about your participation in them. Try to use different tenses in your sentences.

Mark is going to study this weekend. I am, too.

1 _____
2 _____
3 _____
4 _____

All about me

1 **Match the words with the definitions.**

> charismatic   conceited   considerate   down to earth
> happy-go-lucky   ~~pretentious~~   quick-witted   spontaneous

1 Trying to appear more serious or important than you really are. _pretentious_

2 Careful not to upset people; thinking of others. _____

3 Having too much pride in yourself and your abilities and importance. _____

4 Able to reply in a clever or funny way without thinking for too long. _____

5 Done or happening suddenly; not planned. _____

6 Not caring or worried about life and the future. _____

7 Sensible, realistic and practical. _____

8 Able to attract and influence other people. _____

2 **Decide which adjectives from exercise 1 could apply to the people in the following sentences.**

1 Although she has passed all her exams with good marks so far, she knows that she still has a lot more work to do if she wants to go to university. _down to earth_

2 He could persuade people to do what he wanted with a few well-chosen words and a smile. _____

3 In the novel, the writer tries to deal with great philosophical themes but he doesn't really understand them himself! _____

4 Think about what he's going to do next year? He doesn't even plan what he's going to do the next day! _____

5 I've won every chess match I've played in the competition and I'm sure I'll be the school champion. _____

6 She lived life to the full and was always having fun without a lot of planning. _____

7 I wasn't feeling well, so my teacher kindly phoned my parents and then drove me home. _____

8 Quick as a flash, he came up with a smart remark. _____

3 **Answer the questions in the quiz.**

Find out how other people see you with our super personality quiz!

1 When do you feel at your best?
  a In the morning
  b During the afternoon and early evening
  c Late at night

2 When you enter a room full of people, do you make …
  a a loud entrance in the hope that everyone notices you?
  b a quiet entrance and look around for someone you know?
  c an extremely quiet entrance in the hope that nobody notices you?

3 When you talk to people, do you …
  a have one or both your hands on your hips?
  b have your hands held in front of you?
  c stand with your arms folded?

4 When something amuses you, how do you react?
  a With a loud appreciative laugh
  b With a laugh but not a particularly loud one
  c With a smile

5 How do you usually walk?
  a Fast, with your head up and looking people in the eye
  b Quite quickly, but not looking at anyone in particular
  c At a moderate pace with your head down

6 How do you feel when you are working very hard and someone interrupts you?
  a You're happy to have a break.
  b It depends on the moment.
  c You feel extremely annoyed.

4 **Now read what your answers mean.**

Mostly a answers
You are charismatic and a leader. However, although people like you for your outgoing character, they also see you as considerate.

Mostly b answers
Your friends see you as sensible and down to earth. You enjoy the company of your friends but you have a balanced outlook on life and know when it's time to work hard.

Mostly c answers
Your friends see you as careful and meticulous and they would be shocked if you were ever spontaneous. You appear shy but when people get to know you, they realize that they have made a friend that they can trust.

●●●●● **CHALLENGE!** ●●●●●
Think of two more questions for the personality quiz.
1 _____
2 _____

Ellipsis in comparisons

1 Complete the sentences with the words in the box.

are   do   did   is   ~~last week~~   necessary

1 There won't be as many people at the meeting as
   last week   .

2 Conceited people are more likely to overestimate their
   chances of success than modest people _____.

3 We studied more English novels during the course than
   the other class _____.

4 The inspector interviewed more people than was
   _____.

5 Psychology tests don't test job candidates as efficiently
   as interviews _____.

6 The book is more interesting than the film version
   _____.

2 Decide which sentence (a or b) provides the correct form of
ellipsis.

1 Some personality tests are more successful than other
   personality tests are successful.
   a Some personality tests are more successful
      than other. ☐
   b Some personality tests are more successful than
      others are. ☐

2 Tom works harder than it is advisable to work.
   a Tom works harder than is advisable. ☐
   b Tom works harder than it is. ☐

3 Charismatic people use their charm more than
   down to earth people use their charm.
   a Charismatic people use their charm more than
      down to earth people use. ☐
   b Charismatic people use their charm more than
      down to earth people do. ☐

4 We arrived earlier than we were told to arrive.
   a We arrived earlier than we were told. ☐
   b We arrived earlier than we were. ☐

5 He wanted to write more pages than it was
   possible to write.
   a He wanted to write more pages than possible
      to write. ☐
   b He wanted to write more pages than was possible. ☐

6 A lot of students are happier about doing homework
   than other students are happy about doing homework.
   a A lot of students are happier about doing
      homework than other students are. ☐
   b A lot of students are happier about doing
      homework than other students are happy about. ☐

3 Rewrite the sentences using ellipsis.

1 English cities are more spread out than other European
   cities are spread out.
   English cities are more spread out than other European
   cities are.

2 They failed more exams than it is allowed to fail.

3 Healthy people are less likely to suffer from heart
   problems than unhealthy people are likely to suffer from
   heart problems.

4 He ate more food than he was offered to eat.

5 We studied more units than my brother's class studied.

6 Angela often tries to help others more than it is possible
   to help.

4 Read the text and cross out or replace any unnecessary
words.

One popular personality test involves asking job candidates
to put a list of colours in order of preference. Candidates
choosing red ~~as their favourite colour~~ are considered to be
more energetic than candidates choosing other colours.
People who put yellow in first place are happier about
working in a team than other candidates are happy about
working in a team. A person who likes blue usually reacts
more calmly to problems than it is normal to react.
Ambitious candidates don't place the colour grey as high in
their lists as other candidates place the colour grey in their
lists. A person who chooses green first often persists more
with their work than it is usual to persist. Finally,
candidates who put black in last place are more organized
at work than other candidates are organized at work.

⬤⬤⬤⬤⬤ CHALLENGE! ⬤⬤⬤⬤⬤

Compare two books you have read recently. Use ellipsis
where possible.

The detective novel was more interesting than the science fiction book.

A comparison and contrast essay

Preparation

1 **Read the essay. In what way do Frank and the writer have similar personalities?**

Although Frank and I are not brothers, we've spent so much time together since we were born that we could be. We met when we were three years old at Highfield Road nursery school and we became instant friends. At least that's what our mothers tell us as we only have vague memories of our time there. What we do know is that while we were at the nursery together, Frank and I created the foundations for a friendship that has lasted until university.

Physically, Frank and I are very different. Frank is tall and blond and looks as if he's from Scandinavia. ¹_____. However, when it comes to personality, we have a lot in common. We both enjoy being the life and soul of the party and I think more than one person has got fed up with our loud behaviour! However, ²_____, we also take our studies seriously. We both have good heads on our shoulders for maths and science and after spending all our school lives in the same classroom together, we are now on the same degree course at university.

Despite sharing a lot of characteristics, there are also some differences. In my free time I love playing sports and I'm a big fan of basketball in particular. ³_____. Furthermore, ⁴_____, I prefer going to the cinema to escape from the real world. You'd never get Frank into a cinema even if you offered to pay for him!

To sum up, we are very similar in many ways and after so much time together, we understand each other really well. Apart from being good fun, Frank is also the most trustworthy person I know outside of my family and the first person I would call if I needed help.

2 **Complete the essay with the following sentences.**

A whereas Frank is an avid reader

B while we know how to enjoy ourselves

C On the other hand, I'm quite small and dark-haired and people think I'm from the Mediterranean.

D In contrast, Frank prefers more peaceful activities and he enjoys taking computers apart and putting them together again.

3 **Choose the best answers.**

1 (While) / **On the other hand** my dad likes to go to the seaside, my mum prefers to go to the countryside.

2 The northern Spanish are used to rain. **Whereas / On the other hand,** the southern Spanish rarely see it.

3 Andy loves travelling **in contrast / whereas** his brother hates leaving the family home.

4 My sister really enjoys doing personality tests. **In contrast / While,** I think they are a waste of time.

5 I don't read novels very often. **On the other hand / Whereas,** I read a lot of poetry.

Writing task

4 **Think of two people in your family or circle of friends and make notes on the following questions.**

- What are the similarities / differences in their physical appearances?
- What are the similarities / differences in their personalities?
- What experiences have they shared?

5 **In your notebook write an essay that compares and contrasts the physical appearance and personality of two people. Write 200–250 words.**

- Describe when and where they met.
- Describe their relationship.
- Compare their appearances and personalities; what are the similarities and / or differences?
- Write a conclusion.

Check your work

Have you

☐ thought about the reason for their first meeting?
☐ thought about the most noticeable physical characteristics of those people?
☐ thought about the most noticeable personality characteristics of those people?
☐ covered all the points in the plan?
☐ used linking words to compare and contrast points?

1 **Answer the questions.**

1 Ellipsis is used to omit words and avoid _____.

2 We use _____ when the first statement is negative and the response is also negative.

3 We use ellipsis after *than* or _____ in comparative sentences.

4 Replace the words in bold with one word: We haven't been here as long as they**'ve been here**. _____

5 One form of ellipsis involves omitting the main verb and just using the _____ verb.

6 Replace the words in bold with one word: He's more annoyed about the results than you **are annoyed about the results**. _____

7 In ellipsis in comparative sentences, verbs without an auxiliary verb are replaced by _____.

8 We use _____ when the first statement is positive and the response is also positive.

9 Complete the exchange: 'I hated that film.' 'I _____ too.'

10 If the response _____ the original statement, we don't use *either* or *too*.

Your score ____ /10

2 **Choose the best continuation or response for each sentence. In some cases, both are correct.**

1 Doctors sometimes prescribe more medicine
  a than is necessary. ☐ b than it is necessary. ☐

2 I think speaking in public is difficult.
  a I think, too. ☐ b I do, too. ☐

3 We don't really like her novels.
  a I don't, either. ☐ b I do. ☐

4 Students living away from home need more money than students living at home
  a need. ☐ b do. ☐

5 Andy eats more chocolate than
  a advisable. ☐ b is advisable. ☐

6 Sue wants to live abroad for a while.
  a Alice does, too. ☐ b Alice doesn't. ☐

7 We stay up later than our cousins
  a do. ☐ b stay up. ☐

8 I didn't do as well in the exams as
  a last term. ☐ b before. ☐

9 Sam hasn't phoned the school about the results yet.
  a I have, too. ☐ b I haven't, either. ☐

10 Kate thinks the meeting will be useful.
  a I don't. ☐ b I don't, either. ☐

Your score ____ /10

3 **There are mistakes in eight of the sentences. Find the mistakes and correct them. Where there are two sentences, do not make any changes to the first sentence.**

1 Alan hasn't written his project yet. Oh, I haven't, too.

_____

2 Footballers earn a lot more money than most people are.

_____

3 Diana really dislikes listening to pop music. I do, too.

_____

4 He's more interested in science than his brother does.

_____

5 Novelists writing in English sell more books than novelists writing in French sell.

_____

6 Sam didn't do the test. I did, too.

_____

7 Most factory owners are wealthier than their workers do.

_____

8 Spontaneous people are less likely to have doubts than more cautious people have.

_____

9 They didn't have to revise as hard as the other class did.

_____

10 Angela has been to the exhibition. I haven't, either.

_____

Your score ____ /10

4 **Complete the text with one word in each gap.**

A lot of people have taken personality tests when they have applied for a job. I have, ¹_____. Who hasn't? According to some experts, they reveal more about job candidates than interviews ²_____. However, a few experts think that job candidates have to face more tests than is ³_____. I ⁴_____ too. These experts think that interviews aren't as useful at discovering what someone is really like as tests ⁵_____. I don't ⁶_____. I think that if you want to know if someone is more suitable for a job than another candidate ⁷_____, you have to speak to them. A few experts even want personality tests banned. I ⁸_____. I just don't think that they should be used as much as they ⁹_____ now. A good interview is a better way of judging what a person is like than a personality test ¹⁰_____.

Your score ____ /20

Total ____ /50

1 Complete the vocabulary quiz with words from Unit 5.

QUIZ

1 A down to _____ person is practical and sensible.

2 If two people are like chalk and _____, they are not similar at all.

3 An _____ person is unfriendly and doesn't want to take part in anything.

4 _____ is a more formal word for brother or sister.

5 A _____ decision is made without thinking about it a lot.

6 A _____ person thinks about other people.

7 A person who is not hurt by criticism is often described as _____-skinned.

8 If you keep _____ on someone, you watch over them.

9 Someone with a short _____ becomes angry easily.

10 _____ is a more formal way of saying *determined*.

11 A _____ person thinks that their beliefs are right.

12 *Trustworthy* is a synonym for _____.

13 Something that is more important than other things over _____ them.

14 If you go towards something, you _____ towards it.

15 A kind, friendly person can be described as 'as nice as _____'.

16 A _____ person is too proud of their own abilities.

17 Someone who stops other people from enjoying themselves is a *wet* _____.

18 If you _____ something, you support it in public.

19 To _____ something means to mention it to support an idea or theory.

20 What adjective describes someone who can influence people easily because of their personality?

_____

Your score [ ] /20

2 Complete the words and expressions in the article.

Most people would agree that it is an advantage to be good-looking. Studies seem to support that view, and they have shown that we ¹_____ look the failings of attractive people's characters and regularly allow them to get away with ²_____. We assume that a good-looking person is more ³_____worthy than others and we tend to look ⁴_____ to attractive people simply because they have a pleasant appearance. However, although good-looking people are not automatically born with nice personalities, their looks do affect their characters. From an early age, they find themselves in the ⁵_____light more and tend to learn to be ⁶_____-assured in public.

However, the same studies have revealed that it's not all good. Attractive people who don't want to be the ⁷_____ and soul of the party are often labelled as rude and unfriendly instead of being seen as ⁸_____ violets. Furthermore, it seems that we believe that 'beautiful people' don't have very good heads on their ⁹_____ for intellectual matters. Conventional ¹⁰_____ labels good-looking people as nice but not particularly intelligent. To sum up, whatever we look like, we all have to overcome the prejudices of society.

Your score [ ] /10

Total [ ] /30

READING

Before reading: Farming

1 Match the words with the definitions.

crop ~~edible~~ germinate grain harvest oats
seed variety

1 Suitable or safe to eat. _edible_
2 A cereal plant like a grass which is used in baking and cooking and also to feed animals. _____
3 The small hard part of a plant from which a new plant of the same kind can grow. _____
4 A type of plant, etc. _____
5 The seeds of wheat, rice, etc. _____
6 To cause a seed to start growing. _____
7 To collect the grain, fruit, etc. that has grown on a farm. _____
8 The total amount of one variety of grain, etc. that a farmer grows at one time. _____

2 Read the text quickly. How long can the longest-surviving seeds last for?

3 Use your own words to say what the numbers refer to.

1 100 _The tunnel that goes to the vaults in the Svalbard Global Seed Bank is 100 metres long._
2 2008 _____
3 526,000 _____
4 18 _____
5 20–30 _____

4 Are the sentences true or false? Correct the false sentences.

1 The seeds are more valuable than precious metals, precious stones or currency. _T_
2 The seeds are only for use in an emergency. ___
3 The vault also keeps examples of fully-grown fruit and vegetables. ___
4 The freezing conditions make it difficult to keep the seeds in good condition. ___
5 All the seeds last for the same length of time. ___
6 New seeds are produced from fruit and vegetables that are grown from seeds in the vaults. ___

Seeds for the future

On a remote Norwegian island near the Arctic Circle, there is a hundred-metre tunnel that leads to a series of vaults securely locked beneath the centre of a mountain. Inside the vaults is something more precious than gold, diamonds or money: over half a million seeds. You may wonder why seeds need to be protected with such a high degree of security. But just imagine if a global catastrophe were to happen, and the world's food supply were permanently wiped out; the seeds in these vaults could be released and new crops could be grown from them.

The vaults constitute the Svalbard Global Seed Bank, which became operational in February 2008. The seed bank preserves single specimens of 526,000 varieties of the world's edible plants, including varieties of barley, wheat, and oats as well as seeds that can produce fruits and vegetables. The isolated location of the seed bank was carefully chosen so that the seeds would be far from harm in the event of a war, natural disaster, or other calamity. Furthermore, the ideal temperature for keeping the seeds is –18 degrees Celsius, which is easier to maintain in the glacial temperatures of the Arctic permafrost. Although seed banks already exist around the world, they are not as secure and Svalbard will provide the ultimate back-up.

In spite of the fact that the seed bank provides the best chance of survival for the world's crops, seeds can still die. Some crops, such as peas, may survive for 20–30 years in frozen conditions before they lose their ability to germinate and grow. Others, such as sunflower and some grains, can survive for hundreds of years. However, eventually all seeds will lose their ability to make food. Before this happens, a few seeds are taken from the stored samples and planted. New seeds are then harvested and preserved. As a result of this process, the original variety of plant can be perpetuated, possibly lasting forever.

Hopefully, the world will never need the Svalbard Global Seed Bank, but we should feel a little more secure knowing that it exists.

VOCABULARY

From farmland to the supermarket

1 Complete the text with the correct form of the words in the box.

> consensus   differ   donate   fertilizer   harvesting
> herbicide   intervention   lease   ~~mission~~   pioneering
> sacrifice   sustainable   switch   venture   well being

For years, food scientists have had an important ¹ mission _____ :
to find a way to feed the world. As a result of their work,
scientists' ² _____ techniques in plant production have
developed a new type of food: genetically modified (GM) food.
Through scientific ³ _____ in plants, changes are made to
their DNA so that they become more resistant to disease. Some
GM crops, such as cotton, contain their own ⁴ _____ that
kill other plants that attack them. Other GM crops can be grown
in difficult conditions where poor farmers don't have the good
⁵ _____ they need to help their seeds develop into crops.
Therefore, the ⁶ _____ of some crops even in bad years
is assured. This is especially important for many small farmers
who don't own the land they work on, but have to pay for a
⁷ _____ .

However, there is little ⁸ _____ among scientists on
the benefits of GM foods, and many experts' views
⁹ _____ greatly from the positive picture painted by the
producers of GM seeds. In the first place, we still don't know
what effect GM foods will have on people's ¹⁰ _____ .
Some scientists think people's health might be affected
negatively in the long term. Furthermore, many of those involved
in ¹¹ _____ farming projects claim that their natural crops
are contaminated and have to be ¹² _____ when GM food
crops are grown near their farms. Finally, GM seeds are only
produced by a few business ¹³ _____ which have a
monopoly on the market. In some cases,
companies have ¹⁴ _____ free GM
seeds to farmers to encourage them to
¹⁵ _____ to GM food production.
However, if they want to continue they always
have to return to the same supplier to buy their
GM seeds, whereas in the past they were free
to use their own natural seeds.

Types of food

2 Match the words with the definitions.

> ~~artichoke~~   bay leaf   cinnamon   ginger   okra
> pomegranate   parsley   tangerine

1   artichoke _____ : a green vegetable with a lot of thick
    pointed leaves. You can eat the bottom part of the
    leaves.
2   _____ : the green seed cases from a tropical
    plant that are eaten as a vegetable or used to thicken
    soups and other dishes.
3   _____ : a round fruit with thick smooth skin that
    is red inside and full of seeds.
4   _____ : a plant with small curly leaves that are
    used in cooking and for food decoration.
5   _____ : a green leaf that is often hard and dried
    and used in cooking to add flavour.
6   _____ : a sweet brown powder that is made from
    the bark of a tree.
7   _____ : a root that tastes hot and is used in
    cooking.
8   _____ : a fruit like a small sweet orange with a
    skin that is easy to take off.

Idioms: food

3 Complete the sentences with correct form of the idioms
in the box.

> have your cake and eat it   sour grapes   fishy
> to eat your words   ~~a fish out of water~~   make a meal of it

1   Everybody on the trip could ski and I couldn't, so I felt
    like a fish out of water .
2   I don't think it's so great to play for the school team –
    and that's not just _____ because I wasn't
    chosen.
3   Mike says he was in the classroom when it happened
    but nobody remembers seeing him there. If you ask me
    there's something _____ going on here.
4   When my sister had to clean the house she really
    _____ ! She complained so much and it wasn't a
    big job.
5   If Sue and Ann want to get better grades, they can't
    expect to do no work! They can't _____ .
6   John said I'd never be accepted by the university, but
    when I tell him I'm going to do a degree in medicine
    he'll have _____ .

Cleft sentences (1): *it*

1 Choose the correct answers. In some cases both are correct.

1 It's the tomatoes **are tasteless** / **that are tasteless**
2 It's a good night's sleep **you need** / **that you need**.
3 It's children **that love hamburgers** / **love hamburgers**.
4 It's fast food **I think children should eat less of** / **that I think children should eat less of**.
5 It's Spanish food **that we like most of all** / **we like most of all**.
6 It's the waitress **that has your credit card** / **has your credit card**.

2 Rewrite the sentences using the words in brackets.

1 Cheese gives you headaches. (chocolate)
   No, it's chocolate that gives me headaches.
2 Foreign food isn't allowed into the country. (GM foods)
   _____
3 The Indian restaurant prepares really good take-away food. (Chinese restaurant)
   _____
4 Your dad said you should go on a diet. (doctor)
   _____
5 The supermarket sells such good vegetables. (greengrocer's)
   _____
6 Potatoes have lots of vitamin C. (oranges)
   _____
7 Coffee is your favourite drink. (tea)
   _____
8 Fruit is very fattening. (sweets)
   _____

3 Rewrite the sentences as cleft sentences by focusing on the words in bold. Omit *that* where possible.

1 Some scientists think **GM crops** can help produce more food.
   It's GM crops some scientists think can help produce more food.
2 **Primary schools** should provide free meals.
   _____
3 Sports people need **a diet high in carbohydrates**.
   _____
4 George loves **French cooking**.
   _____
5 **The restaurants** want to stay open later.
   _____
6 Andy always takes **the last piece of cake**.
   _____

4 Complete the dialogue with cleft sentences with preparatory *it*. Use the words in brackets and omit the relative pronoun where possible.

Ann I hear you're cooking lunch for your family this weekend. (dinner)
Sue [1] *No, it's dinner I'm cooking.*
Ann Are your aunt and uncle coming? (my cousins)
Sue No, [2] _____.
Ann Oh. Is it true that you're going to prepare beefburgers? (big pizza)
Sue No, it isn't. [3] _____
Ann I see. Are you using a recipe from a cook book? (a website)
Sue No. [4] _____.
Ann And you're serving a cake for dessert. (ice cream)
Sue No, [5] _____.
Ann Are you going to the cinema afterwards? (theatre)
Sue No, [6] _____.
Ann Well, I hope it all goes well.
Sue Thanks.

●●●●● CHALLENGE! ●●●●●

Write six cleft sentences with preparatory *it* about your favourite meals and drinks.

It's cheese on toast that I love to eat for lunch every day.

1 _____
2 _____
3 _____
4 _____
5 _____
6 _____

In the kitchen

1 **Match the words with the definitions.**

> casserole   colander   food processor
> garlic press   ladle   pestle and mortar
> ~~potato peeler~~   whisk   wok

1 A special knife for taking the skin off fruit and vegetables. _potato peeler_

2 A large pan that is shaped like a bowl and used for cooking. _____

3 A large dish with a lid for cooking meat and vegetables in liquid for a long time in the oven. _____

4 A small heavy bowl and a small heavy tool with a round end, used for crushing food or other substances into powder. _____

5 An electric machine that can mix food and also cut food into small pieces. _____

6 A small device in which a plant with a strong taste and smell is crushed. _____

7 A metal or plastic bowl with a lot of small holes in it that is used for removing water from food that has been boiled or washed. _____

8 A large deep spoon with a long handle. _____

9 A tool that you use for beating eggs, etc. very fast. _____

2 **There are mistakes in six of the sentences. Find the mistakes and correct them.**

1 My mum always takes the skin off apples with a ~~whisk~~. _potato peeler_

2 First, beat the eggs and milk together with a ladle. _____

3 Put the meat and vegetables in a food processor and leave them to cook at a low heat for two hours. _____

4 You can't drain rice with that colander. The holes are too big. _____

5 Crush the spices and herbs together in a garlic press. _____

6 Use a potato peeler to finely chop the lamb and vegetables. _____

7 Stir-fry the vegetables and beef quickly in a wok at a high temperature. _____

8 And finally serve two or three colanders of the sauce onto each plate. _____

3 **Answer the questions in the quiz.**

Your diet can affect your energy levels, your studies and, most importantly, your health. Find out with our quiz if it's time for you to make some changes to what you put in your stomach!

1 What is your attitude to breakfast?
   a It's the best way to start the day.
   b I manage a slice of toast.
   c If I have time, I have a hot drink.

2 How often do you eat chocolate or sweets?
   a Never. They ruin your teeth.
   b At the weekends or on special occasions.
   c All the time when I'm online or in front of the TV.

3 When you're thirsty, what do you drink?
   a A glass of water, milk or fruit juice; something refreshing and healthy.
   b Tea or coffee with a little sugar.
   c A fizzy drink like cola. It gives you lots of energy.

4 How often do you eat fruit and vegetables?
   a A meal without fruit or vegetables isn't a proper meal.
   b Perhaps one or two pieces a day.
   c They're too much work. I prefer pre-cooked meals.

5 Do you enjoy fast food?
   a No. It's poor quality and a waste of money.
   b I like it once in a while, especially at weekends when I'm with friends.
   c I love it and would eat it three times a day!

6 If you have to cook for yourself, what do you do?
   a I use fresh ingredients and my imagination to create a tasty meal.
   b I defrost something that my mum has cooked and left in the freezer.
   c I heat up a pre-cooked meal in the microwave.

4 **Now read what your answers mean.**

Mostly a answers
You're certainly aware of what makes up a good diet and what doesn't. You also seem to have an interest in cooking, which will make you even more aware of the nutritional value of different food. However, don't worry about eating the occasional take-away; you won't die!

Mostly b answers
You've got a pretty good idea of what you should and shouldn't eat and drink, but you can't always resist unhealthy food. Why don't you take a bit more interest in cooking? It's a great way of finding out what goes into meals and discovering what you really like to eat.

Mostly c answers
Wow, it seems you don't care at all about your health! Remember a poor diet can have bad long-term effects. It can also affect your energy levels and your studies. Why not try and cut out a few of the snacks or pre-cooked meals you eat and replace them with healthier meals? You'll immediately feel like a new person!

● ● ● ● ●   **CHALLENGE!**   ● ● ● ● ●

Write down a list of everything that you've eaten in the last three days and decide if there are any ways you can improve your diet.

_____
_____
_____

Cleft sentences (2): *what*

1 Complete the text with *is* or *what*.

Good decoration ¹is_____ ²_____ gives a good impression when you go to a new restaurant for the first time. Furthermore, ³_____ new clients also appreciate ⁴_____ good service. But of course, food ⁵_____ ⁶_____ people are interested in when they eat out. A recommendation from a friend ⁷_____ ⁸_____ persuades people to try a new restaurant for the first time. ⁹_____ a lot of restaurateurs believe helps bring in new clients ¹⁰_____ advertising in the local press, but ¹¹_____ really works ¹²_____ someone telling their friends about the great meal they had when they ate out.

2 Write cleft sentences with *what*, using the questions and answers.

1 What makes pasta dishes so popular? Easy preparation.
  Easy preparation is what makes pasta dishes so popular. / What makes pasta dishes so popular is easy preparation.

2 What gives this dish its flavour? Okra.
  _____

3 What makes Dad happy every morning? A big breakfast.
  _____

4 What impressed everyone? The variety of dishes.
  _____

5 What keeps Jack in such good form? Regular exercise.
  _____

6 What attracts new customers to the café? Good sandwiches.
  _____

3 Write the alternative cleft sentence form of each sentence.

1 What Mike wanted was an easy life.
  An easy life was what Mike wanted.

2 The great coffee is what makes this bar popular.
  _____

3 What we like best is Italian food.
  _____

4 The cooking is what makes my job enjoyable.
  _____

5 What Ray does is entertain the guests.
  _____

6 The sauce was what made that dish so tasty.
  _____

7 What we appreciate most is good service and a nice atmosphere.
  _____

8 The cost is what puts people off eating here.
  _____

4 Write cleft sentences that begin with *what* to say what the kitchen equipment does. Use the verbs in the box.

| ~~crush~~ drain peel serve stew stir-fry |

1 garlic press: *What it crushes is garlic.*_____
2 potato peeler: _____
3 colander: _____
4 ladle: _____
5 casserole: _____
6 wok: _____

●●●●● CHALLENGE! ●●●●●

Write cleft sentences beginning with *what* to describe the jobs five pieces of equipment in your house do.

microwave: *what it heats up very quickly is food.*

1 _____
2 _____
3 _____
4 _____
5 _____

An informative article

Preparation

1 Read the essay. What effect did the arrival of tomatoes in Europe have?

The world's favourite dish

A Ask people where pizza comes from and most of them will tell you 'Italy'. The rest will probably answer 'The United States'. However, the truth is that the dish had existed for centuries in countries like Egypt and Greece before the word 'pizza' first appeared over 400 years ago in Naples, the Italian city that is considered the birthplace of pizza.

B Originally, pizza wasn't even a dish. Bakers used to test the temperature of their ovens to see if they were ready to bake bread by putting a thin flat slice of dough (uncooked bread) into the oven. If the dough cooked quickly, then the oven was ready. In other words, pizza was a baker's tool and not a popular recipe. So how did it become one of the world's most popular dishes?

C The 'baker's tool' of flat bread used to be given away or sold very cheaply to the poor. However, it was the arrival of the tomato from South America in the late 16th century that really helped create the modern pizza. Tomatoes were also inexpensive and the people of Naples started putting them on their flat bread. With time, bakers added ingredients, for example, herbs, spices, garlic and small salty fish, and produced their own pizza recipes. To put it another way, the reason why pizza became popular was because it was a cheap, tasty meal.

D However, it was the visit of Queen Margherita of Italy to Naples that made pizza popular all over the country. She was curious about the dish she saw everybody eating and a local baker made a special Margherita pizza with tomato, herbs and Mozzarella cheese to represent the colours of the Italian flag, that is to say, red, green and white. As a result, pizza became popular with all social classes. In later years Italian emigrants to countries such as the USA took their cheap, nutritious pizza recipes with them and turned pizza into the world's most popular dish.

2 Which paragraph …

1 explains how pizza-making began? B
2 describes the development of pizza? ___
3 describes an event that popularized pizza? ___
4 explains where pizza comes from? ___

3 Find three examples of exemplification and three examples of clarification in the text.

Exemplification	Clarification
¹ countries like Egypt and Greece	4 _____
2 _____	5 _____
3 _____	6 _____

4 Match the beginnings (1–7) with the endings (a–g) to make sentences.

1 Does he have the right restaurant work experience? In e
2 In agriculture, for ___
3 The best thing about pizza is that there are so many different types. That ___
4 You should eat foods rich in vitamin C such ___
5 That sum of money is to cover costs like ___
6 These vegetables are a bit raw. To put it ___
7 Restaurants can easily become more environmentally-friendly by ___

a as tomatoes and oranges.
b eating out and drinks on the trip.
c instance, thousands of jobs are being lost because of technology.
d using and recycling glass drinks bottles instead of plastic ones, for example.
e other words, can he work in a busy kitchen?
f another way, could you cook them a little longer?
g is to say that you never get bored of eating them.

Writing task

5 Think of a popular dish and do some research on it.

- Where is it from originally?
- What are the main ingredients?
- How and why did it become popular?
- Who is / was it popular with?

6 Use a mind map to make notes and organize your ideas.

7 In your notebook write an essay that describes the history and development of a popular dish. Organize your materials into three paragraphs. Write 200–250 words.

- Explain the origins of the dish.
- Describe the dish and its ingredients.
- Describe why and how it's popular.

Check your work

Have you

- [ ] researched the history of the dish?
- [ ] made notes on the ingredients of the dish?
- [ ] thought about who it is popular with and why?
- [ ] used a number of words and phrases for exemplification and clarification?

1 **Complete the sentences or answer the questions.**

1 We can start a cleft sentence with _____ it.

2 The expression *the man* _____ can be used in a cleft sentence that includes a question word.

3 What doesn't change in a cleft sentence that includes a question word? _____

4 We can leave out _____ when writing a cleft sentence about a direct object.

5 We can use *what* and other _____ words in cleft sentences.

6 Where can we put the words that we want to emphasize in a cleft sentence with *what*? _____

7 The words and phrases that we want to emphasize in a cleft sentence with *it* are made into a _____ clause.

8 The expression *the day* _____ can be used in a cleft sentence that includes a question word.

9 How do we join the words that we want to emphasize to the relative clause in a cleft sentence that includes a question word? _____

10 *It* is the _____ of a cleft sentence.

Your score	/10

2 **Tick the best continuation for each sentence. In some cases, both are correct.**

1 What I enjoy most
   a is a three-course meal. ✓
   b that's a three-course meal. ☐

2 A Chinese restaurant is what
   a he is going to open. ☐
   b we want to go to. ☐

3 It's TV programmes about cooking
   a that I can't stand. ☐
   b he likes. ☐

4 It's fruit
   a is imported that is expensive. ☐
   b you should eat more of. ☐

5 Indian dishes are
   a that the British eat the most when they go out. ☐
   b what the British eat the most when they go out. ☐

6 What costs more
   a is fresh fish. ☐
   b fresh fish. ☐

Your score	/6

3 **There are mistakes in five of the sentences. Find the mistakes and correct them.**

1 It is the food I bought from the supermarket.

   _____

2 A whisk is what should you use.

   _____

3 Is spending time with friends that I enjoy the most.

   _____

4 What we like to drink that is very sweet coffee.

   _____

5 It's the cooking time what we need to control.

   _____

6 What the chef does first is slice all the vegetables.

   _____

7 It's the cold depresses me.

   _____

8 What I hate most is peeling potatoes.

   _____

Your score	/8

4 **Rewrite the sentences as cleft sentences. Emphasize the words that are in bold.**

1 These tomatoes **taste of soil**.
   What _____

2 **The head chef** always cooks our meal.
   It's _____

3 You should eat **a good diet**.
   A good diet _____

4 **The supermarket** sells good bread.
   It's _____

5 **My mum** cooks tasty dishes.
   What _____

6 Not many people know anything about **German cuisine**.
   It's _____

7 **I** use a food processor to make cakes.
   A food processor _____

8 **We** buy our fruit and vegetables at the market.
   What _____

Your score	/16

Total	/40

1 Complete the vocabulary quiz with words from Unit 7.

QUIZ

1 We stir-fry vegetables, meat and fish in a _____.

2 Complete the idiom: *to have your* _____ *and eat it*.

3 There is _____ when a group of people accept a decision or opinion.

4 _____ is used to make plants grow well.

5 Complete the idiom: *eat my* _____.

6 _____ is a herb which is used to flavour and decorate dishes.

7 We beat eggs with a _____.

8 A _____ is a type of small orange.

9 Complete the idiom: *a* _____ *out of water*.

10 A _____ is a job that someone thinks is important to do.

11 We crush parsley and other herbs with a _____.

12 To _____ is to give money or goods to organizations without asking for anything in return.

13 A _____ is a legal agreement to rent land or a vehicle for a period of time.

14 Complete the idiom: *make a* _____ *of it*.

15 We crush garlic with a _____.

16 An _____ is a green vegetable with pointed leaves.

17 When you go to a restaurant a waiter _____ you.

18 A _____ is a business activity.

19 We drain pasta with a _____.

20 Complete the idiom: *sour* _____.

Your score ____ /20

2 Complete the article with the correct words (a–d).

In 2010, Mexican cuisine was included on UNESCO's cultural heritage list. According to UNESCO, Mexican food production differs [1]_____ many others because the whole food chain, from planting to [2]_____ to cooking, involves all the community. In many other countries, the [3]_____ of technology has distanced local people from the food production process. Furthermore, Mexican food is good for the [4]_____ of the environment and people. Although Mexican farmers use [5]_____ and pesticides like farmers all over the world do, they also use [6]_____ farming practices which respect the environment. Moreover, Mexican cooking often involves slowly [7]_____ ingredients in [8]_____ for a long time, a process that greatly improves the nutritional value of the meals. Quicker meals include [9]_____ vegetables and pieces of meat that have been [10]_____ thinly, a cooking process that doesn't produce heavy, unhealthy dishes. So the next time you want to go out for a meal, why not try a Mexican restaurant?

	a	b	c	d
1	to	at	with	from
2	pioneering	harvesting	serving	slicing
3	intervention	consensus	mission	sacrifice
4	well being	healthy	goodness	process
5	medicine	drugs	herbicides	poison
6	sustainable	renewable	recyclable	wasteful
7	peeling	serving	crushing	stewing
8	ladle	casseroles	garlic press	colander
9	chopping	whisking	stir-frying	switching
10	sliced	pressed	donated	leased

Your score ____ /10

Total ____ /30

READING

1 Complete the idioms in the sentences using the words in the box.

> cloud   ground   leaps   ~~moon~~   roll   through

1 Alice was over the _moon_ about being picked for the volleyball team.
2 Tom sailed _____ his driving test first time.
3 Sam hit the _____ running when he started university and made a good impression immediately.
4 The school team has won ten games in a row so they're obviously on a _____.
5 Her Chinese has improved in _____ and bounds and now she can even write it.
6 Mike was on _____ nine when he heard he had passed all his exams.

2 Read the text quickly. In what part of the USA was Bruno Furtado attending university?

3 Choose the correct answers.

1 Bruno was accepted by an American university because
   a he was a brilliant student.
   b of his sporting talent.
   c he loved the USA.
2 What irritated Bruno was having to
   a explain to everyone what a coconut was.
   b do without something he was used to.
   c work hard academically.
3 Coconut water is considered
   a to be the best drink of its kind.
   b to contain too much sugar and salt.
   c to be nearly as good as American health drinks.
4 Bruno's teammates
   a refused to try coconut water.
   b only ate and drank things that were sweet.
   c didn't really understand his problem.
5 Coconut water is now
   a less popular because there is clean drinking water.
   b considered fashionable with poor communities.
   c used by a charity organization to raise funds.

In a nutshell

Bruno Furtado comes from Brazil and is a brilliant sportsman. When he applied for a scholarship to study at a prestigious American university, he was quickly accepted on the grounds of his ability to play football for the university team. He was over the moon about attending such a well-regarded institution, and since he had been to the United States many times, he felt comfortable about living there.

After one year, Bruno was doing well academically, and his football team had been on a roll, winning nearly all of their matches. However, one thing slightly annoyed Bruno about life in America – he couldn't find his favourite health drink. In fact, no one in Southern California had even heard of coconut water.

The juice that comes straight out of a coconut has some amazing properties and is now widely recognized as the ultimate energy drink. Not only does it have the right balance of sugar, salt and vitamins for a healthy workout, but also it is totally natural. Bruno knew that coconut water was the best way to provide the energy and vitamins his body needed after the extreme physical exertion required in the football matches.

Bruno tried a popular sports beverage recommended by the team trainer, but he didn't feel happy or healthy drinking it. It was ultra-sweet and just didn't have the same restorative powers as Brazilian coconut water. Bruno's teammates couldn't sympathize with him because they all drank the American sports beverages and felt

fantastic. In time, Bruno adapted to the American energy drinks, but he still enjoyed coconut water on his trips home to Brazil.

Then, in his final year of university, Bruno made a pleasant discovery. A Brazilian foundation had begun selling coconut water in the United States in an effort to raise money to provide clean drinking water for poor communities in Brazil. Bruno was surprised to find that coconut water was becoming a trendy drink amongst American athletes – including members of his own football team!

Conversational styles – what sport are you?

1 Complete the text with the correct form of the words in the box.

> camaraderie   deference   dribble   etiquette   grab
> hit it off   hold the floor   overgeneralization   overlap
> pitch   rapport   reticent   simultaneously   tackle   ~~toss~~

Once the referee has ¹ tossed the coin in the air and the captains have decided who kicks off, football fans are only interested in one thing: seeing their stars ² _____ the ball past their opponents or race back to ³ _____ and stop the other team's attackers. If the players performed well, the ⁴ _____ of the fans' cheers reaches its highest point. At such moments, it must be hard for these young men not to believe that they are special, although most would be ⁵ _____ about voicing such thoughts. Furthermore, when the match is over, the exaggerated respect and ⁶ _____ that journalists show the successful team adds to the idea that footballers are extraordinary people. However, there is one club where the players manage to be ⁷ _____ successful and modest: FC Barcelona.

When FC Barcelona's trainer or players ⁸ _____ at press conferences, it becomes clear that the rules of the club's ⁹ _____ forbid displays of big-headedness, even though the players' spectacular victories have ¹⁰ _____ the sports page headlines from their rivals over the last few years. Most of Barcelona's players have come through the club's youth training programme and the ¹¹ _____ is there for all to see. However, the club's school, La Masia, builds more than a good ¹² _____ and understanding between the young players. It teaches them that talent is not enough for success; it has to ¹³ _____ with hard work and respect for others. The few players the club does buy are bought not only for their skills but also for their willingness to adapt to the club's philosophy, and as a result they soon ¹⁴ _____ with their new companions on and off the pitch.

The world of sports journalism is a world of ¹⁵ _____, half-truths and exaggeration, but when commentators say the Barça players are perfect role models for young sports enthusiasts everywhere, nobody disagrees.

Verbal communication

2 Correct the mistake in each sentence.

1 He's always ~~protesting~~ about his colleagues' private lives. gossiping

2 Ann leaned over and chatted something in her best friend's ear. _____

3 The accused discussed his innocence throughout the whole of the trial. _____

4 Stop gossiping! If you want to complain, say it clearly! _____

5 She spends hours on the internet discussing to her friends. _____

6 The head of department wants to mutter the company's plans with everybody in the office. _____

Idioms with *hit*

3 Choose the correct answers.

1 Although we hit **the buffers** / (**the road**) at 6 am., we didn't arrive until the evening.

2 His first novel was a big success, but his career hit **the buffers / it big** when his second book only sold a thousand copies.

3 Sara hit **it big / the hay** when a buyer saw her exhibition and bought two paintings for an important businessman.

4 Mike hit **the road / the roof** when I lost his mobile phone.

5 Erica hit **the nail on the head / the ground running** when she said the school needs a gymnasium.

6 You've got to get up very early tomorrow so I think you should hit **it big / the hay**.

7 Mike hit **the roof / the ground running** in his new job after working for ten years in the same field.

4 Complete the sentences with the correct parts of the idioms from exercise 3.

1 When he was 16, he hit _it big_ and won a number of international tennis tournaments.

2 Well, I'm tired and I've got an exam tomorrow, so I'm going to hit _____.

3 You've hit _____, because that's exactly what the boss thinks.

4 Mum and Dad will hit _____ when they find out that the teacher sent me to see the headmaster.

5 My career as a lawyer hit _____ when I lost three consecutive cases.

6 Jack will the hit _____ when he starts his new job. It's just what he's always wanted to do.

7 I've got to hit _____ soon if I want to avoid the rush hour traffic.

Participle clauses

1 Decide which sentence has the same meaning as the participle clause.

1 Having studied hard, he expected to pass his exams.
   a While he had studied hard, he expected to pass his exams. ☑
   b Because he had studied hard, he expected to pass his exams. ☐

2 Opening the door to his flat, Tom could smell his mother's cooking.
   a Since he opened the door to his flat, Tom could smell his mother's cooking. ☐
   b When he opened the door to his flat, Tom could smell his mother's cooking. ☐

3 Being good at languages, Diane soon learnt a few useful phrases in Korean.
   a As she was good at languages, Diane soon learnt a few useful phrases in Korean. ☐
   b While she was good at languages, Diane soon learnt a few useful phrases in Korean. ☐

4 Knowing very little about Indian culture, Jack was worried about offending his hosts.
   a After he knew very little about Indian culture, Jack was worried about offending his hosts. ☐
   b Since he knew very little about Indian culture, Jack was worried about offending his hosts. ☐

2 Complete the sentences with the correct participle forms of the verbs in the box.

ask	be	~~eat~~	enjoy	feel	live	use	want

1 _Eating_ his lunch slowly, Tom listened to the radio.
2 _____ in London for the day, we can visit the National Gallery.
3 _____ in Berlin for five years, Kate learned to speak fluent German.
4 Not _____ well, she went to see the doctor.
5 _____ the concert a lot, Alice applauded enthusiastically after each piece.
6 Not _____ to fly, we took the train.
7 _____ her mobile phone, Amy didn't hear the bell ring for class.
8 _____ for directions, John mispronounced the name of the street.

3 Which participle clauses in exercise 2 express reasons and which express time relations? One of the sentences expresses both.

Reasons: ___, ___, ___, ___, ___
Time relations: _1_, ___, ___, ___

4 Use participle clauses to join the sentences. In some cases, more than one answer is possible.

1 I left my books at school. I didn't have much to carry home.
   Leaving / Having left my books at school, I didn't have much to carry home.

2 We live in Switzerland. We speak four languages.
   _____

3 Jack had looked at different models. Jack bought a touch-screen phone.
   _____

4 Rachel had finished the exams. Rachel went on holiday to her grandparents.
   _____

5 David knows about Chinese customs. David didn't have any problems working in Beijing.
   _____

5 Replace the bold words with participle clauses.

Because they are [1]_Being_ very formal, the Japanese sometimes think people from other parts of the world are a little rude when they meet them. **Because I had never met** [2]_____ a Japanese person before, I was a bit nervous, so I asked a colleague for advice. He said that **when you meet** [3]_____ a Japanese person for the first time, you should wait to be introduced. Then, **as you say** [4]_____ your name, lower your head to the other person. Furthermore, **since they think** [5]_____ business cards represent their owner, the Japanese exchange them with a lot of ceremony. **When you offer** [6]_____ your card, you should give it with both your hands. **While you receive** [7]_____ one, you should accept it with both your hands too and then spend some time looking at it. **Now that I've written** [8]_____ this down, I feel more confident about meeting Japanese people in the future.

● ● ● ● ● ● **CHALLENGE!** ● ● ● ● ●

Write sentences using participle clauses about the way people should behave when they meet people for the first time in your country.

Speaking to someone for the first time, you should use their full name and their title.

_____

Proverbs

1 Match the beginnings (1–10) with the endings (a–j) to make proverbs.

1	Absence makes	a	make light work.
2	Actions speak	b	hesitates is lost.
3	Clothes make	c	you leap.
4	Don't judge a book	d	out of mind
5	He who	e	spoil the broth.
6	Look before	f	than the sword.
7	Many hands	g	the heart grow fonder.
8	Out of sight,	h	the man.
9	The pen is mightier	i	louder than words.
10	Too many cooks	j	by its cover.

2 Rewrite the sentences with proverbs that have the opposite meaning.

1 I don't think you should wait. He who hesitates is lost!

 I think you should wait. Look before you leap!

2 My friends won't miss me. Out of sight, out of mind.

_____

3 I don't like working in a team. Too many cooks spoil the broth.

_____

4 Appearance is very important. Clothes make the man.

_____

5 Don't do anything! The pen is mightier than the sword.

_____

3 Read the text. What can expressions tell us about the people who created them?

4 Complete the text with the words in the box.

American   Dutch   Indian   Irish   New York   Rome

●●●●●● CHALLENGE! ●●●●●

List a few expressions in your language that refer to buildings, places, nationalities, countries, etc. Explain in a short sentence what the meaning of each expression is.

_____

_____

_____

A HISTORY OF ENGLISH PROVERBS

For most people, the proverbs and sayings of another language can prove difficult to master. However, students realize that even if these expressions are often hard to remember and use, it is at least useful to study them in order to recognize them in the future. Furthermore, these expressions also tell us something about the history and culture of the native speakers who coined them. A lot of sayings in English reveal much about British and American people's attitudes to other countries and to themselves. Here are a few examples of English expressions that refer to different places and nationalities.

[1]_____ **wasn't built in a day**

An idiom popular with people who don't want to be pressured while they're working. They are saying indirectly that all great things take time and patience to create.

It's all double [2]_____ **to me!**

This idiom is used when someone comes across language or speech that is difficult or impossible to understand. As native English-speakers are notoriously bad language learners, almost any language could be used in this expression, but it no doubt comes from Britain's long trading relationship with these neighbours.

The luck of the [3]_____

An expression referring to Britain's closest neighbours, although history shows that they were not very lucky in their dealings with the British.

An [4]_____ **summer**

An idiom often used in Britain when there is a period of warm weather in early autumn. It originates from Britain's past as a colonial power.

A [5]_____ **minute**

Not surprisingly when you think about the city it refers to, this saying suggests that there are less than 60 seconds in a minute!

The [6]_____ **dream**

This idiom represents the hopes of millions of immigrants who left their homes looking for better material comforts. It is still popular today, both with people born there and newcomers.

Participle clauses after conjunctions and prepositions

1 Choose the correct answers.

1 If **finding** /(**found**), your umbrella will be taken to the lost property office.

2 While **travelling** / **travelled**, we stopped for a break.

3 Don't open the door until **indicating** / **indicated** by the bell.

4 When **introducing** / **introduced**, give your full name.

5 If **approaching** / **approached** by a taxi driver, ask to see his licence.

6 When **waving** / **waved** for a taxi, whistle at the same time.

7 Once **seating** / **seated** in class, I take out my books.

2 Complete the sentences with the correct present or past participle forms of the verbs in brackets.

1 Before _guessing_ (guess) the answer, try and work it out from the context.

2 He won't help you until _____ (ask).

3 You can find the way with the GPS on your mobile if _____ (lose).

4 Despite _____ (live) in France, he still couldn't say a word in French after a year.

5 He's grown up a lot since _____ (leave) home.

6 While _____ (walk) in the park, I saw a couple of my classmates.

3 Complete the sentences with the correct present or past participle forms of the verbs in brackets.

Wherever you are, when [1] _travelling_ (travel) by plane the rules are the same. After [2] _____ (proceed) through check-in, everyone has to pass the security check. Before [3] _____ (go) through the scanner, you have to take off your belt, watch and sometimes your shoes. If [4] _____ (hold) up by slow people, some travellers can get nervous about missing their plane so have everything ready. When [5] _____ (enter) the scanner, if it makes a beep-beep noise, you'll probably be searched by a security guard. If [6] _____ (approach) by a police officer, you'll be asked to open your suitcase. Only speak when [7] _____ (speak) to if you want to avoid it taking longer than necessary. On [8] _____ (close) your suitcase you can relax; the worst part of the journey is over!

4 Complete the sentences with the correct present or past participle forms of the verbs in the box.

| allow | ~~arrive~~ | ask | close | do | eat | enter | stay |

1 On _arriving_ at the hotel, please go straight to the reception desk.

2 When _____ in the hotel restaurant, please give the waiter your room number.

3 If _____, the door will be opened by the night porter when you ring the bell.

4 When _____, the receptionist will be happy to give some advice on local sights.

5 On _____ your bedroom, place the card in the slot to switch on the lights.

6 Our cleaners only enter the rooms when _____ to by our guests.

7 Despite _____ our best to provide excellent service, please tell us if you're not happy with anything.

8 While _____ at the hotel, please feel free to use all our services.

●●●●● CHALLENGE! ●●●●●

Use participle clauses after conjunctions and prepositions to write five sentences about the rules for using transport in your home town.

When getting on a bus, it's considered polite to let elderly people
and mothers with children get on first.

1 _____

2 _____

3 _____

4 _____

5 _____

Travel advice

Preparation

1 Read the essay. When do New Yorkers get angry?

Travelling to the Big Apple

New York welcomes about ten million tourists a year in search of exciting experiences, and most of them have an ¹ action-packed stay. However, to ensure a truly memorable trip to the Big Apple, follow our ² _____ on how to behave like a real New Yorker.

First of all, tourists should be aware that time is ³ _____ to New Yorkers and, as a result, they walk at a very fast pace and expect everybody around them to do the same. Nothing makes them more ⁴ _____ than someone walking slowly, especially if they are ⁵ _____ on their way to or from work. If you do want to take in the sights, leave space on the sidewalk for people to pass. Furthermore, avoid stopping suddenly otherwise you'll find the person walking closely behind you ⁶ _____ bumping into you. This might also result in you receiving a less than ⁷ _____ comment!

However, when they are not racing around the city, New Yorkers are friendly. They usually introduce themselves by their first name and will immediately begin to use yours. This shouldn't be seen as ⁸ _____ behaviour, but as a way of creating an ⁹ _____ atmosphere and communicating friendliness.

Finally, a word about dress: New York is a very cosmopolitan city and you can find fashions from all over the world. However, in some restaurants and theatres there are dress codes and it is ¹⁰ _____ to check before reserving a table or seats. Furthermore, if you're also going to do business in New York, make sure you have some smart clothes with you.

So there you have it; follow our advice and you'll soon feel completely at home in the world's greatest city!

2 Complete the text with the words in the box.

> ~~action-packed~~ advisable agreeable commuters
> discourteous furious inadvertently precious
> pleasant tips

3 Complete the sentences with the words from exercise 2.

1 I thought the shop assistant was rude and _discourteous_ .
2 The weather was very pleasant and we spent an _____ evening in Central Park.
3 His coffee break is very _____ to him and he gets angry if he has to miss it.
4 It's _____ to book your plane tickets as soon as possible before they are all sold.
5 Tom _____ deleted all the files and lost all his work. Now he's got to do it again.
6 We were late and the teacher was _____ with us.
7 We had a really _____ day and did loads of things.
8 Mum gave some good _____ and ideas on how to cook this lamb dish.
9 You can't get on the underground in the morning because it's packed with _____.
10 She plays a _____ character in the play that the audience likes a lot.

Writing task

4 Think about advice you would give to somebody visiting your country / city. Make notes on the following.

- Street life
- Meeting people
- Style of dress

5 Ask yourself the following questions.

- How do people in my town act when they are on the streets? Do they move quickly or slowly? Is it a place to meet people? Is it a place to do business?
- How do they greet new people? How do they address them? Why?
- How do they dress? Are there different ways of dressing for different places and occasions? Are visitors expected to dress in the same way?

6 In your notebook write a piece of travel advice. Think of more expressive language to replace words that you frequently use.

Check your work

Have you

☐ made some notes on the three areas?
☐ thought of some expressive language?
☐ organized your material into four paragraphs?

SELF CHECK 8: GRAMMAR

1 Complete the sentences or answer the questions.

1 Participle clauses can be used to express reasons and _____.

2 What two structures can be followed by a present participle? _____

3 Write three prepositions or conjunctions that can be followed by present participles. _____

4 What can be used as present participles but are not usually used in continuous tenses? _____

5 Although a present participle is in the present, it can refer to the _____.

6 Complete the sentence with the correct form of the verb *take*: Having _____ so long in the shower, she didn't have time for breakfast.

7 What has to be the same in both clauses when you use a participle clause in a sentence? _____

8 Where does a participle clause appear in a sentence: at the beginning, in the middle or both? _____

9 Complete the sentence with the correct form of the verb *discuss*: When _____, the topic causes a lot of arguments.

10 What are omitted in participle clauses that introduce a reason or a time relation? _____

Your score /10

2 Choose the correct answers.

1 **Since having arrived / Having arrived** home, Jack decided to do his homework.

2 **On / Until** leaving, please take all valuables with you.

3 **Been / Being** hungry, he cooked himself a pizza.

4 **Talking / After talking** on the phone, Mary didn't hear the teacher enter the classroom.

5 **Once / Despite** seated in the cab, you can ask the taxi driver to go anywhere in the city limits.

6 You should buy some souvenirs **when / as** visiting Paris.

7 When **told / telling** to get on, you should move quickly.

8 Andy looked at the photos, **thought / thinking** about the great holiday he'd had.

9 Having **read / reading** the book years ago, I can't remember the story now.

10 Don't pay anything **until / while** asked to.

Your score /10

3 There are mistakes in seven of the sentences. Find the mistakes and correct them.

1 Tried to open the door with the wrong key, Tom broke the lock.

_____

2 If stopping at the airport by the police, you'll have to show your passport.

_____

3 Despite living on his own, he doesn't know how to cook.

_____

4 Seen the film a couple of times, I don't fancy seeing it again.

_____

5 Having not studied English at school, Pierre didn't understand what they were saying.

_____

6 After served lunch, we were a lot happier.

_____

7 Because not wanting to travel by plane, he couldn't go on the school trip.

_____

8 On having heard the news, the crowd cheered.

_____

Your score /8

4 Rewrite the sentences using participle clauses.

1 Because he was living in Greenland for a year, Professor Watson was able to study the customs of the Inuit people.

_____

2 After she opened the door, she found some letters on the floor.

_____

3 Before you go to bed, remember to phone your parents.

_____

4 When you are invited to lunch by your host, you must accept.

_____

5 Since they had worked abroad for years, they quickly adapted to their new home country.

_____

6 If you are asked to carry something in your suitcase, say you haven't got enough space.

_____

Your score /12

Total /40

1 Complete the vocabulary quiz with words from Unit 8.

QUIZ

1 Complete the proverb: *look before you* _____.

2 If you _____, you talk about other people's private lives.

3 People who share a good understanding of each other have a good _____.

4 _____ means two or more things happening at the same time.

5 If you _____ something into the air, you throw it.

6 Complete the idiom: *out of sight*, *out of* _____.

7 _____ is the formal rules of a society or an organization.

8 _____ is the display of respect someone has for someone or something.

9 When you hold the _____, it's your turn to speak at a meeting.

10 When you _____ something, you pull it off someone else with your hands.

11 If you _____, you deliberately speak in a very low voice so that not many people can hear you.

12 Complete the proverb: *the pen is mightier than the* _____.

13 _____ refers to a high or low sound.

14 Footballers _____ their opponents and take the ball from them.

15 When one thing partly covers another, it _____ it.

16 Complete the idiom: *hit the nail on the* _____.

17 _____ people don't like talking about themselves.

18 You _____ when you express your disagreement with others.

19 When you feel very tired, you want to hit the _____.

20 Complete the proverb: *absence makes the heart grow* _____.

Your score ____ /20

2 Complete the text with the correct words (a–d).

Sport and personality

They say that ¹_____ speak louder than words and, according to some experts, the sport that a person plays can tell you a lot about their personality. Not surprisingly, people who enjoy the ²_____ of others are drawn to team sports. Team players are often outgoing people who hope to hit it ³_____ with their teammates off the pitch as well as on it. Having people to ⁴_____ to is as important to them as the ability to ⁵_____ past the other team with the ball.

Introverts, on the other hand, believe that ⁶_____ many cooks spoil the broth and prefer individual sports. Players of sports such as golf or snooker require a lot of self-motivation and you'll see them ⁷_____ motivational phrases to themselves. They are often in control of their emotions and are unlikely to ⁸_____ the roof if they make a mistake. But don't make the mistake of judging a ⁹_____ by its cover. They are just as passionate about their sports as team players but while team players are enjoying the company of their team mates, the individualists secretly dream of still hitting it ¹⁰_____ one day.

1	a words	b people	c actions	d children
2	a friends	b camaraderie	c tactics	d gossip
3	a off	b on	c in	d out
4	a discuss	b shout	c chat	d meet
5	a tackle	b protest	c toss	d dribble
6	a too	b to	c enough	d so
7	a muttering	b screaming	c referring	d telling
8	a make	b hit	c do	d break
9	a magazine	b newspaper	c book	d laptop
10	a successful	b big	c high	d up

Your score ____ /10

Total ____ /30

9 Being green

READING

Before reading: Dealing with rubbish

1 **Match the phrasal verbs with the definitions.**

cut down on   ~~do away with~~   fall apart   give away
grow out of   pick up   set up   sign up to

1 To get rid of something or stop using something.
do away with

2 To stop doing or using something as you get older.
_____

3 To establish a new business, organization, etc.
_____

4 To agree to become involved in an organized activity.
_____

5 To do less of something or use smaller amounts of something. _____

6 To offer something to someone without asking for payment. _____

7 To break into pieces. _____

8 To collect or go and get something. _____

2 **Read the text quickly. What must a user of Freecycle do in their first post to the site?**

3 **Choose the correct answers.**

1 What can you find in landfills?
   a Only things that have fallen apart.
   b Brand new DVDs that haven't been watched.
   c Consumer goods still in working condition.

2 Why did Deron Beal set up Freecycle?
   a He was worried about the amount of waste he saw.
   b It was part of his work.
   c His company needed some office furniture.

3 What was the response to Deron Beal's email?
   a Only his close friends were interested.
   b His idea spread quickly.
   c His friends sent him their old furniture.

4 What must Freecycle users do?
   a Go and collect the goods that they have accepted.
   b Only charge for transport.
   c Never say you need something.

5 What does the Freecycle website say?
   a It hopes to spread to other parts of the world soon.
   b Millions of its members visit landfills and rescue material every day.
   c It finds a new home for huge volumes of consumer goods every day.

changing the world one gift at a time

What do you do with those old DVDs that you have watched hundreds of times, but you just can't bear to throw out in the rubbish? What about a games console that you have grown out of? You have moved on to something new but your old console is in perfect working condition. Our consumer-led lifestyle means that we often want to dispose of things before they have fallen apart and become useless. Many people simply throw things away, and as a result, there are millions of items in landfill that are in good working order.

In 2003, Deron Beal was working for an organization to promote waste reduction in Tucson, Arizona. He was disconcerted by the amount of useful things being thrown away, so he sent out an email to several friends, offering free office furniture that the organization no longer needed and was planning to discard. The response was encouraging – people wanted to take the unwanted items and re-use them. In addition, they forwarded the email to their friends and soon lots of people were signing up to the email group.

Beal's idea of getting rid of your own 'junk' by giving it away to someone who needed it soon caught on, and he named his group Freecycle. Many of the subscribers began offering their own free items, including furniture, clothing, toys and appliances. Beal created some simple rules for Freecycle users: you can either post what you have to give away, or what you need, but the first post must be an offer of something you would like to get rid of. All goods must be free to anyone willing to take them, and the taker must make the arrangements to pick up and transport them.

Within months, the Freecycle concept had spread to other parts of the world and people were setting up their own groups. Today, there are believed to be as many as 4,700 Freecycle groups linking millions of members in over 75 countries. According to the Freecycle website, there are estimated to be 500 tonnes of material saved from landfills every day.

A tiny step to save the environment

1 Complete the sentences or answer the questions.

1 If something is *portable*, it means you can _____ it.
   (a) carry   **b** drink   **c** buy

2 When you _____ *size* something, you make it smaller.
   a small   **b** down   **c** shrink

3 A _____ is a machine that produces electricity.
   a loft   **b** fold-up   **c** generator

4 If something is _____, it lasts for a long time.
   a durable   **b** exorbitant   **c** incentive

5 Someone who is _____ is not worried about problems.
   a unimaginable   **b** incentive   **c** undaunted

6 A *fold-*_____ chair is a chair that can be made smaller when it isn't in use.
   a across   **b** in   **c** up

7 To _____ something means to bear it or not be changed by it.
   a withstand   **b** withhold   **c** within

8 Something that is *exorbitant* is …
   a expensive.   **b** cheap.   **c** reasonable.

9 An *incentive* _____ you to do something.
   a wants   **b** encourages   **c** reminds

10 If you _____ *rid of* something, you throw it away.
   a go   **b** get   **c** take

11 To _____ things means to put them into the correct groups.
   a classify   **b** class   **c** classification

12 To _____ people means to provide a place where they can stay.
   a home   **b** room   **c** accommodate

13 A *loft* is a space at the _____ of the building.
   a top   **b** bottom   **c** side

14 The word _____ refers to things related to goods or money.
   a material   **b** economical   **c** purchase

15 Something that is difficult to imagine is _____imaginable.
   a dis   **b** un   **c** ill

Negative adjectives for impact

2 Complete the sentences with the prefixes *in-* or *un-*.

1 The motorcycle accident left him _in_capacitated for nearly a year.

2 The difference in price was ___significant so I bought the slightly more expensive one.

3 The sofa was a very ___wieldy object to try and get up the stairs.

4 Although he was quite ___ept at sport, he always played for the team because of his determination.

5 The ___trepid climbers reached the summit despite the terrible weather.

6 For some ___explicable reason he's resigned from his job!

7 He has an ___canny ability to memorize facts and figures.

3 Choose the correct adjectives.

1 It was an (uncanny) / insignificant experience. It was the first time we had met, but he knew everything about me!

2 Jane has refused the company's offer of a pay rise! It really is **intrepid / inexplicable**!

3 He might be an **intrepid / unwieldy** explorer but he seems frightened of his neighbours.

4 Sue was so **incapacitated / inept** with her hands at school that it's hard to believe she's now a surgeon.

5 This enormous old suitcase is so **unwieldy / uncanny**. Why don't you buy some new luggage?

6 Although the injuries left him **incapacitated / inept** in terms of sport, he could still attend classes.

7 He came to the meeting but his contribution was so **inexplicable / insignificant** I can't remember it.

Types of home

4 Match the houses with the definitions.

bungalow   caravan   detached house   ~~mansion~~
semi-detached house   terraced house

1 A very large expensive house, often in the countryside.
   mansion

2 A small house that forms part of a row of small houses.
   _____

3 A long vehicle for travelling and living in. _____

4 A house, often quite large, that is not connected to other houses. _____

5 A house with only one floor. _____

6 A house that is connected to a similar house on one side.
   _____

Inversion

1 Choose the correct answers.

1 Never ~~have we thought~~ / we have thought about living in a tiny house.

2 Seldom **think people** / **do people think** about the consequences of throwing away consumer goods.

3 Under no circumstances **should spend we** / **should we spend** money on new office furniture.

4 **At any time** / **At no time** has the company shown an interest in being more environmentally friendly.

5 Not until everybody reduces their energy consumption **the environment will** / **will the environment** benefit.

6 No sooner had he told us about the benefits of hybrid cars **than** / **but also** we bought one.

7 Rarely **have we had** / **have we** such an opportunity to do something for the environment.

8 Not only are they going to go to work by bicycle, but **are they also** / **they are also** going to sell their car.

2 Complete the sentences with one word.

1 No _sooner_ had we started using energy-efficient light bulbs than we noticed a reduction in our bill.

2 Not _____ does the company give away its computers on Freecycle, but it also uses recycled paper.

3 _____ no circumstances will we buy a big car.

4 Not _____ the committee produces its report should we change anything.

5 Hardly had they finished school _____ they joined a summer volunteer group to clean the beaches.

6 _____ after reading about environment issues did I decide to do something.

3 Use inversion to rewrite the following sentences. Make any other changes that are necessary.

1 We shouldn't fail to cut down on energy consumption under any circumstances.
   Under no circumstances should we fail to cut down on energy consumption.

2 The company started to recycle materials only after the workers complained.
   _____

3 He had hardly sent the email than he received lots of replies agreeing with his idea.
   _____

4 So many people have seldom been interested in green issues.
   _____

5 I never eat meat.
   _____

6 I realized how good energy-efficient light bulbs were only after using them.
   _____

7 We never expected Freecycle to be so successful.
   _____

8 They weren't interested in helping at any time.
   _____

4 Complete the speech with the words and tense in brackets.

'... In the first place, under no circumstances ¹_should students throw_ (students / throw – should) used paper into the rubbish bins. Please use the new recycling bins. Seldom ²_____ (we / have – present perfect) such a good opportunity to recycle, so please don't waste it. Secondly, at no time ³_____ (you / ask – should) for more food than you really need in the school canteen. Not only ⁴_____ (we / want – present simple) to avoid wasting the food we don't eat, but we can also donate the food we don't use to charity organizations. Finally, no sooner ⁵_____ (we / form – past perfect) the school environment committee than the headmaster ordered energy-saving bulbs for the whole school. However, only by all students being more energy-conscious ⁶_____ (we / reduce – future with *going to*) the school's carbon footprint. So please switch off all lights and electrical devices when you are not using them. Now, let's look at transport ...'

● ● ● ● ● CHALLENGE! ● ● ● ● ●

Use inversion to write sentences saying what your classmates can do to be more environmentally friendly.

Under no circumstances should you leave the light on if you are the last person to leave the classroom.

_____

_____

Green issues

1 **Match the words with the definitions.**

> biodegradable   break down   charge up   eco-friendly
> emissions   greenhouse gas   landfill   on standby   ~~toxic~~

1 Poisonous. toxic_____

2 Something that has been made to do the least possible damage to the environment. _____

3 A place where rubbish is buried. _____

4 To become weaker and be destroyed. _____

5 A substance that is believed to cause the gradual warming of the planet. _____

6 Something that breaks down easily and doesn't harm the environment. _____

7 When an electrical device is ready to be used if necessary.

   _____

8 Amounts of gas, heat, etc. that are sent out by cars, factories, etc. _____

9 To put electricity into an electrical device. _____

2 **Complete the sentences with the correct form of the words from exercise 1.**

1 Try not to send your old plastics to landfill_____ sites because they are not _____ and take a very long time to _____. However, you should never burn them because the fumes they produce are _____ and cause health problems.

2 Avoid leaving electrical devices _____ as they continue to consume energy even if you're not using them. Also try not to _____ devices such as MP3 players until their batteries are almost completely empty. In this way, you'll be more _____ and consume less of the planet's scarce energy resources.

3 _____ from vehicles produce carbon dioxide and increase the _____ that are heating up the planet.

3 **Read the text. What has caused the increase in the use of air conditioning?**

4 **Are the sentences true or false? Correct the false sentences.**

1 Surfing the internet affects the environment. T__

2 The IEA says we should buy fewer electronic devices. ___

3 Air conditioning hasn't always been an energy-efficient system. ___

4 Energy efficiency increases the use of electronic devices.

   ___

5 Ecologists want to see higher taxes on electronic devices.

   ___

6 People probably wouldn't mind paying more taxes to save the planet. ___

Curbing our energy consumption

There are thousands of popular websites that are forums for people who share the view that human industrial activity and our thirst for energy have caused global warming. Yet the existence of these sites highlights the contradiction between what many of us think and what most of us really do. The energy required to run the world's computers and the internet now produces a bigger carbon footprint than air travel. We all want to improve the environment but we are so addicted to electrical devices such as mobile phones, computers and flat screen TVs that household energy consumption has as much as doubled in the last twenty years. The International Energy Agency says that electrical gadgets now consume more energy than washing machines and fridges, with the consequent increase in greenhouse gases. The answer, the IEA say, is in using more energy-efficient devices. But is that really true?

Not according to a growing number of ecologists. They claim that energy-efficient devices encourage greater consumption, and they use air conditioning as an example. Air conditioning systems originally needed a lot of energy to function and had a very big impact on people's electricity bills. The result was that they were only switched on when temperatures became unbearably hot. However, because of improvements in technology, air conditioning has become much cheaper to run and people now leave it on all the time. Furthermore, the use of air conditioning has spread across the planet, even to countries with relatively cool climates such as Britain. Not only does energy efficiency encourage people to use air conditioning more, but it has also dramatically increased the number of systems in the world. As a result, air conditioning now consumes much more of the world's resources.

So just what is the solution? Some ecologists claim that the only way to stop people from using so much energy is to make it more expensive. If governments increase taxes, their argument goes, people will reduce their consumption, and it seems that recent experience shows that they are right. The financial crisis that hit the world towards the end of the first decade of the new millennium saw some European countries reporting the first drop in energy consumption for years. Perhaps the most eco-friendly action that governments could take is to hit their citizens in their pockets. It might not be popular with voters, but the planet would appreciate it.

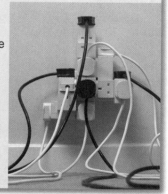

●●●●●● **CHALLENGE!** ●●●●●●

Make a list of the electrical devices that you own and that are in your home. Organize them into three groups:

• Devices that are essential

• Devices that you could use less

• Devices that you could survive without

Emphatic use of *as...as*

1 Choose the correct answers.

1 There are as **much** / **many** as fifteen students in my class who walk to school.

2 Some newspapers say as **few** / **many** as one in 500,000 citizens of industrialized countries have reduced their carbon footprint.

3 As **many** / **little** as two thousand delegates flew to the conference on global warming in Mexico.

4 The new DVD recorder weighs as **few** / **little** as 500 grams.

5 They have sold as **much** / **many** as a thousand of the new mobile phones in this store in one week.

6 As **few** / **much** as two leopards have been born in captivity.

7 As **few** / **little** as £150 will buy you a new notebook.

8 An average person loses as **many** / **much** as 1.4 litres of sweat per hour during exercise.

2 Complete the text with *many*, *much*, *few* and *little*.

Current global warming has been caused by as
[1] few_____ as 15 countries. People in these industrialized countries say they didn't know they were damaging the environment until recently. However, their energy consumption has increased by as [2] _____ as 100% in the last 20 years. As [3] _____ as 4 billion of the world's 5 billion mobile phones, and most electrical devices such as computers and MP3 players, are used by people in developed countries. Today, as [4] _____ as 5% of the world's energy is used to run computers and recharge electrical devices but as [5] _____ as 20% of this energy is used by citizens in developing countries. Organizations such as Greenpeace say people in industrialized countries have to reduce their energy consumption by as [6] _____ as 80% but as [7] _____ as 1 in 500,000 households have managed to do this. The world's poorest people – as [8] _____ as 4.5 billion – use only 20% of the world's resources, but they are the ones who will suffer the most from the consequences of global warming.

3 Rewrite the sentences with the words in brackets.

1 It takes three hours to manufacturer a car on a modern production line. (little)

_____

2 There were three hundred students at the meeting. (many)

_____

3 Three students had done the homework. (few)

_____

4 A new bicycle can cost £50. (little)

_____

5 That family produces three bags of rubbish a day! (much)

_____

6 He has five mobile phones that he uses for work. (many)

_____

4 Use the emphatic *as … as* structure and the student's notes to write sentences about the results of a survey of a class of twenty students.

4 students – recycle five kilos or more of waste material a week
3 students – come to school by car
14 students – cycle to school
4 students – spend only £1 a week
2 students – don't charge up electrical devices such as mobile phones
All students – use computers for at least ten hours a week

1 Four students recycle as much as five kilos of waste material a week.

2 _____

3 _____

4 _____

5 _____

6 _____

●●●●● CHALLENGE! ●●●●●

Use the emphatic use of *as … as* to write five sentences about your use of computers and other electronic devices.

I charge up my mobile phone for as much as three hours a week.

1 _____

2 _____

3 _____

4 _____

5 _____

A report: cause and effect

Preparation

1 Read the essay. What has been the main benefit of an increased number of visitors to Barcelona?

THE POSSIBLE EFFECTS OF INCREASED TOURISM

In recent years, the city of Barcelona has become a very popular destination for both people attending conferences and tourists. Its modern infrastructure combined with its pleasant climate and beaches have attracted both business people and pleasure-seekers, and their presence has made an impact on the local economy. Local shopkeepers and restauranteurs have increased their income and, as a result of the greater economic activity, the local council is planning to try and attract even more visitors. A _____ However, not everyone is keen to see the tourism sector grow further and many feel that the already visible adverse effects of mass tourism will only get worse.

The city has increased the amount of energy that it uses dramatically in recent years and the local electricity system has collapsed under the strain on more than one occasion. While the city has invested heavily in hotels and transport, the energy companies have done little to update their equipment and further demand would considerably affect the normal running of the system, and therefore the city. B _____

More visitors would also reverse the good work that has been done to improve the city's transportation system and to encourage local residents to use the city's bicycle renting scheme. C _____ What is more, more vehicles on the roads would also mean more pollution in the atmosphere and possibly a threat to people's health, especially for children and the elderly.

Finally, a greater number of visitors may also affect local emergency services. Hospitals and clinics in the city centre are already stretched to the limit in the summer dealing with cases of extreme sunburn, heat stroke and minor injuries caused on the beach. D _____ An increase in visitors might mean that medical and police resources from other parts of the city would have to be diverted to tourist areas and this may reduce the quality of the service in the rest of the city.

At present, Barcelona has the resources to meet the needs of both local residents and visitors. However, an increase in the number of tourists would undoubtedly have negative effects on the quality of life for the city's population.

2 Complete the text with the following sentences.

1 Furthermore, the need for more energy would mean a rise in pollution from local power stations.
2 An increase in the use of taxis and private coaches would cause traffic congestion and would greatly reduce the quality of life for local people.
3 Moreover, tourists unfortunately attract pickpockets and the local police spend a lot of their valuable time dealing with this problem.
4 The city has built various conference centres and hotels to accommodate visitors and thousands of jobs have been created in the tourist industry.

3 Which of the sentences in exercise 2 are main consequences or effects and which are secondary?

Main consequences / effects: 2 , ___
Secondary consequences / effects: ___ , ___

Writing task

4 Complete the effects diagram with the phrases a–f.

a You can keep up to date with what is happening in the world.
b They have to be charged up regularly.
c You can ask for help when in a difficult situation or an emergency.
d You can keep in constant contact with friends and family.
e Most phones allow you to connect to the internet.
f They have increased energy consumption.

Consequence 1 ☐	→	Secondary consequence ☐
Consequence 2 ☐	→	Secondary consequence ☐
Consequence 3 ☐	→	Secondary consequence ☐

5 Add your own main consequences and secondary consequences about the positive effects of the mobile phone on society.

6 In your notebook write a cause and effect report on the following topic.

The effect of the mobile phone on society has been more positive than negative.

Check your work

Have you

☐ thought of positive and negative points?
☐ added some main and secondary consequences of your own?
☐ organized your material into four paragraphs?

1 Answer the questions.

1 What do we use inversion for? _____

2 Which structure do we use with countable nouns to express a lower limit? _____

3 What do we put at the beginning of a sentence that has inversion? _____

4 Write two examples of restrictive words that can be used on their own in inversion. _____

5 Which structure do we use with uncountable nouns to express an upper limit? _____

6 What is the order of the subject and the affirmative auxiliary verb in a sentence that has inversion?
_____

7 Which structure do we use with uncountable nouns to express a lower limit? _____

8 A negative adverbial expression must contain one of which two words? _____

9 Which structure do we use with countable nouns to express an upper limit? _____

10 Which structure do we use with countable words such as *hours*, *kilograms* or *pounds*? _____

Your score ☐ /10

2 Choose the best continuation for each sentence. In some cases, both are correct.

1 Some notebooks weigh as
   a little as 300 grams. ☐
   b few as 300 grams. ☐
2 There were as
   a many as twenty people at the meeting. ☐
   b few as twenty people at the meeting. ☐
3 Not only are they expensive
   a but they're also badly made. ☐
   b than they're also badly made. ☐
4 Some newspapers say computers in the future will cost as
   a many as £50. ☐
   b little as £50. ☐
5 No sooner
   a did I arrive, than the phone rang. ☐
   b had I arrived, than the phone rang. ☐
6 Hardly had the organization been set up,
   a that it became incredibly popular. ☐
   b than it became incredibly popular. ☐

Your score ☐ /6

3 There are mistakes in five of the sentences. Find the mistakes and correct them.

1 Only in a few companies all the workers print documents on recycled paper.
_____

2 There are as few as twenty tigers still living on the reserve.
_____

3 You can take as much than you want but don't take more than you need.
_____

4 The school needs so many as thirty computers for its new technology room.
_____

5 Seldom down-sizing has increased a company's costs.
_____

6 Hardly had Jane finished the report but she spotted a few typing mistakes.
_____

Your score ☐ /6

4 Rewrite the sentences with the words in brackets. Make any other changes that are necessary.

1 I heard the news and I sent an email to my friends. (sooner)
_____

2 It should take two minutes to grill a steak. (little)
_____

3 Staff salaries account for 60% of the company's costs. (much)
_____

4 There will be 3,000 ecologists on the demonstration. (many)
_____

5 He didn't realize that he was wasting so much energy. (little)
_____

6 Some hybrid cars can only carry two people. (few)
_____

7 He's going to change jobs and also he's going to leave home. (only)
_____

8 We weren't aware of the damage we were causing. (time)
_____

Your score ☐ /8

Total ☐ /30

1 Complete the vocabulary quiz with words from Unit 9.

QUIZ

1 The negative prefix used with *explicable* is

_____.

2 A _____ is a house with only one floor.

3 Someone who is _____ is not skilled or effective at what they do.

4 _____ means something is very expensive.

5 If something is _____, it lasts a long time.

6 Something that is _____ is easy to carry.

7 A _____ is an enormous house with lots of rooms.

8 CO_2 is an example of a _____ gas.

9 The negative prefix used with *daunted* is _____.

10 Something that is _____ can kill you.

11 An _____ usually motivates people to do something.

12 The negative prefix used with *capacitated* is

_____.

13 When we go shopping we buy _____ goods.

14 If you are _____, you are still determined to do something despite problems.

15 When you _____ things, you put them into groups.

16 A _____ site is where rubbish is buried.

17 A _____ piece of furniture can be made smaller so it can be easily put away.

18 The negative prefix used with *canny* is _____.

19 A _____ is found under the roof of a house.

20 A _____ is a type of mobile home.

Your score ____ /20

2 Complete the words and expressions in the article.

Them and us

Trying to be an [1]_____-friendly member of society can be a difficult task. For most of us, it is not a realistic option to [2]_____-size to a tiny house or a mini hybrid car. Neither is the task of getting [3]_____ of our possessions so that we can live in nine square metres. Most of us have filled all the space in our terraced or [4]_____-detached houses and dream of moving to a bigger place so we can live more comfortably. Furthermore, most people haven't got time to dedicate to taking such an [5]_____trepid green step. School, work and family commitments mean that we can only make [6]_____significant gestures towards being greener. We try to use [7]_____degradable products and avoid charging [8]_____ our mobiles too frequently and leaving electrical devices [9]_____ standby, but modern life doesn't allow us to do much more. Furthermore, the [10]_____imaginable scenarios of disaster that are predicted for the future of the planet frighten some people so much that they'd prefer not to think about the environment at all!

Your score ____ /10

Total ____ /30

10 Child's play

READING

1 Match the words with the definitions.

classics   critic   epic   literary   lyrical   prolific
verse   ~~volume~~

1 One book in a set of books related by topic.
   volume

2 Producing a great amount or number of something.
   _____

3 Someone who gives their opinion about films,
   books, music, etc. in a newspaper, on a radio
   programme, etc. _____

4 The study of ancient Greek and Roman culture,
   especially the languages and literature.
   _____

5 One of the parts which a poem or song is divided
   into. _____

6 Connected with literature. _____

7 A poem, book or film which is long and contains a
   lot of action, usually dealing with a historical
   subject. _____

8 Expressing thoughts and feelings in a beautiful way.
   _____

2 Read the text quickly. Why did Keats decide to become a
doctor?

3 Answer the questions.

Which paragraph talks about …
1 Keats's feelings about being a doctor? D
2 a form of poetry that Keats invented? ____
3 a negative personal experience? ____
4 the way young people's talent often shows itself? ____
5 what Keats achieved while he was alive? ____

4 Are the sentences true or false? Correct the false
sentences.

1 People are more familiar with certain types of prodigies
   than others. T
2 Keats's work wasn't published before his death. ____
3 Keats was from a wealthy background. ____
4 Keats was considered a talented surgeon. ____
5 Keats didn't have time to dedicate to his work as a
   surgeon. ____
6 Keats's work hasn't had any effect on other poets. ____

A Prodigy of English Literature

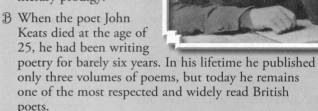

A Everyone must be
familiar with prodigies
who have discovered
new mathematical
formulas or principles of
physics. The other type
of prodigy that typically
springs to mind is the
musical one who can
compose and play
complicated piano
sonatas from a young
age. But what about the
literary prodigy?

B When the poet John
Keats died at the age of
25, he had been writing
poetry for barely six years. In his lifetime he published
only three volumes of poems, but today he remains
one of the most respected and widely read British
poets.

C Born in 1795 to parents of relatively modest means,
Keats attended a boarding school near his
grandparents' home north of London. He showed an
interest in classics and history, and in 1809, won his
first academic prize for high marks in school exams.
As a result of the death of his parents, Keats left
school and became a surgeon's apprentice. Shortly
after completing his apprenticeship, Keats further
demonstrated his aptitude for medicine by earning an
appointment as a junior surgeon in a London hospital.

D However, the medical field did not captivate Keats in
the way that poetry did. He felt compelled to create
poems, and resented the amount of time medicine
required. By the age of 20, Keats had decided to
dedicate himself to writing and announced to his
guardian that he was giving up his medical career.

E Keats was a prolific writer, and in 1819 he composed
six odes in a short period of time that have become
some of his most famous poems. An ode is a type of
poem that focuses on a particular event or individual,
and describes it intellectually rather than emotionally.
The odes represent Keats's attempt to create a new
type of short, lyrical poem, which influenced later
generations of poets and writers. Many critics believe
Keats's work shows an insight and wisdom beyond his
years. I find it difficult to imagine what Keats could
have accomplished had he not died from tuberculosis
at such a young age.

VOCABULARY

Rising stars

1 Answer the questions with the correct forms of the words in the box.

> acclaimed adamant ~~aptitude~~ call upon cherish
> chip in launch level-headed ovation prestigious
> tie under pressure unprecedented victory virtuoso

When Peter Helfgott decided that his five-year-old son, David, had an ¹ _aptitude_ for playing the piano, he was starting him off on a career that would eventually see David play at some of the world's most famous and ² _____ concert halls. By the time he was ten, David was considered a ³ _____ and he started winning prizes in his home country of Australia. When he was 19 he left for London, where he was to be ⁴ _____ on a career that would take him all over the world. However, he soon felt stressed and ⁵ _____ from his new responsibilities and returned home with mental health problems. Fortunately for David, he met a ⁶ _____ woman who became his wife, and her sensible personality soon helped him return to a more relaxed lifestyle.

However, David's life changed dramatically when a film was made about his experiences as a music prodigy. The film, *Shine*, was an ⁷ _____ success for a story about classical music; indeed, there is a ⁸ _____ at eighth place between *Shine* and a Jennifer Lopez production in the list of most successful films ever about a musician. However, *Shine* wasn't just a ⁹ _____ for the director and actors. As a result of all the publicity, David was ¹⁰ _____ to perform all over the world and each performance he gave finished with a standing ¹¹ _____ from his adoring audience. However, it wasn't all good news. Unfortunately, he had lost a lot of his childhood ability and his piano playing, which had once been so highly ¹² _____, was criticized as being very poor. Indeed, music critics said he had very little talent and objected to his habit of ¹³ _____ with comments during the quiet moments of the pieces he was playing. Further problems came from his sister Margaret. She claimed that the film had damaged the image of their dead father, whose memory she still loved and ¹⁴ _____. She was ¹⁵ _____ about repairing the damage done and she eventually wrote a book about how good their father had been and how disloyal David was.

Music

2 Match the words with the definitions.

> anthem composer conductor flute opera pianist
> symphony synthesizer ~~violin~~

1 A musical instrument made of wood with four strings which is held against the neck and played by moving a bow across the strings. _violin_
2 A musical instrument shaped like a thin pipe. The musician holds it sideways and blows across a hole at one end. _____
3 An electronic keyboard instrument for reproducing and combining different recorded sounds, often copying other musical instruments or voices. _____
4 Someone who directs the performance of musicians. _____
5 A dramatic musical play in which most of the words are sung. _____
6 A song which has importance for a particular country and is often sung on a special occasion. _____
7 A person who writes classical music. _____
8 A person who plays a large musical instrument with a row of black and white keys. _____
9 A long complicated piece of music for an orchestra, usually with four parts. _____

Phrasal verbs and idioms with *get*

3 Replace the words in bold with the correct form of the phrasal verbs and idioms in the box.

> ~~get across~~ get at get by get into get over get rid of
> get to grips with get to the bottom of get up to

1 I never understand what he means because he doesn't **communicate** his ideas very well. _get across_
2 You shouldn't **throw away** your old electrical gadgets. You should recycle them. _____
3 The government will **investigate and find a solution to** the problem. _____
4 I didn't like the book at first, but now I'm **becoming interested in** the story. _____
5 We manage to **survive** on very low salaries. _____
6 Ann is always **criticizing** her younger sister. _____
7 He **recovered from** the shock of the car crash and is now driving again. _____
7 What did you **do** during your week in Paris? _____
8 I'm beginning to **understand what I have to do for** the project. _____

GRAMMAR

Phrasal verbs

1 **Choose the correct answers.**

1 My mum **signed up** / (**turned down**) the job offer because she would have to be away from home a lot.

2 The company I work for has recently been **taken over** / **drawn up** by a German car manufacturer.

3 All of tomorrow's matches have been **taken on** / **called off** because of the bad weather.

4 I knew they were good singers, but I didn't realize that they'd **handed over** / **signed up** with a record company.

5 She's **come up with** / **come in for** an amazing plan to raise money for the school trip to Paris.

6 I said that I would help clear the attic, so I can't **take over** / **go back on** my promise.

7 We've **drawn up** / **turned down** a list of gifts that we think people might want to buy for our wedding.

8 The coach has **come up with** / **come in for** a lot of criticism for the team's run of poor results.

9 The shopkeeper **handed the thief over** / **called the thief off** to the police.

10 Kate **took too much work over** / **took too much work on** and she was under a lot of pressure.

2 **Complete the phrases by forming phrasal verbs with the words in the boxes.**

bring	call	come	hand	~~live~~	set
take	water				

~~down~~	down	off	off	on	over	up
up with						

1 <u>live down</u> an embarrassment
2 _____ _____ more work
3 _____ _____ _____ a brilliant idea
4 _____ _____ on a journey
5 _____ _____ a meeting
6 _____ _____ important documents
7 _____ _____ a topic in a conversation
8 _____ _____ your views

3 **Complete the sentences with the correct form of the phrasal verbs in the box.**

bring up	figure out	get away with	live down	pass up
~~put up with~~	set off	water down		

1 I can <u>put up with</u> your bedroom being untidy, but I hate finding your dirty socks everywhere!

2 Some people never pay on the underground because they can _____ it.

3 What time will we have to _____ to catch the train tomorrow?

4 The students have _____ their demands in the hope of ending the dispute quickly.

5 Can you help me with exercise 3? I can't _____ the answer at all!

6 He's such a bore! He's always _____ his great exam marks and saying what a good student he is.

7 What? She's not going? I can't believe she's _____ the chance to spend a month in Brazil.

8 I'm never going to _____ tripping over on the stage when I went to collect my degree certificate!

4 **Complete the text with the correct adverbs.**

When a group of Chinese businessmen took ¹<u>over</u> United football club, they decided to buy the best players in the world. Young star Toni Piazzi was at the top of their list, and it was an opportunity he couldn't pass ²_____. The club agreed to pay him an incredible amount of money and they drew ³_____ a contract with his agent. Toni happily signed ⁴_____ for United for three years. However, he rarely played for the team and he had to put ⁵_____ with watching the games from the substitutes' bench. He spoke to his agent and asked him to figure ⁶_____ a way of leaving United. His agent spoke to an Italian team but United said they wouldn't let him get ⁷_____ with not fulfilling his contract. When the fans heard that Toni wanted to go ⁸_____ on his contract, he came ⁹_____ for a lot of criticism. Now, not only doesn't he play, but the fans also shout at him as he walks to the bench! It will take him a long time to live this ¹⁰_____.

●●●●● **CHALLENGE!** ●●●●●

Find three new phrasal verbs and write an example sentence and a definition for each one. You could choose three phrasal verbs that are used to talk about one particular topic, e.g. music, sport, studying.

1 _____
2 _____
3 _____

Educational needs

1 Match the beginnings (1–8) with the endings (a–h) to make sentences.

1 Your homework was quite mediocre _h_
2 I don't believe the promises of these accelerated language learning sites ___
3 I failed all my maths exams last year ___
4 Obviously the war has been a serious impediment ___
5 Schools often fail to cater for the needs of gifted children ___
6 Education for special needs offers help to children ___
7 My parents give me an allowance for when I'm at university ___
8 Few people doubt that Mozart ___

a by concentrating on average children.
b and now I'm doing a remedial course.
c but during the summer holidays I work to augment my income.
d who suffer physical or mental disabilities.
e was a musical genius.
f to the country's economic progress.
g that say you'll learn 500 new words every week.
h and I can only give you 5 out of 10.

2 Complete the sentences with words from exercise 1.

> Although it might be difficult to believe, being a ¹gifted_____ child can be an ²_____ to having a pleasant childhood. Their ability to learn at an ³_____ rate means that they speed ahead of their classmates but then have to wait for their more ⁴_____ companions to catch up. This can create and ⁵_____ a sense of frustration in talented children. Others find that being labelled the ⁶_____ of the class means that they are seen as different and might be bullied. Furthermore, a few ⁷_____ students are excellent in one or two subjects but need ⁸_____ lessons in other areas and special attention for their disabilities. As can be seen, talent is a gift that needs to be handled carefully.

3 Read the text. What does the writer suggest are not essential activities for students who are revising?

4 Match the titles (A–E) with the paragraphs (1–5).

A Get organized! _3_
B Sleep on it! ___
C The end is in sight! ___
D Brain training! ___
E Take a reality check! ___

Exam revision tips

1 You're almost there! The academic year is coming to an end and the summer holidays are just around the corner. However, before you can relax, there is one final task: the end-of-year exams. Not only will the results of these exams have a big influence on how you enjoy your break, but they will also shape your future. So, make sure you get the best results you can by following our revision tips.

2 Revision is hard work. Don't waste time with websites that promise to make studying easy; they won't! Don't bother revising with your friends; everybody has their own way of studying and you'll probably end up chatting. Be honest with yourself. Only one person can do your revision: you!

3 Revision takes time. Draw up a revision timetable and allocate sufficient time for studying each subject properly. Also leave enough time for the other commitments in your life that you can't put off until after the exams. After all, activities such as shopping trips and football matches are not essential and you'll survive for a few weeks if you don't do them.

4 A good timetable will help make sure that you allow the right amount of time for your brain to recover. Experiments have shown that students remember more when they go to bed early. Apparently, while our bodies rest, our brains take on the challenge of putting everything we've learnt during the day into the correct 'files' in our memories. But all-night study doesn't give our brains the time to organize everything and, as a result, although we've studied more, we remember less.

5 Exercise doesn't just keep you in good physical condition; it also improves your mental powers. Studies have shown that students who exercise three times a week increase their learning capacity by 15% and they also achieve better exam results. So remember to include a pair of trainers as part of your essential exam preparation materials!

We can't guarantee you'll pass all your exams if you follow our tips, but we're sure that they'll help you to do better. Good luck!

●●●●●● CHALLENGE! ●●●●●●

Write four tips of your own for revising for exams.

_____
_____
_____
_____

Phrasal verbs with objects

1 Choose the correct continuation for each sentence. In some cases, both are correct.

1 We need to sort
   a out the travel arrangements. ☑
   b the travel arrangements out. ☑

2 Will you pick
   a up them? ☐
   b up the children? ☐

3 Back away
   a from me now! ☐
   b me from now! ☐

4 He will never live
   a down that defeat. ☐
   b it down. ☐

5 Did you remember to throw
   a away it? ☐
   b away the rubbish? ☐

6 We'll have to wait
   a out the storm. ☐
   b it out. ☐

2 Add a suitable pronoun to the phrasal verb, in the correct position.

1 I'm afraid you can't play the match tomorrow. They've called off. _called it off_

2 Nobody knew about the story because none of the big TV channels picked up on. _____

3 He always talks about his paintings. I wish he wouldn't bring up every time we meet. _____

4 We saw a big dog in the street and decided to back away from slowly! _____

5 If your plane arrives at six, I'll pick up outside the airport at six-thirty. _____

6 I'm afraid you've given your word and I won't let you go back on! _____

7 So we've decided what's going in the contract and the secretary will draw up tomorrow. _____

8 He says he's lost my DVDs, but I've told him he'll have to come up with soon. _____

3 Complete each sentence with a suitable pronoun and particle. These must be in the correct order.

1 I've got so many old photos but I don't want to throw _them out_.

2 If you've got problems, I'll help you sort _____.

3 I've been studying this text for ages but I still can't figure _____.

4 Tom is really lazy but he gets away _____.

5 The two countries have agreed on a peace treaty and now they're going to draw _____.

6 Once you've made a promise never go back _____.

7 They haven't sold enough tickets for the festival, so they've called _____.

8 I signalled that I wanted to leave but you didn't pick up _____.

4 Rewrite the sentences, replacing the words in bold with a phrasal verb from the box and a suitable pronoun.

> cut off   figure out   get away with   pass up   pick up on   set up   ~~take on~~   throw away

1 I've agreed to **do the extra work.**
   I've agreed to take it on.

2 How did he manage to **escape making his bed**?
   _____

3 You shouldn't **get rid of these chairs.**
   _____

4 Someone is coming to **install the new computers.**
   _____

5 Don't **miss the opportunity to live abroad for a year.**
   _____

6 I always have difficulty **solving maths problems.**
   _____

7 The storm **stopped Ray and Roger from having a phone conversation.**
   _____

8 We didn't **notice what was happening.**
   _____

●●●●● **CHALLENGE!** ●●●●●

Write five sentences with phrasal verbs about challenges that you have faced in your life.

I once walked through a field of bulls and I knew I had to appear confident and not back away from them if they came towards me.

1 _____
2 _____
3 _____
4 _____
5 _____

A summary

Preparation

1 Read the essay. Why do children who are labelled as gifted often fail later in life?

It would seem that some parents are obsessed with producing a child with above-average levels of intelligence. In recent years the sale of 'educational' CDs that pregnant mothers can play to encourage their unborn babies to be the next Mozart or Einstein have gone up dramatically. However, the number of geniuses hasn't. In fact, the experts claim that only 2% of children can be classified as exceptionally gifted and a new report suggests that their superior talent disappears when they become adults.

In a study that lasted from 1974 until 2010, the progress of 210 talented children was followed. The children had been identified as gifted in music, maths and art at the ages of six and seven, but professor Joan Freeman discovered that only 3% of them were successful later on. The big question, of course, is why did so many talented children fail to turn into talented adults?

Joan Freeman and other experts have offered a number of explanations. In the first place, once a child has been identified as gifted, they are often taken away from normal schools where they were usually happy. They are then placed with older children and put under pressure by their parents and teachers to 'perform'. These new environments often have the opposite effect and instead of helping the child to develop, turn them into mediocre students.

Another theory suggests that gifted children are rarely gifted throughout their whole lives. Their talent for learning quickly slows down and disappears as they get older and other children catch up with them. This then leads to frustration, as schoolwork that they had done effortlessly becomes difficult. Furthermore, while their less talented classmates have learned the value of hard work, the onetime classroom 'geniuses' haven't, and they soon start to fall behind.

This is unpleasant news for anybody that has been labelled as 'gifted' at school. However, for the other 98% of the population it's good to know that if you're not born a genius, life still offers opportunities for those who are willing to work for them.

2 Choose the best summary for the text.

a Some parents are obsessed with producing a 'genius'. However, the number of geniuses hasn't gone up. A study from 1974 until 2010 showed that only 3% of gifted children become gifted adults. Professor Joan Freeman and other experts have offered a number of explanations for this. This is unpleasant news for anybody that has been labelled as 'gifted' at school.

b Very few children are gifted, and a study of 210 talented children found that only 3% of them continue to do well later in life. Suggested reasons for this are that gifted children are pressurized to do well and are unhappy about not studying with children of their own age. Other experts believe children are only 'gifted' temporarily and that other students eventually reach their level.

c The writer thinks a lot of parents are too worried about turning their children into geniuses. However, a new report says that most clever children do not continue to stand out as being more intelligent in their working lives. Furthermore, they don't know how to work hard. I agree that this is good news for the 98% of us who are not gifted!

3 Which summary …

1 includes opinions? ___
2 uses too many words and phrases from the original text? ___
3 focuses on facts? ___

4 Look at the reading text on page 76 and underline the main ideas and important facts.

5 Study the parts of the text that you've underlined and think about how you are going to express these ideas in your own words.

6 In your notebook write a summary of 100 words of the text.

Check your work

Have you

☐ underlined the main points or important information in the text?
☐ cut out the writer's opinions?
☐ reduced the number of details?
☐ used your own words?

SELF CHECK 10: GRAMMAR

1 **Answer the questions or complete the sentences.**

1 What does a two-part phrasal verb consist of?
_____

2 When can a phrasal verb be separated? _____

3 Write a three-part phrasal verb that means *to change an agreement*. _____

4 When is it not possible to place the object after the adverb in a two-part phrasal verb? _____

5 Write a two-part phrasal verb that means *take control of something*. _____

6 Phrasal verbs are _____ because their meaning cannot always be understood from the separate parts of the verb.

7 Which type of phrasal verb can't be separated?
_____

8 Write a two-part phrasal verb that means *cancel an arrangement or an event*. _____

9 What does a three-part phrasal verb consist of?
_____

10 Write a three-part phrasal verb that means *notice*.
_____

Your score ___ **/10**

2 **Decide if both sentences in each pair are correct. If just one sentence is correct, say which one.**

1 a I avoided bringing up the subject at the meeting. ☐
  b I avoided bringing the subject up at the meeting. ☐

2 a Diana handed the papers over to the police. ☐
  b Diana handed over them to the police. ☐

3 a We're trying to come up with a new filing system. ☐
  b We're trying to come a new filing system up with. ☐

4 a Sara is not the kind of person who backs a difficult situation away from. ☐
  b Sara is not the kind of person who backs away from a difficult situation. ☐

5 a An Italian company has taken it over. ☐
  b An Italian company has taken over my dad's computer business. ☐

6 a The newspapers picked up on the story but the TV companies didn't. ☐
  b The newspapers picked up on it but the TV companies didn't. ☐

Your score ___ **/6**

3 **There are mistakes in seven of the sentences. Find the mistakes and correct them.**

1 Their team never stops shouting at the referee but they always get away it with.
_____

2 They're going to draw off the picnic because of the bad weather.
_____

3 It was a terrible moment and I don't think I'll ever live it over.
_____

4 He couldn't afford to go on the trip so he had to pass up it.
_____

5 If you go back on your promise, you'll get a bad reputation.
_____

6 I could see what was about to happen but Angela didn't pick anything up on.
_____

7 There was a big traffic jam and we decided to wait out it.
_____

8 I don't want to get away this old table. We can still find a use for it.
_____

Your score ___ **/8**

4 **Rewrite the words in bold, using a phrasal verb and a pronoun.**

1 Joe was telling us about the film when Sue **interrupted him**.
_____

2 I'll **collect you** in the car after training.
_____

3 I missed training last week and the trainer **mentioned it** before the game.
_____

4 It's a good plan and we managed to **produce it** in five minutes over a cup of coffee.
_____

5 It's a big responsibility but Ann's agreed to **undertake it**.
_____

6 All the equipment is in the van but we'll need a couple of hours to **install it**.
_____

Your score ___ **/6**

Total ___ **/30**

1 Complete the vocabulary quiz with words from Unit 10.

QUIZ

1 If you get _____ someone, you criticize them.
2 What do you call someone whose work is neither very good nor very bad? _____
3 Which electronic instrument can reproduce the sounds of lots of other instruments? _____
4 We _____ the people and things that are important to us.
5 Someone who _____ in interrupts a conversation to say something.
6 Someone who is under _____ feels stressed.
7 To call _____ someone is to ask them to do something in a formal way.
8 If you get _____ something, you start enjoying doing it.
9 Something that is _____ has never been experienced before.
10 A _____ is extremely skilled at playing a musical instrument.
11 A _____-headed person is usually calm and can deal with difficult situations.
12 A _____ occurs when an audience shows its appreciation for a musician's performance.
13 A _____ writes pieces of music.
14 If you want to discover why something happened, you have to get to the _____ of it.
15 You _____ a new activity or organization.
16 National _____ are usually played before international sporting events.
17 A _____ occurs when two teams finish a game with the same number of points.
18 What do you call a person who plays the piano?
   _____
19 Students with special needs often require _____ education.
20 Someone who is _____ receives praise for their work.

Your score [ ] /20

2 Choose the correct answers.

Helen Keller

We expect our schools to detect [1]**virtuoso / gifted** children's talents easily and to provide them with the education that will make the most of their personal [2]**mediocre / aptitudes** and abilities. But when someone suffers from [3]**impediments / remedial** such as blindness and deafness then it is obviously much harder to detect their talent. When Helen Keller became deaf and blind at the age of two, her mother was [4]**acclaimed / adamant** that her daughter's condition wouldn't hold her back. She wanted Helen to receive an education for her special [5]**needs / augment** that would enable her to get [6]**into / by** in day-to-day life. But Helen did much more than get to [7]**grips / rid** with her situation.

Helen's teacher, Anne Sullivan, got her ideas [8]**across / at** by spelling words on Helen's hand with her finger. As soon as Helen realized that Ann was teaching her how to communicate, she went through a process of [9]**accelerated / launched** learning, catching up on the five years she'd spent in darkness and silence. Her progress didn't stop there, and in 1904 she received a degree from the [10]**cherished / prestigious** Radcliffe College, the first deaf blind person to graduate from university.

Your score [ ] /10

Total [ ] /30

Before reading: Loaning words

1 Complete the text with the words in the box.

> contemporary   deeds   folklore   immortal   literary
> mother tongue   struggle   transition

Although epic poems, traditional stories and ¹_____ have given us ²_____ heroes, it is the written word rather than the characters described that has lasted. Even today, as we ³_____ through the difficult ⁴_____ from printed paper to electronic screen, those brave acts and ⁵_____ of ancient ⁶_____ heroes are amongst the first works to be digitized so that future generations can enjoy the earliest works written in their ⁷_____. The fact that they are so old gives these stories an extra quality that the ⁸_____ works of today's writers cannot compete with.

2 Read the text. Why do languages take loanwords from other languages?

3 Are the sentences true or false? Correct the false sentences.

1 There are more Arabic speakers than English speakers. ___
2 Arabic and English have been used in business between countries. ___
3 Arabic words in the English language are used for a variety of things. ___
4 Most Arabic words in English came directly from Arabic. ___
5 Today's loanwords from English come often from American English. ___
6 Loan words enter other languages more quickly today. ___

●●●●●● **CHALLENGE!** ●●●●●●

Find five words in your language that are loanwords from other languages. What kind of things do they refer to, e.g. food, media? Are these words new or have they been around for a long time? Do you think people will continue to use them in your language in the future? Why / Why not?

_____
_____
_____

LOANWORDS

At first glance, the languages of Arabic and English appear to have very little in common. However, in terms of importance and history, both of them share certain features. English, with just over 300,000 million native speakers, and Arabic, with around 200,000 million, are two of the world's most widely spoken languages. Furthermore, both languages have been spoken by nations that created empires and, as a result, have also been the languages of international commerce and science. As a consequence of this, both Arabic and English have had an impact on other languages, including on each other.

Arabic loanwords in English often refer to the scientific and technological advances made during the time of the Islamic Empire. There are over 150 Arabic loanwords in English, giving English speakers the names of a wide range of objects, from foodstuffs to household furnishings, from tools to musical instruments. Most of these words passed through other languages such as French and Spanish before being incorporated into English, as the inventions and developments taking place in the Islamic Empire spread across Europe. These words have remained because they described new objects and ideas, things that people had never seen or experienced before and didn't have a name for.

Today, a number of English loanwords are used in Arabic for the same reason. The development of information technology in the English-speaking USA has given the world new devices and tools never seen before. Furthermore, this new technology has enabled these loanwords to be incorporated into Arabic and other languages very quickly and in great numbers. In the past, the process was much slower, allowing cultures to adapt to new things. Loanwords were accepted to name new ideas and objects, but different cultures had time to invent terms to describe how they worked and what they did. Today, that time isn't available.

However, the dramatic increase in the speed at which things change might also mean that these English loanwords will be short lived. Will the world still be 'downloading', using 'search engines' and 'texting' in twenty years' time, or will new technology have made these words obsolete? And will English still be the language of technology or will science be speaking in another tongue entirely?

Before reading: The plugged-in family

1 Match the definitions with the words in the box.

> attribute common contribution device researcher
> issue multi-tasking usage

1 a machine which has been invented to carry out a particular purpose _____

2 a subject or problem that people are discussing _____

3 a particular quality or feature _____

4 someone who makes a detailed study of a subject _____

5 an ability to do more than one thing at the same time _____

6 something that occurs frequently or is the same for a lot of people _____

7 the consumption of a product or service _____

8 something that you do or give to help achieve something with other people _____

2 Read the text. Who adapted the quickest to the new situation? How?

3 Are the sentences true or false? Correct the false sentences.

1 The three Maushart children spent their leisure time in the same way as most teenagers. ___

2 Susan wasn't happy with the way her children spoke to each other. ___

3 Susan felt electronic media had become a substitute for her children's real lives. ___

4 Meal times became long and boring. ___

5 The youngest daughter started to do better at school. ___

6 The family are adamant that they won't ever use electronic media again. ___

●●●●● CHALLENGE! ●●●●●

Carry out a short survey on the use of electronic media in your house. After you've done the survey, write a short report about the situation in your house.

	Me	Person A	Person B	Person C
Types of media.				
Total hours used.				

The plugged-in family

Susan Maushart's three teenage children enjoyed relaxing in the same way as millions of their peers all over the world: listening to music on their iPods, using the internet, playing computer games and watching TV. Nothing unusual you might think, for children of the 21st century. However, Susan wasn't happy about the way she and her three children spent their free time staring at screens instead of talking to each other, so she took a drastic decision: she decided to pull the plug on all the media technology in her house.

It won't come as a surprise to hear that Susan's decision to ban all electronic devices for six months, including mobile phones, wasn't popular. However, she felt that instead of just using electronic media occasionally, everybody in the house was actually living their lives through it. Her daughters, Sussy, 14, and Anni, 18, would spend the whole time social networking and 15-year-old son Bill shut himself in his bedroom with his Playstation. Even Susan herself would disappear into her bedroom with her laptop to finish off 'important' work. They all lived in the same house but they hardly spoke to each other. Would her ban bring them together again?

It was Sussy who had the most difficulty dealing with the new situation. She replaced her hours in front of her computer with hours on the household's landline telephone. Anni would run off to the local library to use the computers to do her school work. However, Bill had few problems adapting to the family's new lifestyle and he used his free time to learn how to play the saxophone. Little by little, the two sisters began to appreciate the benefits of chatting at length with the family after meals and playing board games together. Furthermore, Sussy started getting much better grades at school, an unexpected consequence that convinced her that the ban had been a good thing.

Susan lifted the ban after six months, admitting that such a situation wasn't realistic for people living in the modern world. However, although the electronic devices are back on, the family is adamant that they won't let them take over their lives again.

1 Complete the sentences with the correct forms of the words in the box.

> cater   craving   fancy   gather   gravitate   haul
> range   shift

1 I have eaten any chocolate for ages and now I've got a _____ for it.
2 I always _____ towards the student's café when I need a break from my studies.
3 Are you working on the night _____ this week?
4 Do you _____ going to the cinema tomorrow evening?
5 Now children, _____ round and I'll tell you the story of Robin Hood.
6 The fishermen _____ the enormous fish out of the water into the boat.
7 The government has introduced a _____ of measures to tackle unemployment.
8 This restaurant _____ for students and therefore it's really cheap.

2 Read the text. Where does chicken tikka masala originate from?

3 Answer the questions.

1 What are the effects of globalization on food?
_____
2 How did curry first arrive in Britain?
_____
3 How did it spread across the country?
_____
4 Why might an Asian waiter not be familiar with chicken tikka masala?
_____
5 What has happened since 1999?
_____
6 What might you find in Canada, Australia and New Zealand?
_____

●●●●●● CHALLENGE! ●●●●●●

Write a few sentences about a dish from your country that you think would be popular in other countries. Say what the ingredients are, how you cook it and why people would like it.

Foreign food?

What do you think the most popular dish in Britain is? Fish and chips, perhaps? How about roast beef? Well, it's neither of those, although both dishes continue to be popular. In fact, the British are crazy about curry, and their favourite curry of all is a dish called chicken tikka masala.

When we think about globalization and food, it's often fast food and chain restaurants that come to mind, as these have spread to so many countries. However, if you are interested in knowing what effects our changing world has had on people's eating habits, then the British obsession with the curry is a good place to start.

Curry has been present in British kitchens since the 18th century, when people returning from their work for the British Empire in India brought the recipe home with them. However, it was the arrival of thousands of Bangladeshi immigrants in east London and industrial cities like Birmingham and Glasgow after the Second World War that really made curry popular. The Bangladeshis first opened restaurants to feed their compatriots but the dishes on offer soon became popular with the locals. Today, there are now over 12,000 restaurants serving numerous types of curries and other dishes from India and Pakistan as well as Bangladesh.

But not only have Asians introduced the British to their cuisine, they've also invented dishes to suit their tastes. Enter a restaurant in Asia and order chicken tikka masala and your request is most likely to be met with blank expressions from the waiters. According to some sources, chicken tikka masala is a dish that was created by Indian restaurants in London for their British customers, and until recently, it was unheard of on the Asian sub-continent. However, in Britain it's certainly been a success. Apart from being the dish that is most frequently asked for in restaurants, there is even a pizza with a chicken tikka masala topping and chicken tikka masala-flavoured packets of crisps. However, perhaps the most surprising thing is that, since 1999, the dish has been exported by Britain to India, Pakistan and Bangladesh.

Curry is now an integral part of British cuisine and British curry houses have created a restaurant style that is now being exported to Canada, Australia and New Zealand. Furthermore, a dish which was adapted in an attempt attract British diners has changed a nation's eating habits and become a global favourite.

Before reading: Chinese flowers

1 Match the definitions with the words in the box.

| diverse   flavour   hardships   precisely   prosperity |
| renewal   scrub   shrine |

1 the state of being successful and having a lot of money

_____

2 a particular taste _____

3 in an exact manner _____

4 the act of increasing the life of something _____

5 a place which is holy because of a connection with a holy person or object _____

6 things which make life difficult or unpleasant

_____

7 to rub something hard in order to clean it

_____

8 varied _____

2 Read the text. Why do you think some fireworks are named after plants and trees?

3 Answer the questions.

1 What did the Chinese originally use gunpowder for?

_____

2 Who were fireworks first used for?

_____

3 Who called fireworks 'Chinese flowers'?

_____

4 What are pellets and what do they make?

_____

5 What did the Chinese use the Beijing Olympics to demonstrate?

_____

6 How did they make the virtual fireworks look real?

_____

●●●●●● CHALLENGE! ●●●●●●

Write a short description about the last firework display you saw. Where and when did it take place? What was it for? What types of fireworks were used? What did you think of it?

Chinese flowers

What can make a night-time event truly spectacular? The answer is fireworks. Fireworks are an ancient invention that has become an essential ingredient in any celebration or festival all around the world. But who invented them and where do they come from?

China is the birthplace of fireworks and they were developed after the Chinese had discovered gunpowder in the 9th century. It was the military uses of gunpowder that first interested the Chinese, but by the 12th century they had started to create less powerful 'rockets' and 'bombs' that were used to entertain the Ming dynasty during the celebrations of Chinese New Year. At first, fireworks were a rich man's toy and it wasn't until much later that ordinary people started using them to celebrate weddings and births. Naturally, such a magnificent invention soon spread across the globe and when they reached the Arabic-speaking world, they were called 'Chinese flowers'.

The name 'Chinese flowers' was an apt choice, as many of the patterns created by fireworks mimic the shapes and forms of nature. In fact, three of the most popular, palm, willow and chrysanthemum, bear the names of trees and plants. To create these figures, small explosives, known as pellets, are arranged into a shape and then surrounded with gunpowder. When the gunpowder explodes, the pellets are blown outwards, exploding a few seconds later to make the colourful pattern.

Although fireworks are now manufactured all over the world, the Chinese are still a leading force in the business and they used the opening ceremony of the 2008 Beijing Olympic Games to demonstrate this. They also used the event to introduce the world to a new type of fireworks: virtual fireworks. As the ceremony came to an end, TV viewers around the world watched in awe as fireworks representing giant footprints exploded around the stadium. However, the ones they saw on their TV screens had been recorded months before. To make it look real, typical Beijing weather had been added to the firework sequence on a computer, and the image was shaken to make it appear as if it had been filmed from a helicopter camera. Having given the world the real thing, have the Chinese now introduced us to the beginning of the end of real fireworks?

1 Complete the sentences with the correct form of the words in the box.

> better-suited   convenience   equip   fabric
> low-income   opt   permanently   stereotypically

1 Films set in London _____ show Big Ben in the opening sequences.

2 They've finished building the new school but now they have to _____ it so it can be used.

3 Their new house has every modern _____ you can imagine.

4 I wish my dad would stop eating so much. He's going to damage his health _____.

5 Seats on public transport are usually covered in a hard wearing _____.

6 With your qualifications we think you would be _____ to another type of job.

7 We offered the workers more money or fewer hours and they _____ for the money.

8 The state must do more for _____ people who need financial help.

2 Read the text. What is it possible to do if you live and work in the underground city?

3 Read the text. What do the numbers refer to?

1 13
_____

2 1962
_____

3 12
_____

4 200
_____

5 2,000
_____

6 80
_____

7 28
_____

8 100,000
_____

●●●●● **CHALLENGE!** ●●●●●

Write a few sentences about the disadvantages that living underground would have for people. Think about health, leisure activities, etc.

Going underground

The Canadian city of Montreal is home to almost 2 million citizens but a visitor to the city in winter could be forgiven for thinking that they had arrived in a ghost town. However, with temperatures that regularly drop to –13 C°, it's perhaps not surprising that the streets are empty. Nonetheless, people have to go shopping if they want to eat and drink and the centres of other Canadian cities are busy, so just where do the locals of Montreal disappear to? The answer is just a few metres beneath the visitor's feet.

Since 1962, Montreal has been building an underground city that continues to grow and grow. At present, there are more than 32 km of tunnels and seven underground stations spread over an area of 12 km², making the Underground City the world's largest complex of its kind. As many as 500,000 people head there every day to escape Montreal's freezing winters. Once inside, they can shop at 1,700 stores, eat at over 200 restaurants and see films in more than 30 cinemas.

However, the Underground City is much more than an enormous shopping centre. Students go to university in the Underground City, business people attended conventions at the three exhibition centres and there are museums and even a sports stadium. There are also 2,000 apartments and it is home to 80% of the city's office space, so if you live near an underground line, it's possible to work, shop and go out without ever seeing the outside world!

Given the success of the Underground City, other Canadian cities have developed their own sites. Toronto has the PATH centre, home to 28 km of tunnels lined with shops and with 100,000 daily visitors, while the city of Halifax offers its residents the Downtown Halifax Link that provides underground office space and cinemas. All of these centres have been built in an attempt to provide city dwellers with a way of enjoying life in spite of the freezing Canadian winters. Who knows, we may see a city in a much hotter environment doing the same one day!

FUNCTIONS BANK

Asking for clarification

Why is that exactly?

Could you explain what you mean by that?

Does this mean that people will stop travelling?

So you mean more people will go on cycling holidays?

Using polite language

I was wondering if….

I would recommend …

Might I … ?

Did you want to …?

Would you mind … ?

If you could …

Making positive suggestions

Why don't you … ?

Supposing you … ?

Provided that you …

Imagine if you hadn't …

So long as you …

Making complaints

I'm ringing to complain about …

I'm really unhappy with the service.

It's simply not good enough to …

Sorry, but actually I'd like to …

That's just not acceptable.

It's absolutely ridiculous!

I'd like to speak to the manager.

How can I help you?

Could you tell me precisely what the problem is?

Describing experiences

How can I put it?

How can I describe it?

You just can't imagine.

It was sort of like...

It's a kind of …

It was some type of …

It was like something out of a survival film!

Reaching an agreement

You've got to be joking.

Sorry but I really can't agree with you on that.

I'm afraid we'll have to agree to disagree on that one.

I see your point, but I don't entirely agree.

That's true, but I'm not convinced.

That's a possibility.

I completely agree with you on that.

Yes, I see what you mean.

OK, I'd go along with that.

Presenting an opinion

I'm going to talk about growing your own vegetables and why it's important.

Did you know … ?

An amazing statistic, isn't it?

What I love is …

It's the great range of ingredients that …

And the best thing is, …

Changing the subject

By the way, …

Anyway, going back to my course …

Sorry to interrupt …

That reminds me …

Now, tell me more about …

Showing interest

You're kidding!

You didn't?

Exactly!

Oh, dear. That's terrible.

Presenting an argument

I'll explain in more detail.

To put it another way, …

In other words, …

Let me give you an example.

A good example of this is …

That reminds me about the time …

There are three main points that I'd like to make.

Here's the point I want to make.

And finally, …

An opinion essay

The internet, a researcher's dream?

A lot of students today have access to a computer and Internet connection. This means that they have an incredible research tool at their fingertips that enables them to find sources of information that students a few years ago could only dream of. Nevertheless, to get the most out of the internet, students need to be aware that it is not perfect.

One of the first sources that many students visit is an online encyclopaedia. The fact that these are making print encyclopaedias obsolete suggests that they must be reasonably good, but if you're using a free one, only use it as a starting point. Firstly, you should treat each entry individually; just because one contains accurate information, doesn't mean the next will. Furthermore, make sure the entry you are using provides a lot of references and links to the websites of respected newspapers and journals that will allow you to research your topic further.

With regard to web searches, the most popular websites usually find their way onto the first page of the majority of search engines that appear on your screen; hence a lot of students are taking their information from the same sources. This means that teachers are receiving homework that repeats the same information and lacks originality. Furthermore, just because something is popular doesn't mean it's good or accurate. If you're looking for factually correct information, avoid blogs and message boards and look for sites from official organizations, academic journals, etc. A good search engine will help you find these sites, albeit not so quickly, but the time invested will provide you with original, authoritative information to use.

To sum up, the internet is a fantastic tool for students. However, to get the best out of it, students need to be patient with their searches and not accept the first sites that they find. Furthermore, they need to ask questions about the quality of the material they are reading and the expertise of the people who have provided it. Follow these few simple rules and I'm sure the internet will help you to learn a lot.

- Write four paragraphs. Start with an introduction that explains the current situation of the subject that you are writing about. In the following two paragraphs provide reasons and examples that support or contradict the title.
- Use appropriate linking words to introduces reference, contrast and consequence.
- Use a variety of sentence types. Use complex sentences to show which ideas are more important and which are secondary.
- In the last paragraph, conclude by reinforcing your opinions on the subject.
- Use simple sentences for summing up or getting the reader's attention.
- Use compound sentences to create a balance or contrast of information.

A comparison and contrast essay

- Organize your work into four or five paragraphs. Introduce the people or things that you are going to compare and contrast.
- In paragraph 2, describe one similarity or difference.
- Introduce the main points with expressions such as *The first basic difference* ….
- In paragraph 3, describe a second similarity or difference.
- Use linking words and expressions such as *on the other hand*, *while*, *whereas* and *in contrast* to balance two equally important but contrasting ideas.

For many students, owning a vehicle is a symbol of independence. However, given the prohibitive costs of buying and running a car, the vast majority have to make a choice between two forms of two-wheeled transport: a moped and a bicycle. At first sight, it might seem that once again price would play a big part in helping people come to a decision, but when all the pros and cons are taken into consideration, it is not so clear cut.

The first obvious difference between a moped and a bicycle is the method of propulsion; a moped comes with a motor, whereas on a bicycle you provide it! Many people assume that this increases the cost of mopeds greatly in comparison to bicycles, but this is not true. You can pick up a brand new moped with a 50cc motor for just over £500, while a good bicycle will cost the same. Of course, mopeds need petrol to run, although they are very economical and get 40 to 50 km out of each litre. However, you should also budget for an occasional visit to a mechanic. In contrast, once you've bought a bicycle the little maintenance that is needed can be carried out by the owner.

Both mopeds and bicycles are excellent forms of transport in the city. Whereas car drivers are prisoners of traffic jams, cyclists and moped riders escape them. In an experiment carried out in London involving various forms of public and private transport, the moped rider arrived first at the destination and the cyclist second. However, the cyclist felt exhausted on arriving. The moped rider, on the other hand, didn't.

In conclusion, while price is an important factor, anyone debating which form of transport to use, will take other factors into account. People wanting to keep fit or perhaps because of ecological considerations will choose a bicycle. If getting around town quickly is your main priority, then you'll probably be willing to pay that little bit extra to run a moped.

An informative article

One of the greatest differences between today's teenagers and previous generations is in the way that they use their free time. Today's teenagers spend a lot more time indoors because of electronic gadgets such as computers and game consoles. Furthermore, instead of doing things with friends, some young people prefer the company of their machines. These gadgets can lead to an unhealthy lifestyle and create anti-social behaviour. However, if you're a fan of technology, we've got some good news. According to a recent study, using IT makes you more intelligent! To put it another way, electronic media can be a good thing.

Convincing your parents that using electronic gadgets is better for your brain than other educational activities will probably be difficult, but experiments carried out by an American university have discovered that these new technologies make our brains work more. For instance, the results indicate that searching the web creates a lot more brain activity than reading a book. The researchers came to the conclusion that regular use of technology made young people's brains quicker and more flexible.

Teenagers, however, are not the only ones who benefit from regular exposure to technology. For example, older users can improve their memories by using the internet because web searches exercise the part of the brain used to remember things and make decisions. According to the study, most electronic media can help older people exercise their brains and stop them from losing some of their memory. So tell your parents and grandparents to join you the next time you play a computer game!

However, the study also includes some bad news about excessive use of electronic devices. Despite the fact that regular use of technology makes our brains faster, unfortunately it affects our ability to concentrate negatively. The study revealed that people who frequently use electronic media often find it hard to concentrate on one thing for a long time. The answer? Combine the old with the new. That is to say, combine using new technologies with more conventional sources of information, for example books, encyclopaedias and newspapers. That way, you'll have a healthy brain and happy parents!

- Make sure each of the four paragraphs contains one main point.
- Use clarification to rephrase what you have said before so that the idea is clear to your readers. Introduce clarification with phrases such as *in other words*, *to put it another way* and *that is to say*.
- Introduce examples with a variety of expressions: for example, *for instance*, *such as* and *like*.
- Use clarification to add extra information. Use phrases such as *in other words*, *to put it another way* and *that is to say*.

A report

- Make the focus of your report clear in the first paragraph, so that readers find it easy to follow the logic of your argument in the following paragraphs.
- Use second conditional sentences or auxiliary verbs such as *could*, *would*, *may* or *might* if speculating about the possible effects of a situation.
- Use examples to illustrate your ideas.
- If possible, present alternative outcomes so that the reader feels they are being given all the alternatives.
- Write a brief conclusion that focuses on the future of the situation presented in the introduction.

We are close to the point of peak oil. Peak oil refers to the moment when the maximum amount of oil that can be produced is reached and then production starts to decline. There are varying scientific opinions on the timing of this moment, but nobody disagrees that it will happen soon. When it does, it will probably lead to an increase in the cost of living, as well as having serious consequences for the economy.

Less oil would mean an increase in petrol and electricity prices. Costlier petrol would lead to a rise in the prices of just about every product you can imagine. Nearly everything we eat, wear or use is transported in vehicles that run on petrol-driven motors. Furthermore, a lot of power stations convert oil into electrical energy, so we would also see the cost of electricity going up and as a result this would have a very negative effect on businesses.

Of course, the consequences of the fall in oil production don't have to be so dramatic. Many car manufacturers are already producing either hybrid vehicles, with both a small petrol engine and an electric motor, or vehicles that run on electric motors. Naturally, electricity will still be needed, but there have been great advances in alternative energy forms such as wind and solar power. Hopefully these sources will become efficient enough in the future to provide us with the energy we need.

However, as well as governments switching to alternative energy, citizens must also take part in solving the problem. Many people tend to use their own vehicles even when they have public transport at their disposal. If people used busses, trains and the underground more, we could greatly reduce the amount of oil consumed. Furthermore, the high levels of air pollution in big cities would decrease and the health of urban dwellers would improve.

Most governments and many private businesses are preparing for the day oil runs out. However, if we all collaborated, we could make the transition from an oil-dependent society to one which is run on alternative energy much less difficult.

adventurous /əd'ventʃərəs/ _____

all-inclusive /ˌɔːl ɪn'kluːsɪv/ _____

appeal (to) ☞0 /ə'piːl/ _____

atmosphere ☞0 /'ætməsfɪə(r)/ _____

atrocious /ə'trəʊʃəs/ _____

baggage ☞0 /'bægɪdʒ/ _____

bank holiday
/ˌbæŋk 'hɒlədeɪ/ _____

bargain ☞0 /'bɑːgɪn/ _____

bargain hunting
/'bɑːgɪn ˌhʌntɪŋ/ _____

be intent on sth
/ˌbiː ɪn'tent ˌɒn/ _____

boardwalk /'bɔːdwɔːk/ _____

breeze /briːz/ _____

budget ☞0 /'bʌdʒɪt/ _____

business class
/'bɪznəs ˌklɑːs/ _____

business traveller ☞0
/'bɪznəs ˌtrævələ(r)/ _____

canal /kə'næl/ _____

chalet /'ʃæleɪ/ _____

charming /'tʃɑːmɪŋ/ _____

cheetah /'tʃiːtə/ _____

clatter /'klætə(r)/ _____

comedian /kə'miːdiən/ _____

cosy /'kəʊzi/ _____

crave /kreɪv/ _____

creak /kriːk/ _____

cuisine /kwɪ'ziːn/ _____

custom ☞0 /'kʌstəm/ _____

decade ☞0 /'dekeɪd/ _____

deserted ☞0 /dɪ'zɜːtɪd/ _____

destination /destɪ'neɪʃn/ _____

dine /daɪn/ _____

disposable /dɪ'spəʊzəbl/ _____

dominate ☞0 /'dɒmɪneɪt/ _____

dot /dɒt/ _____

downmarket /daʊn'mɑːkɪt/ _____

downscale /daʊn'skeɪl/ _____

dramatically ☞0 /drə'mætɪkli/ _____

dreadful /'dredfl/ _____

elevator ☞0 /'elɪveɪtə(r)/ _____

enchanting /ɪn'tʃɑːntɪŋ/ _____

exclude ☞0 /ɪk'skluːd/ _____

extravagant /ɪk'strævəgənt/ _____

fabulous /'fæbjələs/ _____

facility ☞0 /fə'sɪləti/ _____

five-star /'faɪv ˌstɑː(r)/ _____

flock /flɒk/ _____

fondue /'fɒnduː/ _____

frighteningly /'fraɪtnɪŋli/ _____

frosty /'frɒsti/ _____

fulfil (your) ambition
/fʊlˌfɪl (jɔːr) æm'bɪʃn/ _____

gag /gæg/ _____

gazelle /gə'zel/ _____

giraffe ☞0 /dʒə'rɑːf/ _____

glide /glaɪd/ _____

guide ☞0 /gaɪd/ _____

gurgle /'gɜːgl/ _____

habitat /'hæbɪtæt/ _____

health concerns ☞0
/helθ kənˌsɜːnz/ _____

hippo /'hɪpəʊ/ _____

hiss /hɪs/ _____

holiday ☞0 /'hɒlədeɪ/ _____

holidaymaker
/'hɒlədeɪmeɪkə(r)/ _____

homely /'həʊmli/ _____

hospitable /hɒ'spɪtəbl/ _____

humorous ☞0 /'hjuːmərəs/ _____

incompatible /ɪnkəm'pætəbl/ _____

jeep /dʒiːp/ _____

landscape ☞0 /'lændskeɪp/ _____

lavish /'lævɪʃ/ _____

lift ☞0 /lɪft/ _____

lion /'laɪən/ _____

low-cost /'ləʊ ˌkɒst/ _____

luggage ☞0 /'lʌgɪdʒ/ _____

luxuriant /lʌg'ʒʊəriənt/ _____

luxury hotel /ˌlʌkʃəri həʊ'tel/ _____

market segment
/ˌmɑːkɪt 'segmənt/ _____

marvel /'mɑːvl/ _____

meteorology /miːtiə'rɒlədʒi/ _____

metro /'metrəʊ/ _____

multitude /'mʌltɪtjuːd/ _____

ocean ☞0 /'əʊʃn/ _____

off the cuff /ˌɒf ðə 'kʌf/ _____

off the record ☞0
/ˌɒf ðə 'rekɔːd/ _____

off the wall ☞0 /ˌɒf ðə 'wɔːl/ _____

on tenterhooks
/ˌɒn 'tentəhʊks/ _____

on the boil ☞0 /ˌɒn ðə 'bɔɪl/ _____

on the go ☞0 /ˌɒn ðə 'gəʊ/ _____

on the hoof /ˌɒn ðə 'huːf/ _____

on the off chance
/ˌɒn ði 'ɒf ˌtʃɑːns/ _____

on the one hand ☞0
/ˌɒn ðə 'wʌn ˌhænd/ _____

on the other hand ☞0
/ˌɒn ði 'ʌðə ˌhænd/ _____

/i/ happy	/æ/ flag	/ɜː/ her	/ʊ/ look	/ʌ/ mum	/ɔɪ/ noisy	/ɪə/ here
/ɪ/ it	/ɑː/ art	/ɒ/ not	/uː/ you	/eɪ/ day	/aʊ/ how	/eə/ wear
/iː/ he	/e/ egg	/ɔː/ four	/ə/ sugar	/aɪ/ why	/əʊ/ go	/ʊə/ tourist

opportunity 🔑 /ˌɒpəˈtjuːnəti/ _____

opulent /ˈɒpjələnt/ _____

overcome 🔑 /ˌəʊvəˈkʌm/ _____

pace 🔑 /peɪs/ _____

participant /pɑːˈtɪsɪpənt/ _____

per night 🔑 /pə ˈnaɪt/ _____

per person 🔑 /pə ˈpɜːsn/ _____

ping /pɪŋ/ _____

portray /pɔːˈtreɪ/ _____

predator /ˈpredətə(r)/ _____

purchase 🔑 /ˈpɜːtʃəs/ _____

process 🔑 /ˈprəʊses/ _____

relaxation /ˌriːlækˈseɪʃn/ _____

resort 🔑 /rɪˈzɔːt/ _____

rollerblading /ˈrəʊləbleɪdɪŋ/ _____

routinely /ruːˈtiːnli/ _____

rustle /ˈrʌsl/ _____

rustling /ˈrʌslɪŋ/ _____

safari /səˈfɑːri/ _____

scenery /ˈsiːnəri/ _____

screech /skriːtʃ/ _____

sea 🔑 /siː/ _____

sea view 🔑 /ˌsiː ˈvjuː/ _____

shimmer /ˈʃɪmə(r)/ _____

significantly 🔑 /sɪɡˈnɪfɪkəntli/ _____

ski run /ˈskiː ˌrʌn/ _____

snow pass 🔑 /ˈsnəʊ ˌpɑːs/ _____

sparse /spɑːs/ _____

sport /spɔːt/ _____

stand-up comedy /ˌstænd ˌʌp ˈkɒmədi/ _____

stark /stɑːk/ _____

subway /ˈsʌbweɪ/ _____

surpass /səˈpɑːs/ _____

suspend /səˈspend/ _____

taxi rank 🔑 /ˈtæksi ˌræŋk/ _____

taxi stand 🔑 /ˈtæksi ˌstænd/ _____

travel industry 🔑 /ˈtrævl ˌɪndəstri/ _____

trend 🔑 /trend/ _____

tube 🔑 /tjuːb/ _____

unassuming /ˌʌnəˈsjuːmɪŋ/ _____

underground 🔑 /ˈʌndəɡraʊnd/ _____

uninviting /ˌʌnɪnˈvaɪtɪŋ/ _____

unpolluted /ˌʌnpəˈluːtɪd/ _____

upmarket /ˌʌpˈmɑːkɪt/ _____

upscale /ˌʌpˈskeɪl/ _____

vacation 🔑 /vəˈkeɪʃn/ _____

vacationer /vəˈkeɪʃnə(r)/ _____

vantage point /ˈvɑːntɪdʒ ˌpɔɪnt/ _____

view 🔑 /vjuː/ _____

watering hole /ˈwɔːtərɪŋ ˌhəʊl/ _____

whoosh /wʊʃ/ _____

workshop /ˈwɜːkʃɒp/ _____

Additional vocabulary

_____

_____

_____

_____

_____

_____

_____

_____

_____

_____

_____

_____

_____

_____

_____

_____

_____

_____

_____

_____

_____

_____

_____

_____

/p/ **p**en	/d/ **d**og	/tʃ/ **b**ea**ch**	/v/ **v**ery	/s/ **s**peak	/ʒ/ televi**s**ion	/n/ **n**ow	/r/ **r**adio
/b/ **b**ig	/k/ **c**an	/dʒ/ **j**ob	/θ/ **th**ink	/z/ **z**oo	/h/ **h**ouse	/ŋ/ si**ng**	/j/ **y**es
/t/ **t**wo	/g/ **g**ood	/f/ **f**ood	/ð/ **th**en	/ʃ/ **sh**e	/m/ **m**eat	/l/ **l**ate	/w/ **w**e

abundant /əˈbʌndənt/ _____

acronym /ˈækrənɪm/ _____

albeit /ɔːlˈbiːɪt/ _____

alliteration /əlɪtəˈreɪʃn/ _____

anagram /ˈænəgræm/ _____

apparent ⚷0 /əˈpærənt/ _____

appreciate ⚷0 /əˈpriːʃieɪt/ _____

bough (n) /baʊ/ _____

brainstorm /ˈbreɪnstɔːm/ _____

calculate ⚷0 /ˈkælkjuleɪt/ _____

calculator /ˈkælkjəleɪtə(r)/ _____

care for (some tea) ⚷0 /ˈkeə fə (səm ˈtiː)/ _____

cliché /ˈkliːʃeɪ/ _____

coin (a word) ⚷0 /ˌkɔɪn (ə ˈwɜːd)/ _____

collapse ⚷0 /kəˈlæps/ _____

collect (data) ⚷0 /kəˌlekt (ˈdeɪtə)/ _____

colossal /kəˈlɒsl/ _____

computer science ⚷0 /kəmˌpjuːtə ˈsaɪəns/ _____

computer software ⚷0 /kəmˌpjuːtə ˈsɒftweə(r)/ _____

considering (that) ⚷0 /kənˈsɪdərɪŋ (ðət)/ _____

contemporary ⚷0 /kənˈtempərəri/ _____

couple ⚷0 /ˈkʌpl/ _____

creation /kriˈeɪʃn/ _____

data mining /ˈdeɪtə ˌmaɪnɪŋ/ _____

decade ⚷0 /ˈdekeɪd/ _____

deed /diːd/ _____

define ⚷0 /dɪˈfaɪn/ _____

delete /dɪˈliːt/ _____

denim /ˈdenɪm/ _____

digitally enhance /ˌdɪdʒɪtəli ɪnˈhɑːns/ _____

document ⚷0 /ˈdɒkjument/ _____

electronic mail ⚷0 /ɪlekˌtrɒnɪk ˈmeɪl/ _____

element ⚷0 /ˈelɪmənt/ _____

emoticon /ɪˈməʊtɪkɒn/ _____

entry ⚷0 /ˈentri/ _____

epic poem /ˌepɪk ˈpəʊɪm/ _____

eponymous /ɪˈpɒnɪməs/ _____

extinct /ɪkˈstɪŋkt/ _____

equals sign /ˈiːkwəlz ˌsaɪn/ _____

evoke ⚷0 /ɪˈvəʊk/ _____

executive suite /ɪgˈzekjutɪv ˌswiːt/ _____

explore (the internet) ⚷0 /ɪkˌsplɔː (ðiˈ ɪntənet)/ _____

extend ⚷0 /ɪkˈstend/ _____

extinction /ɪkˈstɪŋkʃn/ _____

fax machine /ˈfæks məˌʃiːn/ _____

feature ⚷0 /ˈfiːtʃə(r)/ _____

finite /ˈfaɪnaɪt/ _____

finite number /ˈfaɪnaɪt ˌnʌmbə(r)/ _____

folklore /ˈfəʊklɔː(r)/ _____

following ⚷0 /ˈfɒləʊɪŋ/ _____

function ⚷0 /ˈfʌŋkʃn/ _____

get (an idea) ⚷0 /ˌget (ən aɪˈdɪə)/ _____

get (data) ⚷0 /ˌget (ˈdeɪtə)/ _____

graduate student /ˈgrædʒuət ˌstjuːdnt/ _____

have (a holiday) ⚷0 /ˌhæv (ə ˈhɒlədeɪ)/ _____

have (an idea) ⚷0 /ˌhæv (ən aɪˈdɪə)/ _____

heroic /həˈrəʊɪk/ _____

hence ⚷0 /hens/ _____

highly unlikely ⚷0 /ˌhaɪli ʌnˈlaɪkli/ _____

hundred and one ⚷0 /ˌhʌndrəd ən ˈwʌn/ _____

immortal /ɪˈmɔːtl/ _____

in a way ⚷0 /ˌɪn ə ˈweɪ/ _____

in broad daylight (idm) /ˌɪn ˌbrɔːd ˈdeɪlaɪt/ _____

incredible /ɪnˈkredəbl/ _____

ingenuity /ɪndʒəˈnjuːəti/ _____

innovative /ˈɪnəvətɪv/ _____

inspiration /ɪnspəˈreɪʃn/ _____

index ⚷0 /ˈɪndeks/ _____

internet age ⚷0 /ˈɪntənet ˌeɪdʒ/ _____

intriguing /ɪnˈtriːgɪŋ/ _____

invent (a word) ⚷0 /ɪnˌvent (ə ˈwɜːd)/ _____

keep sth to a minimum ⚷0 /ˌkiːp ... tu ə ˈmɪnɪməm/ _____

legend /ˈledʒənd/ _____

lexicon /ˈleksɪkən/ _____

like (some tea) ⚷0 /ˌlaɪk (səm ˈtiː)/ _____

limited ⚷0 /ˈlɪmɪtɪd/ _____

locate ⚷0 /ləʊˈkeɪt/ _____

malware /ˈmælweə(r)/ _____

mass ⚷0 /mæs/ _____

mathematician /mæθəməˈtɪʃn/ _____

mother tongue /ˈmʌðə ˌtʌŋ/ _____

mountainous /ˈmaʊntənəs/ _____

/i/ happy	/æ/ flag	/ɜː/ her	/ʊ/ look	/ʌ/ mum	/ɔɪ/ noisy	/ɪə/ here
/ɪ/ it	/ɑː/ art	/ɒ/ not	/uː/ you	/eɪ/ day	/aʊ/ how	/eə/ wear
/iː/ he	/e/ egg	/ɔː/ four	/ə/ sugar	/aɪ/ why	/əʊ/ go	/ʊə/ tourist

national identity 🔊
/ˌnæʃnəl aɪˈdentəti/ _____

native land /ˌneɪtɪv ˈlænd/ _____

nevertheless 🔊 /ˌnevəðəˈles/ _____

obsolete /ˈɒbsəliːt/ _____

obvious 🔊 /ˈɒbviəs/ _____

officemate /ˈɒfɪsmeɪt/ _____

originate /əˈrɪdʒɪneɪt/ _____

pardon me /ˌpɑːdn ˈmiː/ _____

pass away 🔊 /ˌpɑːs əˈweɪ/ _____

perfect 🔊 /pəˈfekt/ _____

phish /fɪʃ/ _____

phishing /ˈfɪʃɪŋ/ _____

pinch /pɪntʃ/ _____

podcast /ˈpɒdkɑːst/ _____

point out 🔊 /ˌpɔɪnt ˈaʊt/ _____

precisely 🔊 /prɪˈsaɪsli/ _____

publication 🔊 /pʌblɪˈkeɪʃn/ _____

preserve 🔊 /prɪˈzɜːv/ _____

radioactive /reɪdiəʊˈæktɪv/ _____

rarely 🔊 /ˈreəli/ _____

refer to 🔊 /rɪˈfɜː ˌtuː, tə/ _____

replacement part
/rɪˈpleɪsmənt ˌpɑːt/ _____

reservation 🔊 /rezəˈveɪʃn/ _____

savoury /ˈseɪvəri/ _____

search engine /ˈsɜːtʃ ˌendʒɪn/ _____

search (the internet) 🔊
/ˌsɜːtʃ (ðiː ˈɪntənet)/ _____

shut down (the computer) 🔊
/ˌʃʌt ˌdaʊn (ðə kəmˈpjuːtə)/ _____

simile /ˈsɪməli/ _____

social networking
/ˌsəʊʃl ˈnetwɜːkɪŋ/ _____

switch on (a light) 🔊
/ˌswɪtʃ ˌɒn (ə ˈlaɪt)/ _____

take (a holiday) 🔊
/ˌteɪk (ə ˈhɒlədeɪ)/ _____

tangerine /tændʒəˈriːn/ _____

telecommunication system
/telikəmjuːnɪˈkeɪʃn ˌsɪstəm/ _____

telex machine
/ˈteleks məˌʃiːn/ _____

term 🔊 /tɜːm/ _____

tire 🔊 /ˈtaɪə(r)/ _____

ton 🔊 /tʌn/ _____

toponymous /tɒˈpɒnɪməs/ _____

touch 🔊 /tʌtʃ/ _____

trace 🔊 /treɪs/ _____

transition /trænˈzɪʃn/ _____

tribe /traɪb/ _____

turn off (the computer) 🔊
/ˌtɜːn ˌɒf ðə kəmˈpjuːtə(r)/ _____

turn on (a light) 🔊
/ˌtɜːn ˌɒn ə ˈlaɪt/ _____

unconquerable
/ʌnˈkɒŋkərəbl/ _____

unconventional
/ʌnkənˈvenʃənl/ _____

unimaginably
/ʌnɪˈmædʒɪnəbli/ _____

unite 🔊 /juˈnaɪt/ _____

web address 🔊 /ˈweb əˌdres/ _____

webinar /ˈwebɪnɑː(r)/ _____

widely 🔊 /ˈwaɪdli/ _____

widespread /ˈwaɪdspred/ _____

wiki /ˈwɪki/ _____

with regard to 🔊
/ˌwɪð rɪˈgɑːd tə/ _____

word processor
/ˈwɜːd ˌprəʊsesə(r)/ _____

zero 🔊 /ˈzɪərəʊ/ _____

zillion /ˈzɪljən/ _____

Additional vocabulary

_____
_____
_____
_____
_____
_____
_____
_____
_____
_____
_____
_____
_____
_____
_____
_____
_____
_____
_____
_____
_____

/p/ pen	/d/ dog	/tʃ/ beach	/v/ very	/s/ speak	/ʒ/ television	/n/ now	/r/ radio
/b/ big	/k/ can	/dʒ/ job	/θ/ think	/z/ zoo	/h/ house	/ŋ/ sing	/j/ yes
/t/ two	/g/ good	/f/ food	/ð/ then	/ʃ/ she	/m/ meat	/l/ late	/w/ we

ability ⚷ /əˈbɪləti/ _____

academic ⚷ /ækəˈdemɪk/ _____

accidental ⚷ /æksɪˈdentl/ _____

account ⚷ /əˈkaʊnt/ _____

affordable /əˈfɔːdəbl/ _____

aggravate /ˈægrəveɪt/ _____

alphabet ⚷ /ˈælfəbet/ _____

anti /ˈænti/ _____

as the story goes ⚷
/əz ðə ˌstɔːri ˈgəʊz/ _____

asset /ˈæset/ _____

assist ⚷ /əˈsɪst/ _____

associate sth with sth ⚷
/əˈsəʊʃieɪt, -sieɪt/ _____

auto /ˈɔːtəʊ, ˈɔːtə/ _____

automobile /ˈɔːtəməbiːl/ _____

bathtub /ˈbɑːθtʌb/ _____

break away ⚷ /ˌbreɪk əˈweɪ/ _____

break down ⚷
/ˌbreɪk ˈdaʊn/ _____

break into ⚷ /ˈbreɪk ˌɪntə/ _____

break off ⚷ /ˌbreɪk ˈɒf/ _____

break out ⚷ /ˌbreɪk ˈaʊt/ _____

break up ⚷ /ˌbreɪk ˈʌp/ _____

breakthrough /ˈbreɪkθruː/ _____

bullet-proof /ˈbʊlɪt ˌpruːf/ _____

by nature ⚷ /ˌbaɪ ˈneɪtʃə(r)/ _____

calculate ⚷ /ˈkælkjuleɪt/ _____

car ownership
/ˈkɑːr ˌəʊnəʃɪp/ _____

childproof /ˈtʃaɪldpruːf/ _____

come to a conclusion ⚷
/ˌkʌm tu ə kənˈkluːʒn/ _____

commission ⚷ /kəˈmɪʃn/ _____

common sense
/ˌkɒmən ˈsens/ _____

confirm ⚷ /kənˈfɜːm/ _____

considerably ⚷
/kənˈsɪdərəbli/ _____

conversely /ˈkɒnvɜːsli/ _____

craft ⚷ /krɑːft/ _____

daily life ⚷ /ˌdeɪli ˈlaɪf/ _____

definition ⚷ /defɪˈnɪʃn/ _____

density /ˈdensəti/ _____

displace /dɪsˈpleɪs/ _____

divide ⚷ /dɪˈvaɪd/ _____

dramatically ⚷ /drəˈmætɪkli/ _____

duty-free /ˈdjuːti ˌfriː/ _____

elaborate /ɪˈlæbərət/ _____

emerge ⚷ /ɪˈmɜːdʒ/ _____

enable ⚷ /ɪˈneɪbl/ _____

engineer ⚷ /endʒɪˈnɪə(r)/ _____

equal to ⚷ /ˈiːkwəl tə/ _____

essential ⚷ /ɪˈsenʃl/ _____

exacerbate /ɪgˈzæsəbeɪt/ _____

expertise /ekspəˈtiːz/ _____

factor ⚷ /ˈfæktə(r)/ _____

fastener /ˈfɑːsnə(r)/ _____

fat-free /ˈfæt ˌfriː/ _____

foolproof /ˈfuːlpruːf/ _____

frustrate /frʌˈstreɪt/ _____

frustration /frʌˈstreɪʃn/ _____

genius /ˈdʒiːniəs/ _____

gifted /ˈgɪftɪd/ _____

go hand in hand ⚷
/ˌgəʊ ˌhænd ɪn ˈhænd/ _____

goldsmith /ˈgəʊldsmɪθ/ _____

hands-free /ˈhænds ˌfriː/ _____

hike /haɪk/ _____

hook ⚷ /hʊk/ _____

if only ⚷ /ˌɪf ˈəʊnli/ _____

in an instant /ˌɪn ən ˈɪnstənt/ _____

inability ⚷ /ˈɪnəbɪləti/ _____

incident ⚷ /ˈɪnsɪdənt/ _____

indeed ⚷ /ɪnˈdiːd/ _____

insight /ˈɪnsaɪt/ _____

inspiration /ɪnspəˈreɪʃn/ _____

intelligence ⚷ /ɪnˈtelɪdʒəns/ _____

interest-free /ˈɪntrəst ˌfriː/ _____

invention ⚷ /ɪnˈvenʃn/ _____

inventor /ɪnˈventə(r)/ _____

irrelevant /ɪˈreləvənt/ _____

latch on (to sth)
/ˌlætʃ ˈɒn (tə ...)/ _____

light bulb /ˈlaɪt ˌbʌlb/ _____

limited (to sth) ⚷
/ˈlɪmɪtɪd (tə ...)/ _____

loop /luːp/ _____

mal /mæl/ _____

manufacturing process ⚷
/mænjuˈfæktʃərɪŋ ˌprəʊses/ _____

microscope /ˈmaɪkrəskəʊp/ _____

microwave oven
/ˌmaɪkrəweɪv ˈʌvn/ _____

mobile phone
/ˌməʊbaɪl ˈfəʊn/ _____

monumental /mɒnjuˈmentl/ _____

more importantly ⚷
/ˌmɔːr ɪmˈpɔːtntli/ _____

origin ⚷ /ˈɒrɪdʒɪn/ _____

out of the question ⚷
/ˌaʊt əv ðə ˈkwestʃən/ _____

ovenproof /ˈʌvnpruːf/ _____

overcome ⚷ /əʊvəˈkʌm/ _____

/i/ happy	/æ/ flag	/ɜː/ her	/ʊ/ look	/ʌ/ mum	/ɔɪ/ noisy	/ɪə/ here
/ɪ/ it	/ɑː/ art	/ɒ/ not	/uː/ you	/eɪ/ day	/aʊ/ how	/eə/ wear
/iː/ he	/e/ egg	/ɔː/ four	/ə/ sugar	/aɪ/ why	/əʊ/ go	/ʊə/ tourist

Additional vocabulary

overlook /ˌəʊvəˈlʊk/

patent /ˈpætnt, ˈpeɪtnt/

performance 🔊 /pəˈfɔːməns/

perseverance /ˌpɜːsɪˈvɪərəns/

persevere /ˌpɜːsɪˈvɪə(r)/

perspiration /ˌpɜːspəˈreɪʃn/

petrol 🔊 /ˈpetrəl/

possess 🔊 /pəˈzes/

potential 🔊 /pəˈtenʃl/

pre-packaged food
/ˌpriː ˌpækɪdʒd ˈfuːd/

printing press /ˈprɪntɪŋ ˌpres/

prove (a case) 🔊
/ˌpruːv (ə ˈkeɪs)/

provide 🔊 /prəˈvaɪd/

provided 🔊 /prəˈvaɪdɪd/

purity /ˈpjʊərəti/

quantity 🔊 /ˈkwɒntəti/

realize the significance
/ˌriːəlaɪz ðə sɪgˈnɪfɪkəns/

satellite navigation device
/ˌsætəlaɪt nævɪˈgeɪʃn dɪˌvaɪs/

satellite technology
/ˌsætəlaɪt tekˈnɒlədʒi/

semi /ˈsemi/

setback /ˈsetbæk/

significant 🔊 /sɪgˈnɪfɪkənt/

smoke-free /ˈsməʊk ˌfriː/

soundproof /ˈsaʊndpruːf/

specifically 🔊 /spəˈsɪfɪkli/

speculate /ˈspekjuleɪt/

struggle 🔊 /ˈstrʌgl/

submerge /sʌbˈmɜːdʒ/

suspicion 🔊 /səˈspɪʃn/

suspicious 🔊 /səˈspɪʃəs/

take a break 🔊
/ˌteɪk ə ˈbreɪk/

tax-free /ˈtæks ˌfriː/

text messaging
/ˈtekst ˌmesɪdʒɪŋ/

the vast majority (of) 🔊
/ðə ˈvɑːst məˌdʒɒrəti/

t**rouble-free** /ˈtrʌbl ˌfriː/

tub /tʌb/

ultra /ˈʌltrə/

underestimate
/ˌʌndərˈestɪmeɪt/

undoubtedly /ʌnˈdaʊtɪdli/

vehicle 🔊 /ˈviːəkl/

volume 🔊 /ˈvɒljuːm/

waterproof /ˈwɔːtəpruːf/

wire 🔊 /ˈwaɪə(r)/

/p/ **p**en	/d/ **d**og	/tʃ/ bea**ch**	/v/ **v**ery	/s/ **s**peak	/ʒ/ televi**si**on	/n/ **n**ow	/r/ **r**adio
/b/ **b**ig	/k/ **c**an	/dʒ/ **j**ob	/θ/ **th**ink	/z/ **z**oo	/h/ **h**ouse	/ŋ/ si**ng**	/j/ **y**es
/t/ **t**wo	/g/ **g**ood	/f/ **f**ood	/ð/ **th**en	/ʃ/ **sh**e	/m/ **m**eat	/l/ **l**ate	/w/ **w**e

account for sth 🔑
/əˈkaʊnt fə/

advert 🔑 /ˈædvɜːt/

advertisement 🔑
/ədˈvɜːtɪsmənt/

advertiser /ˈædvətaɪzə(r)/

advertising campaign 🔑
/ˈædvətaɪzɪŋ kæmˌpeɪn/

amazingly /əˈmeɪzɪŋli/

angle (n) 🔑 /ˈæŋgl/

appeal 🔑 /əˈpiːl/

arrest (v) 🔑 /əˈrest/

associated (with) 🔑
/əˈsəʊʃieɪtɪd, -sieɪt-/

attribute /əˈtrɪbjuːt/

awkward 🔑 /ˈɔːkwəd/

bargain hunter
/ˈbɑːgɪn ˌhʌntə(r)/

be intent on sth
/ˌbiː ɪnˈtent ˌɒn/

big business 🔑
/ˌbɪg ˈbɪznəs/

billboard /ˈbɪlbɔːd/

brand 🔑 /brænd/

broom (n) /bruːm/

cheap offer 🔑 /ˌtʃiːp ˈɒfə(r)/

closet (n) 🔑 /ˈklɒzɪt/

come to an agreement 🔑
/ˌkʌm ˌtu ən əˈgriːmənt/

compared with 🔑
/kəmˈpeəd ˌwɪð/

conduct 🔑 /ˈkɒndʌkt/

constitute (v) /ˈkɒnstɪtjuːt/

consult 🔑 /kənˈsʌlt/

consumer 🔑 /kənˈsjuːmə(r)/

contribution 🔑
/kɒntrɪˈbjuːʃn/

convince 🔑 /kənˈvɪns/

corner the market 🔑
/ˌkɔːnə ðə ˈmɑːkɪt/

critically /ˈkrɪtɪkli/

customer 🔑 /ˈkʌstəmə(r)/

device 🔑 /dɪˈvaɪs/

digital /ˈdɪdʒɪtl/

direct 🔑 /dəˈrekt, dɪ-, daɪ-/

disposable income
/dɪˌspəʊzəbl ˈɪnkʌm/

drum up business
/ˌdrʌm ˌʌp ˈbɪznəs/

earning power
/ˈɜːnɪŋ ˌpaʊə(r)/

economy 🔑 /ɪˈkɒnəmi/

enable 🔑 /ɪˈneɪbl/

endorsement /ɪnˈdɔːsmənt/

estimate 🔑 /ˈestɪmeɪt/

eventually 🔑 /ɪˈventʃuəli/

every waking moment
/ˌevri ˌweɪkɪŋ ˈməʊmənt/

fast-food restaurant
/ˌfɑːst ˈfuːd ˌrestrɒnt/

fiercely (adv) /ˈfɪəsli/

flexible /ˈfleksəbl/

focus 🔑 /ˈfəʊkəs/

generation 🔑 /dʒenəˈreɪʃn/

good buy 🔑 /ˌgʊd ˈbaɪ/

have a say 🔑 /ˌhæv ə ˈseɪ/

hip /hɪp/

hype /haɪp/

impact 🔑 /ɪmˈpækt/

impulse buyer
/ˈɪmpʌls ˌbaɪə(r)/

in some instances 🔑
/ˌɪn ˈsʌm ˌɪnstənsɪz/

in the pipeline
/ˌɪn ðə ˈpaɪplaɪn/

increase 🔑 /ˈɪŋkriːs/

indicate 🔑 /ˈɪndɪkeɪt/

individual 🔑 /ˌɪndɪˈvɪdʒuəl/

influence 🔑 /ˈɪnfluəns/

issue 🔑 /ˈɪʃuː/

jingle /ˈdʒɪŋgl/

key 🔑 /kiː/

leave out 🔑 /ˌliːv ˈaʊt/

lightweight /ˈlaɪtweɪt/

logo 🔑 /ˈləʊgəʊ/

market 🔑 /ˈmɑːkɪt/

marketing department 🔑
/ˈmɑːkətɪŋ dɪˌpɑːtmənt/

mobile 🔑 /ˈməʊbaɪl/

multi-tasking
/ˌmʌlti ˈtɑːskɪŋ/

must-have item
/ˌmʌst ˈhæv ˌaɪtəm/

name 🔑 /neɪm/

negatively /ˈnegətɪvli/

not up to scratch
/ˌnɒt ˌʌp tə ˈskrætʃ/

object 🔑 /əbˈdʒekt/

obsessed /əbˈsest/

on a regular basis 🔑
/ˌɒn ə ˌregjələ ˈbeɪsɪs/

on the other hand 🔑
/ˌɒn ði ˈʌðə ˌhænd/

online /ɒnˈlaɪn/

option 🔑 /ˈɒpʃn/

ordinary 🔑 /ˈɔːdnri/

/i/ happy	/æ/ flag	/ɜː/ her	/ʊ/ look	/ʌ/ mum	/ɔɪ/ noisy	/ɪə/ here
/ɪ/ it	/ɑː/ art	/ɒ/ not	/uː/ you	/eɪ/ day	/aʊ/ how	/eə/ wear
/iː/ he	/e/ egg	/ɔː/ four	/ə/ sugar	/aɪ/ why	/əʊ/ go	/ʊə/ tourist

overcome 🔑 /ˌəʊvəˈkʌm/ _____

participate /pɑːˈtɪsɪpeɪt/ _____

part-time /ˌpɑːt ˈtaɪm/ _____

peril (n) /ˈperəl/ _____

permit 🔑 /ˈpɜːmɪt/ _____

permit 🔑 /pəˈmɪt/ _____

perplexed (adj) /pəˈplekst/ _____

persistent /pəˈsɪstənt/ _____

personal 🔑 /ˈpɜːsənl/ _____

potential 🔑 /pəˈtenʃl/ _____

preference 🔑 /ˈprefrəns/ _____

present 🔑 /prɪˈzent/ _____

previous 🔑 /ˈpriːviəs/ _____

price tag /ˈpraɪs ˌtæg/ _____

pride (n) 🔑 /praɪd/ _____

product placement
/ˌprɒdʌkt ˈpleɪsmənt/ _____

promote 🔑 /prəˈməʊt/ _____

punctuate (v) /ˈpʌŋktʃueɪt/ _____

purchase 🔑 /ˈpɜːtʃəs/ _____

purchasing decision 🔑
/ˈpɜːtʃəsɪŋ dɪˌsɪʒn/ _____

put sth on the line 🔑
/ˌpʊt ... ˌɒn ðə ˈlaɪn/ _____

quarrelling /ˈkwɒrəlɪŋ/ _____

rebel /rɪˈbel/ _____

recall 🔑 /rɪˈkɔːl/ _____

recently 🔑 /ˈriːsntli/ _____

record 🔑 /ˈrekɔːd/ _____

refuse 🔑 /ˈrefjuːs/ _____

relatively little 🔑
/ˌrelətɪvli ˈlɪtl/ _____

represent 🔑 /reprɪˈzent/ _____

respond 🔑 /rɪˈspɒnd/ _____

resurrect (v) /rezəˈrekt/ _____

screen 🔑 /skriːn/ _____

seize (v) /siːz/ _____

seldom (adv) /ˈseldəm/ _____

serious shopper
/ˌsɪəriəs ˈʃɒpə(r)/ _____

set aside 🔑 /ˌset əˈsaɪd/ _____

shopping centre 🔑
/ˈʃɒpɪŋ ˌsentə(r)/ _____

shopping list 🔑 /ˈʃɒpɪŋ ˌlɪst/ _____

shopping spree /ˈʃɒpɪŋ ˌspriː/ _____

significant 🔑 /sɪgˈnɪfɪkənt/ _____

site 🔑 /saɪt/ _____

slack (n) /slæk/ _____

slight (adj) 🔑 /slaɪt/ _____

slogan /ˈsləʊgən/ _____

smart phone /ˈsmɑːt ˌfəʊn/ _____

spectacles (n) /ˈspektəklz/ _____

spending 🔑 /ˈspendɪŋ/ _____

statistic /stəˈtɪstɪk/ _____

steady 🔑 /ˈstedi/ _____

stove lid (n) /ˈstəʊv ˌlɪd/ _____

strategy 🔑 /ˈstrætədʒi/ _____

subject 🔑 /ˈsʌbdʒɪkt/ _____

survey (n) 🔑 /ˈsɜːveɪ/ _____

survey (v) 🔑 /səˈveɪ/ _____

switch (n) 🔑 /swɪtʃ/ _____

switch 🔑 /swɪtʃ/ _____

target 🔑 /ˈtɑːgɪt/ _____

target market 🔑
/ˌtɑːgɪt ˈmɑːkɪt/ _____

technique 🔑 /tekˈniːk/ _____

teenager /ˈtiːneɪdʒə(r)/ _____

terrific deal /təˌrɪfɪk ˈdiːl/ _____

text 🔑 /tekst/ _____

think outside the box
/ˌθɪŋk aʊtˌsaɪd ðə ˈbɒks/ _____

trendy /ˈtrendi/ _____

unprecedented
/ʌnˈpresɪdentɪd/ _____

usage /ˈjuːsɪdʒ/ _____

wasteful with money
/ˌweɪstfl wɪð ˈmʌni/ _____

wearable /ˈweərəbl/ _____

well-off /ˌwel ˈɒf/ _____

wireless device
/ˈwaɪələs dɪˌvaɪs/ _____

Additional vocabulary

_____

_____

_____

_____

_____

_____

_____

_____

_____

_____

_____

_____

_____

_____

_____

_____

_____

/p/ **p**en	/d/ **d**og	/tʃ/ bea**ch**	/v/ **v**ery	/s/ **s**peak	/ʒ/ televi**s**ion	/n/ **n**ow	/r/ **r**adio
/b/ **b**ig	/k/ **c**an	/dʒ/ **j**ob	/θ/ **th**ink	/z/ **z**oo	/h/ **h**ouse	/ŋ/ si**ng**	/j/ **y**es
/t/ **t**wo	/g/ **g**ood	/f/ **f**ood	/ð/ **th**en	/ʃ/ **sh**e	/m/ **m**eat	/l/ **l**ate	/w/ **w**e

abate /ə'beɪt/ _____

absorb 🔑 /əb'zɔːb/ _____

accurate 🔑 /'ækjərət/ _____

acid 🔑 /'æsɪd/ _____

allegedly /ə'ledʒɪdli/ _____

amnesia /æm'niːziə/ _____

anxious 🔑 /'æŋkʃəs/ _____

appendix /ə'pendɪks/ _____

aromatic /ærə'mætɪk/ _____

arthritis /ɑː'θraɪtɪs/ _____

aspirin /'æsprɪn/ _____

associated (with) 🔑
/ə'səʊʃieɪtɪd, -sieɪt-/ _____

asthma /'æsmə/ _____

attitude 🔑 /'ætɪtjuːd/ _____

balanced approach 🔑
/'bælənst ə'prəʊtʃ/ _____

bark /bɑːk/ _____

be under the weather 🔑
/ˌbi: ˌʌndə ðə 'weðə(r)/ _____

bitter 🔑 /'bɪtə(r)/ _____

blood vessel /'blʌd ˌvesl/ _____

brain 🔑 /breɪn/ _____

cancer 🔑 /'kænsə(r)/ _____

clammy /'klæmi/ _____

colonel /'kɜːnl/ _____

complementary
/kɒmplɪ'mentri/ _____

complimentary
/kɒmplɪ'mentri/ _____

contaminate /kən'tæmɪneɪt/ _____

contamination
/kəntæmɪ'neɪʃn/ _____

contribute 🔑 /kən'trɪbjuːt/ _____

council 🔑 /'kaʊnsl/ _____

counsel /'kaʊnsl/ _____

cramps /kræmps/ _____

creature 🔑 /'kriːtʃə(r)/ _____

crush 🔑 /krʌʃ/ _____

cure 🔑 /kjʊə(r)/ _____

deadly /'dedli/ _____

deafening /'defnɪŋ/ _____

diabetes /daɪə'biːtiːz/ _____

diminish /dɪ'mɪnɪʃ/ _____

disease 🔑 /dɪ'ziːz/ _____

dose /dəʊs/ _____

effective 🔑 /ɪ'fektɪv/ _____

experience 🔑 /ɪk'spɪəriəns/ _____

extract /'ekstrækt/ _____

extraction /ɪk'strækʃn/ _____

face mask /'feɪs ˌmɑːsk/ _____

feel lightheaded
/ˌfiːl laɪt'hedɪd/ _____

feel queasy /ˌfiːl 'kwiːzi/ _____

fever 🔑 /'fiːvə(r)/ _____

food for thought 🔑
/ˌfuːd fə 'θɔːt/ _____

foxglove /'fɒksglʌv/ _____

get butterflies in (your) stomach
/ˌget ˌbʌtəflaɪz ˌɪn ˌ(jɔː) 'stʌmək/ _____

give it a try 🔑
/ˌgɪv ˌɪt ə 'traɪ/ _____

have the sniffles
/ˌhæv ðə 'snɪflz/ _____

headache 🔑 /'hedeɪk/ _____

healing power 🔑
/'hiːlɪŋ ˌpaʊə(r)/ _____

heart 🔑 /hɑːt/ _____

herbal medicine
/ˌhɜːbl 'medsn/ _____

high blood pressure 🔑
/ˌhaɪ 'blʌd ˌpreʃə(r)/ _____

hose /həʊz/ _____

humorous 🔑 /'hjuːmərəs/ _____

identify 🔑 /aɪ'dentɪfaɪ/ _____

imply 🔑 /ɪm'plaɪ/ _____

in order to 🔑 /ɪn 'ɔːdə tə/ _____

infer /ɪn'fɜː(r)/ _____

intestine /ɪn'testɪn/ _____

involve 🔑 /ɪn'vɒlv/ _____

irritation /ɪrɪ'teɪʃn/ _____

jungle /'dʒʌŋgl/ _____

kernel /'kɜːnl/ _____

kidney /'kɪdni/ _____

laughter /'lɑːftə(r)/ _____

legend /'ledʒənd/ _____

lethal /'liːθl/ _____

liver /'lɪvə(r)/ _____

loot /luːt/ _____

lose track of time 🔑
/ˌluːz ˌtræk əv 'taɪm/ _____

lungs 🔑 /lʌŋz/ _____

lute /luːt/ _____

malaria /mə'leəriə/ _____

market 🔑 /'mɑːkɪt/ _____

medical school 🔑
/'medɪkl ˌskuːl/ _____

medication /medɪ'keɪʃn/ _____

mosquito /mə'skiːtəʊ/ _____

mouth-watering
/'maʊθ ˌwɔːtərɪŋ/ _____

natural remedy
/ˌnætʃrəl 'remədi/ _____

/i/ happy	/æ/ flag	/ɜː/ her	/ʊ/ look	/ʌ/ mum	/ɔɪ/ noisy	/ɪə/ here
/ɪ/ it	/ɑː/ art	/ɒ/ not	/uː/ you	/eɪ/ day	/aʊ/ how	/eə/ wear
/iː/ he	/e/ egg	/ɔː/ four	/ə/ sugar	/aɪ/ why	/əʊ/ go	/ʊə/ tourist

neutralization
/ˌnjuːtrəlaɪˈzeɪʃn/ _____

neutralize /ˈnjuːtrəlaɪz/ _____

no exception 🔊
/ˌnəʊ ɪkˈsepʃn/ _____

noblewoman /ˈnəʊblwʊmən/ _____

official 🔊 /əˈfɪʃl/ _____

officious /əˈfɪʃəs/ _____

orchard /ˈɔːtʃəd/ _____

otherwise 🔊 /ˈʌðəwaɪz/ _____

oxygen bar /ˈɒksɪdʒən ˌbɑː(r)/ _____

pain-relieving /ˈpeɪn rɪˌliːvɪŋ/ _____

pancreas /ˈpæŋkriæs/ _____

particularly 🔊 /pəˈtɪkjələli/ _____

patent /ˈpætnt, ˈpeɪtnt/ _____

patient 🔊 /ˈpeɪʃnt/ _____

peasant woman
/ˈpeznt ˌwʊmən/ _____

poison 🔊 /ˈpɔɪzn/ _____

pore /pɔː(r)/ _____

potentially 🔊 /pəˈtenʃəli/ _____

pour 🔊 /pɔː(r)/ _____

produce 🔊 /prəˈdjuːs/ _____

quinine /kwɪˈniːn, ˌkwɪ-/ _____

racial /ˈreɪʃl/ _____

racist /ˈreɪsɪst/ _____

recharge your batteries
/riːˌtʃɑːdʒ jɔː ˌbætəriz/ _____

record 🔊 /rɪˈkɔːd/ _____

recovery /rɪˈkʌvəri/ _____

reduce 🔊 /rɪˈdjuːs/ _____

relief 🔊 /rɪˈliːf/ _____

relieve /rɪˈliːv/ _____

remedy /ˈremədi/ _____

research 🔊 /rɪˈsɜːtʃ, ˈriː-/ _____

roadside /ˈrəʊdsaɪd/ _____

run out of steam 🔊
/ˌrʌn ˌaʊt əv ˈstiːm/ _____

sceptical /ˈskeptɪkl/ _____

science fiction /ˌsaɪəns ˈfɪkʃn/ _____

scorching /ˈskɔːtʃɪŋ/ _____

sensible 🔊 /ˈsensəbl/ _____

sensitive 🔊 /ˈsensətɪv/ _____

situation 🔊 /ˌsɪtʃuˈeɪʃn/ _____

slimy /ˈslaɪmi/ _____

sophistication /səfɪstɪˈkeɪʃn/ _____

spleen /spliːn/ _____

sponge /spʌndʒ/ _____

stationary /ˈsteɪʃnri/ _____

stationery /ˈsteɪʃnri/ _____

stomach 🔊 /ˈstʌmək/ _____

stroke 🔊 /strəʊk/ _____

substance 🔊 /ˈsʌbstəns/ _____

suffer (from) 🔊 /ˈsʌfə (frəm)/ _____

surrounding 🔊 /səˈraʊndɪŋ/ _____

swelling 🔊 /ˈswelɪŋ/ _____

tank 🔊 /tæŋk/ _____

tension 🔊 /ˈtenʃn/ _____

thereby /ðeəˈbaɪ/ _____

tolerance /ˈtɒlərəns/ _____

tolerate /ˈtɒləreɪt/ _____

treat 🔊 /triːt/ _____

treatment 🔊 /ˈtriːtmənt/ _____

treatment plan 🔊
/ˈtriːtmənt ˌplæn/ _____

trial and error 🔊
/ˌtraɪəl ən ˈerə(r)/ _____

tropical rain forest 🔊
/ˌtrɒpɪkl ˈreɪn ˌfɒrɪst/ _____

tuberculosis
/tjuːbɜːkjuˈləʊsɪs/ _____

ulcer /ˈʌlsə(r)/ _____

upset 🔊 /ʌpˈset/ _____

variety 🔊 /vəˈraɪəti/ _____

warning 🔊 /ˈwɔːnɪŋ/ _____

well-being /ˌwel ˈbiːɪŋ/ _____

worth every penny
/ˌwɜːθ ˌevri ˈpeni/ _____

Additional vocabulary

_____

_____

_____

_____

_____

_____

_____

_____

_____

_____

_____

_____

_____

_____

_____

_____

_____

/p/ **pen**	/d/ **dog**	/tʃ/ bea**ch**	/v/ **v**ery	/s/ **s**peak	/ʒ/ televi**si**on	/n/ **n**ow	/r/ **r**adio
/b/ **b**ig	/k/ **c**an	/dʒ/ **j**ob	/θ/ **th**ink	/z/ **z**oo	/h/ **h**ouse	/ŋ/ si**ng**	/j/ **y**es
/t/ **t**wo	/g/ **g**ood	/f/ **f**ood	/ð/ **th**en	/ʃ/ **sh**e	/m/ **m**eat	/l/ **l**ate	/w/ **w**e

abreast (of sth) (adv) /ə'brest/ _____

accommodate /ə'kɒmədeɪt/ _____

accommodating
/ə'kɒmədeɪtɪŋ/ _____

acknowledge ➟O /ək'nɒlɪdʒ/ _____

adaptation /ˌædæp'teɪʃn/ _____

advocate /'ædvəkət/ _____

afoot (adj) /ə'fʊt/ _____

aloof /ə'luːf/ _____

around the clock ➟O
/əˌraʊnd ðə 'klɒk/ _____

as nice as pie
/əz ˌnaɪs əz 'paɪ/ _____

at greater risk ➟O
/ət ˌgreɪtə 'rɪsk/ _____

authentic /ɔː'θentɪk/ _____

bamboo (n) /bæm'buː/ _____

be a shrinking violet
/ˌbiː ə ˌʃrɪŋkɪŋ 'vaɪələt/ _____

be a wet blanket
/ˌbiː ə ˌwet 'blæŋkɪt/ _____

birth order ➟O
/'bɜːθ ˌɔːdə(r)/ _____

cap ➟O /kæp/ _____

capricious /kə'prɪʃəs/ _____

carbonated /'kɑːbəneɪtɪd/ _____

career advancement
/kə'rɪər ədˌvɑːnsmənt/ _____

career choice ➟O /kə'rɪə ˌtʃɔɪs/ _____

career guidance counsellor
/kəˌrɪə 'gaɪdəns ˌkaʊnsələ(r)/ _____

career path ➟O /kə'rɪə ˌpɑːθ/ _____

characteristic ➟O
/ˌkærəktə'rɪstɪk/ _____

charismatic /ˌkærɪz'mætɪk/ _____

cite /saɪt/ _____

classic ➟O /'klæsɪk/ _____

classify /'klæsɪfaɪ/ _____

close ➟O /kləʊs/ _____

club ➟O /klʌb/ _____

comfort level ➟O
/'kʌmfət ˌlevl/ _____

compromise /'kɒmprəmaɪz/ _____

conceited /kən'siːtɪd/ _____

confident ➟O /'kɒnfɪdənt/ _____

considerate /kən'sɪdərət/ _____

conventional wisdom
/kənˌvenʃnl 'wɪzdəm/ _____

counselling /'kaʊnsəlɪŋ/ _____

crop ➟O /krɒp/ _____

cultural icon
/ˌkʌltʃərəl 'aɪkɒn/ _____

derisive (adj) /dɪ'raɪsɪv/ _____

determine ➟O /dɪ'tɜːmɪn/ _____

determined ➟O /dɪ'tɜːmɪnd/ _____

determiner /dɪ'tɜːmɪnə(r)/ _____

disciplined ➟O /'dɪsəplɪnd/ _____

distinction /dɪ'stɪŋkʃn/ _____

distinctive /dɪ'stɪŋktɪv/ _____

dogmatic /dɒg'mætɪk/ _____

down-to-earth /ˌdaʊn tu 'ɜːθ/ _____

earning potential ➟O
/'ɜːnɪŋ pəˌtenʃl/ _____

earning power ➟O
/'ɜːnɪŋ ˌpaʊə(r)/ _____

easy-going /ˌiːzi 'gəʊɪŋ/ _____

entire ➟O /ɪn'taɪə(r)/ _____

equally ➟O /'iːkwəli/ _____

establish ➟O /ɪ'stæblɪʃ/ _____

experiment ➟O /ɪk'sperɪmənt/ _____

extroverted /'ekstrəvɜːtɪd/ _____

exultation (n) /ˌegzʌl'teɪʃn/ _____

fearful (of) /'fɪəfl/ _____

feel at ease ➟O /ˌfiːl ət 'iːz/ _____

financial success ➟O
/faɪˌnænʃl sək'ses/ _____

first-born /'fɜːst ˌbɔːn/ _____

founder /'faʊndə(r)/ _____

get away with murder
/ˌget əˌweɪ ˌwɪð 'mɜːdə(r)/ _____

grave (adj) ➟O /greɪv/ _____

gravitate /'grævɪteɪt/ _____

happy-go-lucky
/ˌhæpi ˌgəʊ 'lʌki/ _____

haul /hɔːl/ _____

have a good head on (your) shoulders
/ˌhæv ə 'gʊd ˌhed ˌɒn ˌ(jɔː) ˈʃəʊldəz/ _____

have a very short fuse
/ˌhæv ə ˌveri ˌʃɔːt 'fjuːz/ _____

have an impact on ➟O
/ˌhæv ən 'ɪmpækt ˌɒn/ _____

heart disease ➟O
/'hɑːt dɪˌziːz/ _____

incline (n) /'ɪnklaɪn/ _____

it stands to reason (that) ➟O
/ɪt ˌstændz tə 'riːzn/ _____

keep tabs on /ˌkiːp 'tæbz ˌɒn/ _____

law enforcement
/'lɔːr ɪnˌfɔːsmənt/ _____

life and soul of the party ➟O
/ˌlaɪf ən ˌsəʊl əv ðə 'pɑːti/ _____

like chalk and cheese
/ˌlaɪk ˌtʃɔːk ən 'tʃiːz/ _____

limelight /'laɪmlaɪt/ _____

line ➟O /'laɪn/ _____

living conditions ➟O
/'lɪvɪŋ kənˌdɪʃnz/ _____

/i/ happy	/æ/ flag	/ɜː/ her	/ʊ/ look	/ʌ/ mum	/ɔɪ/ noisy	/ɪə/ here
/ɪ/ it	/ɑː/ art	/ɒ/ not	/uː/ you	/eɪ/ day	/aʊ/ how	/eə/ wear
/iː/ he	/e/ egg	/ɔː/ four	/ə/ sugar	/aɪ/ why	/əʊ/ go	/ʊə/ tourist

locate 🔑 /ləʊˈkeɪt/ _____

look up to 🔑
/ˌlʊk ˈʌp ˌtuː, tə/ _____

manipulative /məˈnɪpjulətɪv/ _____

multi-tasking /ˌmʌlti ˈtɑːskɪŋ/ _____

negotiation /nɪɡəʊʃiˈeɪʃn/ _____

night shift 🔑 /ˈnaɪt ˌʃɪft/ _____

nowadays /ˈnaʊədeɪz/ _____

on demand 🔑
/ˌɒn dɪˈmɑːnd/ _____

open for business 🔑
/ˈəʊpən fə ˌbɪznəs/ _____

opinionated /əˈpɪnjəneɪtɪd/ _____

outgoing /aʊtˈɡəʊɪŋ/ _____

outlying (adj) /ˈaʊtlaɪɪŋ/ _____

overlook /əʊvəˈlʊk/ _____

override /əʊvəˈraɪd/ _____

people skills 🔑 /ˈpiːpl ˌskɪlz/ _____

picket (n) /ˈpɪkɪt/ _____

pitch 🔑 /pɪtʃ/ _____

platform 🔑 /ˈplætfɔːm/ _____

playing with words 🔑
/ˌpleɪɪŋ wɪð ˈwɜːdz/ _____

plug 🔑 /plʌɡ/ _____

pre-fabricated
/ˌpriː ˈfæbrɪkeɪtɪd/ _____

pretentious /prɪˈtenʃəs/ _____

pterodactyl (n) /terəˈdæktɪl/ _____

quack /kwæk/ _____

quick-witted /ˌkwɪk ˈwɪtɪd/ _____

rank 🔑 /ræŋk/ _____

receptive /rɪˈseptɪv/ _____

reliable /rɪˈlaɪəbl/ _____

resolute /ˈrezəluːt/ _____

restriction 🔑 /rɪˈstrɪkʃn/ _____

role 🔑 /rəʊl/ _____

satisfy your cravings
/ˌsætɪsfaɪ jɔː ˈkreɪvɪŋz/ _____

school 🔑 /skuːl/ _____

scratch 🔑 /skrætʃ/ _____

self-assured /ˌself əˈʃʊəd/ _____

senior management 🔑
/ˌsiːniə ˈmænɪdʒmənt/ _____

shoot 🔑 /ʃuːt/ _____

sibling /ˈsɪblɪŋ/ _____

side by side 🔑
/ˌsaɪd baɪ ˈsaɪd/ _____

skyline (n) /ˈskaɪlaɪn/ _____

social scientist 🔑
/ˌsəʊʃl ˈsaɪəntɪst/ _____

sole /səʊl/ _____

specialty /speʃiˈæləti/ _____

spontaneous /spɒnˈteɪniəs/ _____

stand 🔑 /stænd/ _____

stand-offish /ˌstænd ˈɒfɪʃ/ _____

status 🔑 /ˈsteɪtəs/ _____

stork (n) /stɔːk/ _____

stubborn /ˈstʌbən/ _____

substitute 🔑 /ˈsʌbstɪtjuːt/ _____

thick-skinned /ˌθɪk ˈskɪnd/ _____

trustworthy /ˈtrʌstwɜːði/ _____

typically 🔑 /ˈtɪpɪkli/ _____

ultimately 🔑 /ˈʌltɪmətli/ _____

uncompromising
/ʌnˈkɒmprəmaɪzɪŋ/ _____

unpredictable /ʌnprɪˈdɪktəbl/ _____

upbringing /ˈʌpbrɪŋɪŋ/ _____

van (n) 🔑 /væn/ _____

whale-backed (adj)
/ˈweɪl ˌbækt/ _____

wing 🔑 /wɪŋ/ _____

witty /ˈwɪti/ _____

wont (n) /wəʊnt/ _____

Additional vocabulary

_____
_____
_____
_____
_____
_____
_____
_____
_____
_____
_____
_____
_____
_____
_____
_____
_____
_____
_____
_____
_____
_____
_____

/p/ pen	/d/ dog	/tʃ/ beach	/v/ very	/s/ speak	/ʒ/ television	/n/ now	/r/ radio
/b/ big	/k/ can	/dʒ/ job	/θ/ think	/z/ zoo	/h/ house	/ŋ/ sing	/j/ yes
/t/ two	/g/ good	/f/ food	/ð/ then	/ʃ/ she	/m/ meat	/l/ late	/w/ we

additional ⚙-0 /əˈdɪʃənl/ _____

agriculture /ˈægrɪkʌltʃə(r)/ _____

appetite /ˈæpɪtaɪt/ _____

artichoke /ˈɑːtɪtʃəʊk/ _____

atmosphere ⚙-0 /ˈætməsfɪə(r)/ _____

authentic /ɔːˈθentɪk/ _____

bakery goods /ˈbeɪkəri ˌɡʊdz/ _____

bay leaf /ˈbeɪ ˌliːf/ _____

beat ⚙-0 /biːt/ _____

besides /bɪˈsaɪdz/ _____

biodynamic /baɪəʊdaɪˈnæmɪk/ _____

blanket /ˈblæŋkɪt/ _____

braise /breɪz/ _____

casserole /ˈkæsərəʊl/ _____

centimetre ⚙-0 /ˈsentimiːtə(r)/ _____

chamomile /ˈkæməmaɪl/ _____

characteristic ⚙-0 /kærəktəˈrɪstɪk/ _____

charity ⚙-0 /ˈtʃærəti/ _____

chef /ʃef/ _____

chop ⚙-0 /tʃɒp/ _____

cinnamon /ˈsɪnəmən/ _____

coal miner /ˈkəʊl ˌmaɪnə(r)/ _____

cod /kɒd/ _____

colander /ˈkʌləndə(r)/ _____

commission ⚙-0 /kəˈmɪʃn/ _____

community ⚙-0 /kəˈmjuːnəti/ _____

consensus /kənˈsensəs/ _____

consist of ⚙-0 /kənˈsɪst əv/ _____

conventional ⚙-0 /kənˈvenʃənl/ _____

convert ⚙-0 /kənˈvɜːt/ _____

cooking utensils /ˈkʊkɪŋ juːˌtenslz/ _____

coriander /kɒriˈændə(r)/ _____

crop ⚙-0 /krɒp/ _____

crush ⚙-0 /krʌʃ/ _____

cuisine /kwɪˈziːn/ _____

decrease ⚙-0 /dɪˈkriːs/ _____

deep-fry /ˈdiːp ˌfraɪ/ _____

differ /ˈdɪfə(r)/ _____

diner /ˈdaɪnə(r)/ _____

donate /dəʊˈneɪt/ _____

drain /dreɪn/ _____

easy option ⚙-0 /ˌiːzi ˈɒpʃn/ _____

eat my words /ˌiːt ˌmaɪ ˈwɜːdz/ _____

environmentally /ɪnvaɪrənˈmentəli/ _____

ethnic /ˈeθnɪk/ _____

expand ⚙-0 /ɪkˈspænd/ _____

export ⚙-0 /ɪkˈspɔːt/ _____

farmland /ˈfɑːmlænd/ _____

fertilizer /ˈfɜːtɪlaɪzə(r)/ _____

fish out of water /ˌfɪʃ ˌaʊt əv ˈwɔːtə(r)/ _____

fishy /ˈfɪʃi/ _____

flavour ⚙-0 /ˈfleɪvə(r)/ _____

focus (on) ⚙-0 /ˈfəʊkəs/ _____

food processor /ˈfuːd ˌprəʊsesə(r)/ _____

food-conscious /ˈfuːd ˌkɒnʃəs/ _____

foot ⚙-0 /fʊt/ _____

gallon ⚙-0 /ˈɡælən/ _____

ginger /ˌdʒɪndʒə(r)/ _____

guarantee ⚙-0 /ɡærənˈtiː/ _____

harvesting /ˈhɑːvɪstɪŋ/ _____

have her cake and eat it /ˌhæv ˌhɜː ˌkeɪk ən ˈiːt ˌɪt/ _____

health benefit ⚙-0 /ˈhelθ ˌbenəfɪt/ _____

heavy industry ⚙-0 /ˌhevi ˈɪndəstri/ _____

herb /hɜːb/ _____

herbal tea /ˌhɜːbl ˈtiː/ _____

herbicide /ˈhɜːbɪsaɪd/ _____

imperial /ɪmˈpɪəriəl/ _____

in contrast ⚙-0 /ˌɪn ˈkɒntrɑːst/ _____

in other words ⚙-0 /ˌɪn ˈʌðə ˌwɜːdz/ _____

industrial worker ⚙-0 /ɪnˈdʌstriəl ˈwɜːkə(r)/ _____

inexpensive /ɪnɪkˈspensɪv/ _____

ingredient ⚙-0 /ɪnˈɡriːdiənt/ _____

initial ⚙-0 /ɪˈnɪʃl/ _____

intense /ɪnˈtens/ _____

intervention /ɪntəˈvenʃn/ _____

invest ⚙-0 /ɪnˈvest/ _____

kilogram ⚙-0 /ˈkɪləɡræm/ _____

ladle /ˈleɪdl/ _____

latter ⚙-0 /ˈlætə(r)/ _____

lease /liːs/ _____

lentil /ˈlentl/ _____

litre ⚙-0 /ˈliːtə(r)/ _____

long-term future /ˌlɒŋ ˌtɜːm ˈfjuːtʃə(r)/ _____

lose (some) weight ⚙-0 /ˌluːz (səm) ˈweɪt/ _____

make a meal of it ⚙-0 /ˌmeɪk ə ˈmiːl əv ˌɪt/ _____

market research ⚙-0 /ˌmɑːkɪt rɪˈsɜːtʃ, ˈriː-/ _____

menu ⚙-0 /ˈmenjuː/ _____

method ⚙-0 /ˈmeθəd/ _____

metre ⚙-0 /ˈmiːtə(r)/ _____

/i/ happy	/æ/ flag	/ɜː/ her	/ʊ/ look	/ʌ/ mum	/ɔɪ/ noisy	/ɪə/ here
/ɪ/ it	/ɑː/ art	/ɒ/ not	/uː/ you	/eɪ/ day	/aʊ/ how	/eə/ wear
/iː/ he	/e/ egg	/ɔː/ four	/ə/ sugar	/aɪ/ why	/əʊ/ go	/ʊə/ tourist

metric /'metrɪk/ _____

milligram 🔑 /'mɪligræm/ _____

millilitre /'mɪliliːtə(r)/ _____

mint /mɪnt/ _____

mission /'mɪʃn/ _____

mix 🔑 /mɪks/ _____

modern-day /'mɒdn ˌdeɪ/ _____

oat /əʊt/ _____

okra /'əʊkrə, 'ɒkrə/ _____

organic /ɔː'gænɪk/ _____

ounce /aʊns/ _____

packet 🔑 /'pækɪt/ _____

parsley /'pɑːsli/ _____

passionate /'pæʃənət/ _____

peel /piːl/ _____

pestle and mortar
/ˌpesl ən 'mɔːtə(r)/ _____

pint 🔑 /paɪnt/ _____

pioneering /paɪə'nɪərɪŋ/ _____

pomegranate /'pɒmɪgrænɪt/ _____

potato peeler
/pə'teɪtəʊ ˌpiːlə(r)/ _____

pound 🔑 /paʊnd/ _____

pre-measured /'priː ˌmeʒəd/ _____

preparation 🔑 /prepə'reɪʃn/ _____

primarily 🔑 /praɪ'merəli/ _____

product 🔑 /'prɒdʌkt/ _____

profit 🔑 /'prɒfɪt/ _____

pumpkin /'pʌmpkɪn/ _____

questionable /'kwestʃənəbl/ _____

ranging from sth to sth 🔑
/'reɪndʒɪŋ frəm/ _____

realize a dream 🔑
/ˌriːəlaɪz ə 'driːm/ _____

restaurateur /restərə'tɜː(r)/ _____

root vegetable 🔑
/'ruːt ˌvedʒtəbl/ _____

sacrifice /'sækrɪfaɪs/ _____

salad greens 🔑
/'sæləd ˌgriːnz/ _____

seasonal /'siːzənl/ _____

serve 🔑 /sɜːv/ _____

service 🔑 /'sɜːvɪs/ _____

significantly 🔑
/sɪg'nɪfɪkəntli/ _____

silk 🔑 /sɪlk/ _____

slice 🔑 /slaɪs/ _____

soil 🔑 /sɔɪl/ _____

sour grapes /ˌsaʊə 'greɪps/ _____

speciality /speʃi'æləti/ _____

specific requirement 🔑
/spəˌsɪfɪk rɪ'kwaɪəmənt/ _____

spicy 🔑 /'spaɪsi/ _____

stew /stjuː/ _____

stimulate /'stɪmjuleɪt/ _____

stir-fry /'stɜː ˌfraɪ/ _____

sustainable /sə'steɪnəbl/ _____

switch to 🔑 /'swɪtʃ tə/ _____

tagine /tæ'ʒiːn/ _____

tangerine /tændʒə'riːn/ _____

technique 🔑 /tek'niːk/ _____

temperature 🔑
/'temprətʃə(r)/ _____

to put it another way 🔑
/tə ˌpʊt ˌɪt ə'nʌðə ˌweɪ/ _____

tomato 🔑 /tə'mɑːtəʊ/ _____

tractor /'træktə(r)/ _____

traditionally 🔑 /trə'dɪʃənəli/ _____

transform 🔑 /træns'fɔːm/ _____

trend 🔑 /trend/ _____

turnip /'tɜːnɪp/ _____

typical 🔑 /'tɪpɪkl/ _____

variety 🔑 /və'raɪəti/ _____

venture 🔑 /'ventʃə(r)/ _____

well-being /ˌwel 'biːɪŋ/ _____

what a shame 🔑
/ˌwɒt ə 'ʃeɪm/ _____

whisk /wɪsk/ _____

wok /wɒk/ _____

wrap 🔑 /ræp/ _____

yard 🔑 /jɑːd/ _____

Additional vocabulary

_____

_____

_____

_____

_____

_____

_____

_____

_____

_____

_____

_____

_____

_____

_____

_____

_____

_____

_____

_____

/p/ pen	/d/ dog	/tʃ/ beach	/v/ very	/s/ speak	/ʒ/ television	/n/ now	/r/ radio
/b/ big	/k/ can	/dʒ/ job	/θ/ think	/z/ zoo	/h/ house	/ŋ/ sing	/j/ yes
/t/ two	/g/ good	/f/ food	/ð/ then	/ʃ/ she	/m/ meat	/l/ late	/w/ we

absence makes the heart
grow fonder
/ˌæbsəns ˌmeɪks ðə ˌhɑːt
ˌɡrəʊ ˈfɒndə(r)/

actions speak louder than
words 🔊
/ˌækʃnz ˌspiːk ˌlaʊdə ðən
ˈwɜːdz/

appropriate 🔊 /əˈprəʊpriət/

attire /əˈtaɪə(r)/

automatic 🔊 /ˌɔːtəˈmætɪk/

background 🔊 /ˈbækɡraʊnd/

bash /bæʃ/

bosom (n) /ˈbʊzəm/

bus stop /ˈbʌs ˌstɒp/

business associate 🔊
/ˈbɪznəs əˌsəʊʃiət/

by degrees (idm) 🔊
/ˌbaɪ dɪˈɡriːz/

cameraderie /ˌkæməˈrɑːdəri/

cannon (n) /ˈkænən/

captivity (n) /kæpˈtɪvəti/

chamber (n) /ˈtʃeɪmbə(r)/

characterize /ˈkærəktəraɪz/

chat 🔊 /tʃæt/

cleave (v) /kliːv/

clothes make the man 🔊
/ˌkləʊðz ˌmeɪk ðə ˈmæn/

contradict (v) /ˌkɒntrəˈdɪkt/

conversational
/ˌkɒnvəˈseɪʃənl/

convey (v) /kənˈveɪ/

crest (n) /krest/

customary /ˈkʌstəməri/

dash (to pieces) (v)
/ˌdæʃ (tə ˈpiːsɪz)/

deference /ˈdefərəns/

degree 🔊 /dɪˈɡriː/

differ /ˈdɪfə(r)/

discourteous /dɪsˈkɜːtiəs/

discuss 🔊 /dɪsˈkʌs/

distinguish 🔊 /dɪˈstɪŋɡwɪʃ/

don't judge a book by its
cover 🔊
/ˌdəʊnt ˌdʒʌdʒ ə ˌbʊk ˌbaɪ ˌits
ˈkʌvə(r)/

dribble /ˈdrɪbl/

enrol /ɪnˈrəʊl/

error 🔊 /ˈerə(r)/

escalator /ˈeskəleɪtə(r)/

etiquette /ˈetɪket/

exception 🔊 /ɪkˈsepʃn/

extensive 🔊 /ɪkˈstensɪv/

extent 🔊 /ɪkˈstent/

extremity (n) /ɪkˈstreməti/

famished (adj) /ˈfæmɪʃt/

firmament (n) /ˈfɜːməmənt/

foaming (adj) /ˈfəʊmɪŋ/

form a queue /ˌfɔːm ə ˈkjuː/

fortress (n) /ˈfɔːtrəs/

fugitive (n) /ˈfjuːdʒətɪv/

gear 🔊 /ɡɪə(r)/

gender /ˈdʒendə(r)/

gild (v) /ɡɪld/

gossip /ˈɡɒsɪp/

governor (n) 🔊 /ˈɡʌvənə(r)/

grab 🔊 /ɡræb/

guideline /ˈɡaɪdlaɪn/

harbour (n) /ˈhɑːbə(r)/

hardship /ˈhɑːdʃɪp/

he who hesitates is lost 🔊
/ˌhiː ˌhuː ˌhezɪteɪts ˌɪz ˈlɒst/

heap /hiːp/

hit it big 🔊 /ˌhɪt ˌɪt ˈbɪɡ/

hit it off 🔊 /ˌhɪt ˌɪt ˈɒf/

hit the buffers /ˌhɪt ðə ˈbʌfəz/

hit the ground running 🔊
/ˌhɪt ðə ˌɡraʊnd ˈrʌnɪŋ/

hit the hay /ˌhɪt ðə ˈheɪ/

hit the nail on the head 🔊
/ˌhɪt ðə ˌneɪl ˌɒn ðə ˈhed/

hit the road 🔊
/ˌhɪt ðə ˈrəʊd/

hit the roof 🔊 /ˌhɪt ðə ˈruːf/

hold the floor 🔊
/ˌhəʊld ðə ˈflɔː(r)/

homesick /ˈhəʊmsɪk/

illustrate 🔊 /ˈɪləstreɪt/

imposing (adj) 🔊 /ɪmˈpəʊzɪŋ/

in terms of 🔊 /ˌɪn ˈtɜːmz əv/

inanimate (adj) /ɪnˈænɪmət/

instructor /ɪnˈstrʌktə(r)/

intercultural /ˌɪntəˈkʌltʃərəl/

interrupt 🔊 /ˌɪntəˈrʌpt/

it just isn't done 🔊
/ˌɪt ˌdʒʌst ˌɪznt ˈdʌn/

jump the queue
/ˌdʒʌmp ðə ˈkjuː/

lively 🔊 /ˈlaɪvli/

local authority
/ˌləʊkl ɔːˈθɒrəti/

look before you leap
/ˌlʊk bɪˌfɔː ju ˈliːp/

majesty (n) /ˈmædʒəsti/

/i/ happy	/æ/ flag	/ɜː/ her	/ʊ/ look	/ʌ/ mum	/ɔɪ/ noisy	/ɪə/ here
/ɪ/ it	/ɑː/ art	/ɒ/ not	/uː/ you	/eɪ/ day	/aʊ/ how	/eə/ wear
/iː/ he	/e/ egg	/ɔː/ four	/ə/ sugar	/aɪ/ why	/əʊ/ go	/ʊə/ tourist

many hands make light work 🔑
/ˌmeni ˌhændz ˌmeɪk ˌlaɪt ˈwɜːk/

masters course /ˈmɑːstəz ˌkɔːs/

metaphor /ˈmetəfɔː(r)/

meter 🔑 /ˈmiːtə(r)/

mutter /ˈmʌtə(r)/

navigational /ˌnævɪˈgeɪʃnl/

norm /nɔːm/

on silent 🔑 /ˌɒn ˈsaɪlənt/

on the blink /ˌɒn ðə ˈblɪŋk/

open the conversation 🔑
/ˌəʊpən ðə kɒnvəˈseɪʃn/

out of order 🔑
/ˌaʊt əv ˈɔːdə(r)/

out of sight, out of mind 🔑
/ˌaʊt əv ˈsaɪt ˌaʊt əv ˈmaɪnd/

overcharge /ˌəʊvəˈtʃɑːdʒ/

overgeneralization
/ˌəʊvədʒenrəlaɪˈzeɪʃn/

overlap /ˌəʊvəˈlæp/

participate /pɑːˈtɪsɪpeɪt/

pass muster (idm)
/ˌpɑːs ˈmʌstə(r)/

passage (of time) 🔑
/ˈpæsɪdʒ (əv ˌtaɪm)/

personal space 🔑
/ˌpɜːsənl ˈspeɪs/

pharmaceutical
/ˌfɑːməˈs(j)uːtɪkl/

photo album /ˈfəʊtəʊ ˌælbəm/

physical contact 🔑
/ˌfɪzɪkl ˈkɒntækt/

pitch 🔑 /pɪtʃ/

pity (n) 🔑 /ˈpɪti/

plethora /ˈpleθərə/

pretext (n) /ˈpriːtekst/

procedural /prəˈsiːdʒərəl/

prosperity /prɒˈsperəti/

protest 🔑 /prəˈtest/

prow (n) /praʊ/

pursue (v) 🔑 /pəˈsjuː/

rapport /ræˈpɔː(r)/

reflect 🔑 /rɪˈflekt/

remote 🔑 /rɪˈməʊt/

renewal /rɪˈnjuːəl/

resemble /rɪˈzembl/

reticent /ˈretɪsnt/

rugby /ˈrʌgbi/

semester /sɪˈmestə(r)/

session 🔑 /ˈseʃn/

shrine /ʃraɪn/

signal 🔑 /ˈsɪgnəl/

simultaneously
/sɪməlˈteɪniəsli/

socialize /ˈsəʊʃəlaɪz/

somewhat 🔑 /ˈsʌmwɒt/

spectacle (n) /ˈspektəkl/

spontaneous /spɒnˈteɪniəs/

status 🔑 /ˈsteɪtəs/

strict 🔑 /strɪkt/

strike 🔑 /straɪk/

strive (v) /straɪv/

symbolize /ˈsɪmbəlaɪz/

tackle 🔑 /ˈtækl/

taxi stand 🔑 /ˈtæksi ˌstænd/

tempest (n) /ˈtempɪst/

the pen is mightier than the sword
/ðə ˌpen ɪz ˌmaɪtiə ðən ðə ˈsɔːd/

too many cooks spoil the broth ////
/ˌtuː ˌmeni ˌkʊks ˌspɔɪl ðə ˈbrɒθ/

toss /tɒs/

turn taking /ˈtɜːn ˌteɪkɪŋ/

turnkey (n) /ˈtɜːnkiː/

typo /ˈtaɪpəʊ/

underground 🔑
/ˈʌndəgraʊnd/

variation 🔑 /veəriˈeɪʃn/

wave 🔑 /weɪv/

whisper 🔑 /ˈwɪspə(r)/

whistle 🔑 /ˈwɪsl/

wretched (adj) /ˈretʃɪd/

Additional vocabulary

/p/ **p**en	/d/ **d**og	/tʃ/ bea**ch**	/v/ **v**ery	/s/ **s**peak	/ʒ/ televi**si**on	/n/ **n**ow	/r/ **r**adio
/b/ **b**ig	/k/ **c**an	/dʒ/ **j**ob	/θ/ **th**ink	/z/ **z**oo	/h/ **h**ouse	/ŋ/ si**ng**	/j/ **y**es
/t/ **t**wo	/g/ **g**ood	/f/ **f**ood	/ð/ **th**en	/ʃ/ **sh**e	/m/ **m**eat	/l/ **l**ate	/w/ **w**e

accessible /əkˈsesəbl/ _____

accommodate /əˈkɒmədeɪt/ _____

adequate 🔑 /ˈædɪkwət/ _____

adverse effect
/ˌædvɜːs əˈfekt/ _____

air conditioner
/ˈeə kənˌdɪʃənə(r)/ _____

air conditioning
/ˈeə kənˌdɪʃənɪŋ/ _____

air travel 🔑 /ˈeə ˌtrævl/ _____

appliance /əˈplaɪəns/ _____

assemble /əˈsembl/ _____

atmospheric /ætməsˈferɪk/ _____

available 🔑 /əˈveɪləbl/ _____

belongings /bɪˈlɒŋɪŋz/ _____

bench /bentʃ/ _____

biodegradable
/baɪəʊdɪˈgreɪdəbl/ _____

break down 🔑
/ˌbreɪk ˈdaʊn/ _____

breeze /briːz/ _____

bungalow /ˈbʌŋgələʊ/ _____

calculation 🔑 /kælkjuˈleɪʃn/ _____

capital city 🔑 /ˌkæpɪtl ˈsɪti/ _____

caravan /ˈkærəvæn/ _____

carbon footprint
/ˌkɑːbən ˈfʊtprɪnt/ _____

characteristic 🔑
/kærəktəˈrɪstɪk/ _____

charge up 🔑 /ˌtʃɑːdʒ ˈʌp/ _____

chemical 🔑 /ˈkemɪkl/ _____

classify /ˈklæsɪfaɪ/ _____

climate 🔑 /ˈklaɪmət/ _____

committee 🔑 /kəˈmɪti/ _____

construct 🔑 /kənˈstrʌkt/ _____

construction 🔑 /kənˈstrʌkʃn/ _____

consumption /kənˈsʌmpʃn/ _____

corporation /kɔːpəˈreɪʃn/ _____

currently 🔑 /ˈkʌrəntli/ _____

daily 🔑 /ˈdeɪli/ _____

degrees centigrade
/dɪˌgriːz ˈsentɪgreɪd/ _____

demand 🔑 /dɪˈmɑːnd/ _____

demographic trend
/deməˌgræfɪk ˈtrend/ _____

detached house
/dɪˈtætʃt ˌhaʊs/ _____

dioxin /daɪˈɒksɪn/ _____

disposable /dɪˈspəʊzəbl/ _____

donate /dəʊˈneɪt/ _____

downsize /daʊnˈsaɪz/ _____

durable /ˈdjʊərəbl/ _____

eco-friendly /ˌiːkəʊ ˈfrendli/ _____

economical /iːkəˈnɒmɪkl/ _____

elevated /ˈelɪveɪtɪd/ _____

emission /ɪˈmɪʃn/ _____

empirical /ɪmˈpɪrɪkl/ _____

energy 🔑 /ˈenədʒi/ _____

energy efficient 🔑
/ˌenədʒi ɪˈfɪʃnt/ _____

energy-saving 🔑
/ˈenədʒi ˌseɪvɪŋ/ _____

entertain 🔑 /entəˈteɪn/ _____

environmental group 🔑
/ɪnvaɪrənˈmentl ˌgruːp/ _____

equip /ɪˈkwɪp/ _____

evaporate /ɪˈvæpəreɪt/ _____

exorbitant /ɪgˈzɔːbɪtənt/ _____

experimental /ɪksperɪˈmentl/ _____

fold-out /ˈfəʊld ˌaʊt/ _____

fold-up /ˈfəʊld ˌʌp/ _____

full-time /ˌfʊl ˈtaɪm/ _____

generator /ˈdʒenəreɪtə(r)/ _____

get rid of 🔑 /ˌget ˈrɪd əv/ _____

government agency 🔑
/ˈgʌvnmənt ˌeɪdʒənsi/ _____

greenhouse gas
/ˌgriːnhaʊs ˈgæs/ _____

grow up 🔑 /ˌgrəʊ ˈʌp/ _____

humidity /hjuːˈmɪdəti/ _____

incapacitated
/ɪnkəˈpæsɪteɪtɪd/ _____

incentive /ɪnˈsentɪv/ _____

inept /ɪˈnept/ _____

inexplicable /ɪnɪkˈsplɪkəbl/ _____

insignificant /ɪnsɪgˈnɪfɪkənt/ _____

integral /ˈɪntɪgrəl/ _____

intrepid /ɪnˈtrepɪd/ _____

laboratory /ləˈbɒrətri/ _____

ladder /ˈlædə(r)/ _____

landfill /ˈlændfɪl/ _____

light bulb /ˈlaɪt ˌbʌlb/ _____

limitation /lɪmɪˈteɪʃn/ _____

little do we realize 🔑
/ˈlɪtl ˌduː ˌwiː ˌriːəlaɪz/ _____

living space 🔑 /ˈlɪvɪŋ ˌspeɪs/ _____

locate 🔑 /ləʊˈkeɪt/ _____

location 🔑 /ləʊˈkeɪʃn/ _____

loft /lɒft/ _____

mansion /ˈmænʃn/ _____

married couple 🔑
/ˌmærid ˈkʌpl/ _____

mass-market /ˈmæs ˌmɑːkɪt/ _____

material 🔑 /məˈtɪəriəl/ _____

medical facilities
/ˈmedɪkl fəˌsɪlətiz/ _____

/i/ happy	/æ/ flag	/ɜː/ her	/ʊ/ look	/ʌ/ mum	/ɔɪ/ noisy	/ɪə/ here
/ɪ/ it	/ɑː/ art	/ɒ/ not	/uː/ you	/eɪ/ day	/aʊ/ how	/eə/ wear
/iː/ he	/e/ egg	/ɔː/ four	/ə/ sugar	/aɪ/ why	/əʊ/ go	/ʊə/ tourist

modern conveniences
/ˌmɒdn kənˈviːniənsɪz/

namely /ˈneɪmli/

natural resources 🔑
/ˌnætʃrəl rɪˈzɔːsɪz/

negative 🔑 /ˈnegətɪv/

on behalf of sb/sth 🔑
/ˌɒn bɪˈhɑːf əv/

on standby /ˌɒn ˈstændbaɪ/

orchard /ˈɔːtʃəd/

pack up 🔑 /ˌpæk ˈʌp/

period 🔑 /ˈpɪəriəd/

place setting /ˈpleɪs ˌsetɪŋ/

plastic 🔑 /ˈplæstɪk/

plateau /ˈplætəʊ/

portability /pɔːtəˈbɪləti/

portable /ˈpɔːtəbl/

pre-assembled
/ˈpriː əˌsembld/

primarily 🔑 /praɪˈmerəli/

professor 🔑 /prəˈfesə(r)/

purchase 🔑 /ˈpɜːtʃəs/

quality 🔑 /ˈkwɒləti/

range 🔑 /reɪndʒ/

reduce 🔑 /rɪˈdjuːs/

regular 🔑 /ˈregjələ(r)/

respectfully /rɪˈspektfəli/

season 🔑 /ˈsiːzn/

seldom /ˈseldəm/

semi-detached house
/ˌsemi dɪˈtætʃt ˌhaʊs/

significant 🔑 /sɪgˈnɪfɪkənt/

solar heating /ˌsəʊlə ˈhiːtɪŋ/

solar panel /ˌsəʊlə ˈpænl/

square metre 🔑
/ˌskweə ˈmiːtə(r)/

terraced house /ˈterəst ˌhaʊs/

tiny 🔑 /ˈtaɪni/

toxic waste /ˌtɒksɪk ˈweɪst/

toxic /ˈtɒksɪk/

trivial /ˈtrɪviəl/

typically 🔑 /ˈtɪpɪkli/

uncanny /ʌnˈkæni/

undaunted /ʌnˈdɔːntɪd/

under no circumstances 🔑
/ˌʌndə ˈnəʊ ˌsɜːkəmstɑːnsɪz/

unimaginable
/ʌnɪˈmædʒɪnəbl/

unwieldy /ʌnˈwiːldi/

variety 🔑 /vəˈraɪəti/

whereas 🔑 /weərˈæz/

widespread /ˈwaɪdspred/

wildlife habitat
/ˈwaɪldlaɪf ˌhæbɪtæt/

wind-powered /ˈwɪnd ˌpaʊəd/

withstand /wɪðˈstænd/

worldwide /wɜːldˈwaɪd/

Additional vocabulary

/p/ **p**en	/d/ **d**og	/tʃ/ bea**ch**	/v/ **v**ery	/s/ **s**peak	/ʒ/ televi**si**on	/n/ **n**ow	/r/ **r**adio
/b/ **b**ig	/k/ **c**an	/dʒ/ **j**ob	/θ/ **th**ink	/z/ **z**oo	/h/ **h**ouse	/ŋ/ si**ng**	/j/ **y**es
/t/ **t**wo	/g/ **g**ood	/f/ **f**ood	/ð/ **th**en	/ʃ/ **sh**e	/m/ **m**eat	/l/ **l**ate	/w/ **w**e

absurd (adj) /əbˈsɜːd/ _____

academic 🔑 /ˌækəˈdemɪk/ _____

accelerated /əkˈseləreɪtɪd/ _____

acclaimed /əˈkleɪmd/ _____

accomplished /əˈkʌmplɪʃt/ _____

act dumb /ˌækt ˈdʌm/ _____

adamant /ˈædəmənt/ _____

alternative 🔑 /ɔːlˈtɜːnətɪv/ _____

aluminium /ˌæljəˈmɪniəm/ _____

anchor /ˈæŋkə(r)/ _____

anthem /ˈænθəm/ _____

aptitude /ˈæptɪtjuːd/ _____

arithmetic /əˈrɪθmətɪk/ _____

audience 🔑 /ˈɔːdiəns/ _____

augment /ɔːgˈment/ _____

award a contract 🔑
/əˌwɔːd ə ˈkɒntrækt/ _____

back away (from) 🔑
/ˌbæk əˈweɪ/ _____

base camp /ˈbeɪs ˌkæmp/ _____

behaviour 🔑 /bɪˈheɪvjə(r)/ _____

beseech (v) /bɪˈsiːtʃ/ _____

blog (about) /blɒg/ _____

boarding school
/ˈbɔːdɪŋ ˌskuːl/ _____

buzzer /ˈbʌzə(r)/ _____

call off 🔑 /ˌkɔːl ˈɒf/ _____

call upon 🔑 /ˈkɔːl əˌpɒn/ _____

cameraman /ˈkæmərəmən/ _____

cherish /ˈtʃerɪʃ/ _____

chip in with 🔑 /ˌtʃɪp ˈɪn ˌwɪð/ _____

classical /ˈklæsɪkl/ _____

come in for 🔑 /ˌkʌm ˈɪn fə/ _____

come up with 🔑
/ˌkʌm ˈʌp ˌwɪð/ _____

commendable (adj)
/kəˈmendəbl/ _____

composer /kəmˈpəʊzə(r)/ _____

concert hall 🔑 /ˈkɒnsət ˌhɔːl/ _____

conclude 🔑 /kənˈkluːd/ _____

conductor /kənˈdʌktə(r)/ _____

corpse (n) /kɔːps/ _____

courtier (n) /ˈkɔːtiə(r)/ _____

deal 🔑 /diːl/ _____

dejected (adj) /dɪˈdʒektɪd/ _____

denote (v) /dɪˈnəʊt/ _____

draw up 🔑 /ˌdrɔːr ˈʌp/ _____

dumb down /ˌdʌm ˈdaʊn/ _____

enthusiasm 🔑
/ɪnˈθjuːziæzəm/ _____

equip /ɪˈkwɪp/ _____

essentially 🔑 /ɪˈsenʃəli/ _____

eternity (n) /ɪˈtɜːnəti/ _____

even more so 🔑
/ˌiːvn ˈmɔː ˌsəʊ/ _____

executive 🔑 /ɪgˈzekjutɪv/ _____

fabric /ˈfæbrɪk/ _____

felt-like /ˈfelt ˌlaɪk/ _____

filial (adj) /ˈfɪliəl/ _____

flute /fluːt/ _____

genius /ˈdʒiːniəs/ _____

get across 🔑 /ˌget əˈkrɒs/ _____

get along with sb 🔑
/ˌget əˈlɒŋ ˌwɪð/ _____

get at sb 🔑 /ˈget ət/ _____

get by 🔑 /ˌget ˈbaɪ/ _____

get into 🔑 /ˌget ˈɪntuː, ˈɪntə/ _____

get over 🔑 /ˌget ˈəʊvə(r)/ _____

get rid of sth 🔑 /ˌget ˈrɪd əv/ _____

get to grips with sth
/ˌget tə ˈgrɪps ˌwɪð/ _____

get to the bottom of sth 🔑
/ˌget tə ðə ˈbɒtəm əv/ _____

get up to 🔑
/ˌget ˈʌp ˌtuː, tə/ _____

gifted 🔑 /ˈgɪftɪd/ _____

go back on 🔑
/ˌgəʊ ˈbæk ˌɒn/ _____

hand over sth to someone 🔑
/ˈhænd ˌəʊvə/ _____

honour 🔑 /ˈɒnə(r)/ _____

houseboat /ˈhaʊsbəʊt/ _____

impart (v) /ɪmˈpɑːt/ _____

impediment /ɪmˈpedɪmənt/ _____

impious (adj) /ˈɪmpiəs/ _____

impressive 🔑 /ɪmˈpresɪv/ _____

intellectual /ˌɪntəˈlektʃuəl/ _____

intent (n) /ɪnˈtent/ _____

launch 🔑 /lɔːntʃ/ _____

legal age 🔑 /ˈliːgl ˌeɪdʒ/ _____

level-headed /ˌlevl ˈhedɪd/ _____

low-income /ˈləʊ ˌɪnkʌm/ _____

mediocre /miːdiˈəʊkə(r)/ _____

mid-court /ˈmɪd ˌkɔːt/ _____

mourning (n) /ˈmɔːnɪŋ/ _____

multi-million-dollar
/ˈmʌlti ˌmɪljən ˌdɒlə(r)/ _____

murmur /ˈmɜːmə(r)/ _____

nomadic /nəʊˈmædɪk/ _____

non-profit organization
/ˌnɒn ˌprɒft ɔːgənaɪˈzeɪʃn/ _____

obligation (n) /ɒblɪˈgeɪʃn/ _____

obsequious (adj) /əbˈsiːkwiəs/ _____

obstinate (adj) /ˈɒbstɪnət/ _____

/i/ ha**pp**y	/æ/ fl**a**g	/ɜː/ h**er**	/ʊ/ l**oo**k	/ʌ/ m**u**m	/ɔɪ/ n**oi**sy	/ɪə/ h**ere**
/ɪ/ **i**t	/ɑː/ **ar**t	/ɒ/ n**o**t	/uː/ y**ou**	/eɪ/ d**ay**	/aʊ/ h**ow**	/eə/ w**ear**
/iː/ h**e**	/e/ **e**gg	/ɔː/ f**ou**r	/ə/ s**u**g**ar**	/aɪ/ wh**y**	/əʊ/ g**o**	/ʊə/ t**ou**rist

onstage /ɒnˈsteɪdʒ/

opera /ˈɒprə/

opt for /ˈɒpt ˌfɔː(r), fə(r)/

orchestra /ˈɔːkɪstrə/

originate with /əˈrɪdʒɪneɪt ˌwɪð/

ovation /əʊˈveɪʃn/

overtime /ˈəʊvətaɪm/

peevish (adj) /ˈpiːvɪʃ/

performance 🔑 /pəˈfɔːməns/

permanently 🔑 /ˈpɜːmənəntli/

pianist /ˈpiənɪst/

pick up (on) 🔑 /ˌpɪk ˈʌp ˌ(ɒn)/

portable /ˈpɔːtəbl/

preparatory /prəˈpærətri/

preserve (v) 🔑 /prɪˈzɜːv/

pressure 🔑 /ˈpreʃə(r)/

prestigious /preˈstɪdʒəs/

primary school /ˈpraɪməri ˌskuːl/

psychologist /saɪˈkɒlədʒɪst/

recital /rɪˈsaɪtl/

recording contract 🔑 /rɪˈkɔːdɪŋ ˌkɒntrækt/

remedial /rɪˈmiːdiəl/

resolve the situation 🔑 /rɪˌzɒlv ðə sɪtʃuˈeɪʃn/

retrograde (adj) /ˈretrəgreɪd/

semi-detached /ˌsemi dɪˈtætʃt/

show an interest (in) 🔑 /ˌʃəʊ ən ˈɪntrəst/

sign up 🔑 /ˌsaɪn ˈʌp/

significantly 🔑 /sɪgˈnɪfɪkəntli/

smart from sth 🔑 /ˈsmɑːt frəm/

smart move 🔑 /ˌsmɑːt ˈmuːv/

smart set 🔑 /ˈsmɑːt ˌset/

solemn (adj) /ˈsɒləm/

special needs 🔑 /ˌspeʃl ˈniːdz/

stardom /ˈstɑːdəm/

stereotypically /steriəˈtɪpɪkli/

struck dumb /ˌstrʌk ˈdʌm/

successfully 🔑 /səkˈsesfəli/

summit /ˈsʌmɪt/

symphony /ˈsɪmfəni/

symphony orchestra /ˈsɪmfəni ˌɔːkɪstrə/

synthesizer /ˈsɪnθəsaɪzə(r)/

take on 🔑 /ˌteɪk ˈɒn/

take over 🔑 /ˌteɪk ˈəʊvə(r)/

take sth to heart (idm) 🔑 /ˌteɪk … tə ˈhɑːt/

temporary 🔑 /ˈtemprəri/

throne (n) /θrəʊn/

tie 🔑 /taɪ/

trailer /ˈtreɪlə(r)/

trappings (n, pl) /ˈtræpɪŋz/

troubled 🔑 /ˈtrʌbld/

turn down 🔑 /ˌtɜːn ˈdaʊn/

two-digit multiplication /ˌtuː ˌdɪdʒɪt mʌltɪplɪˈkeɪʃn/

under pressure 🔑 /ˌʌndə ˈpreʃə(r)/

unfortified (adj) /ʌnˈfɔːtɪfaɪd/

unprevailing (adj) /ˌʌnprɪˈveɪlɪŋ/

victory 🔑 /ˈvɪktəri/

violin /vaɪəˈlɪn/

violinist /vaɪəˈlɪnɪst/

virtuoso /vɜːtʃuˈəʊsəʊ, -ˈəʊzəʊ/

visage (n) /ˈvɪzɪdʒ/

vulgar (adj) /ˈvʌlgə(r)/

wait out 🔑 /ˌweɪt ˈaʊt/

with ease 🔑 /ˌwɪð ˈiːz/

withdraw (from) 🔑 /wɪðˈdrɔː/

woe (n) /wəʊ/

yurt /jɜːt/

Additional vocabulary

/p/ **p**en	/d/ **d**og	/tʃ/ bea**ch**	/v/ **v**ery	/s/ **s**peak	/ʒ/ televi**si**on	/n/ **n**ow	/r/ **r**adio
/b/ **b**ig	/k/ **c**an	/dʒ/ **j**ob	/θ/ **th**ink	/z/ **z**oo	/h/ **h**ouse	/ŋ/ si**ng**	/j/ **y**es
/t/ **t**wo	/g/ **g**ood	/f/ **f**ood	/ð/ **th**en	/ʃ/ **sh**e	/m/ **m**eat	/l/ **l**ate	/w/ **w**e

IRREGULAR VERBS

Base form	Past simple	Past participle	Base form	Past simple	Past participle
be	was/were	been	make	made	made
beat	beat	beaten	mean	meant	meant
become	became	become	meet	met	met
begin	began	begun	overcome	overcame	overcome
bend	bent	bent			
bite	bit	bitten	pay	paid	paid
blow	blew	blown	put	put	put
break	broke	broken	read	read	read
bring	brought	brought	ride	rode	ridden
build	built	built	ring	rang	rung
burn	burnt	burnt	run	ran	run
buy	bought	bought	say	said	said
can	could	been able to	see	saw	seen
catch	caught	caught	sell	sold	sold
choose	chose	chosen	send	sent	sent
come	came	come	set	set	set
cost	cost	cost	shake	shook	shaken
cut	cut	cut	shine	shone	shone
deal	dealt	dealt	shoot	shot	shot
do	did	done	show	showed	shown/-ed
draw	drew	drawn	shut	shut	shut
drink	drank	drunk	sing	sang	sung
drive	drove	driven	sink	sank	sunk
eat	ate	eaten	sit	sat	sat
fall	fell	fallen	sleep	slept	slept
feed	fed	fed	smell	smelt/-ed	smelt/-led
feel	felt	felt	speak	spoke	spoken
fight	fought	fought	spell	spelt/-ed	spelt/-led
find	found	found	spend	spent	spent
flee	fled	fled	spill	spilt/-ed	spilt/-led
fly	flew	flown	split	split	split
forget	forgot	forgotten	spread	spread	spread
get	got	got	spring	sprang	sprung
give	gave	given	stand	stood	stood
go	went	gone/been	steal	stole	stolen
grow	grew	grown	swim	swam	swum
hang	hung	hung	take	took	taken
have	had	had	teach	taught	taught
hear	heard	heard	tear	tore	torn
hide	hid	hidden	tell	told	told
hit	hit	hit	think	thought	thought
hold	held	held	throw	threw	thrown
keep	kept	kept	understand	understood	understood
know	knew	known	wake	woke	woken
lay	laid	laid	wear	wore	worn
lead	led	led	win	won	won
learn	learnt/-ed	learnt/-ed	write	wrote	written
leave	left	left			
lend	lent	lent			
lose	lost	lost			